306

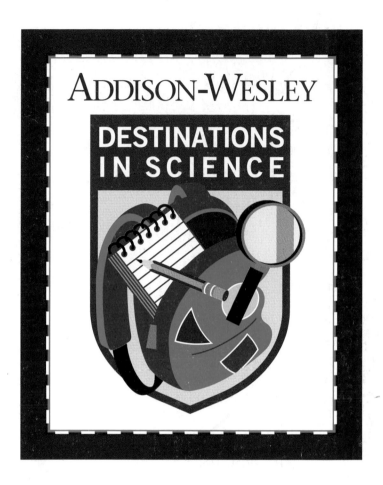

ADDISON-WESLEY

DESTINATIONS IN SCIENCE

Authors
David C. Brummett
Karen K. Lind
Charles R. Barman
Michael A. DiSpezio
Karen L. Ostlund

Contributing Authors
Jim Hopkins
Vallie W. Guthrie
Michael B. Leyden
Gerry M. Madrazo, Jr.
Sheryl A. Mercier
Jerome M. Shaw

Activity Consultant
Doug Herridge

Addison-Wesley Publishing Company
Menlo Park, California ▪ Reading, Massachusetts ▪ New York ▪ Don Mills, Ontario ▪ Wokingham, England ▪ Amsterdam
Bonn ▪ Paris ▪ Milan ▪ Madrid ▪ Sydney ▪ Singapore ▪ Tokyo ▪ Seoul ▪ Taipei ▪ Mexico City ▪ San Juan

Destinations in Science ™ is a trademark of Addison-Wesley Publishing Company, Inc.

Destinations in Science

CONTENTS

Unit A
Classification

Unit B
Cells & Heredity

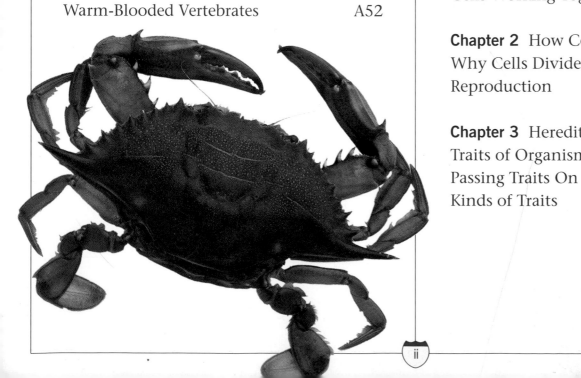

Unit C
Energy & Resources

LANDFILL RECYCLING

Destinations in Science

Unit E
Earth Movements

Unit D
Motion & Energy

Consultants and Reviewers

Special Consultants

Reading
Bonnie Armbruster, Ph.D.
Center for the Study of Reading
University of Illinois at
    Urbana-Champaign

Assessment
Steve Rakow, Ph.D.
Associate Professor of Education
University of Houston–Clear Lake
Houston, Texas

Special Needs
Valerie Wales, M.S.
Coordinator
Special Education Resource Center
Mansfield, Ohio

Multicultural
Gerard Fergerson, Ph.D.
Assistant Professor of Health Policy
New York University

Arlene Maclin, Ph.D.
Director for Research and
    Research Professor of Physics
Hampton University
Hampton, Virginia

Luis Martinez-Perez, Ph.D.
Associate Professor of
    Science Education
Florida International University

Barbara F. May
Language Enrichment Teacher
Thomy Lafon School
New Orleans, Louisiana

A. Barretto Ogilvie, Ed.D.
Dean of Continuing and
    Professional Education
Seattle Central Community College

Jennifer K. Patterson
New Orleans Public Schools
New Orleans, Louisiana

Tone Shimizu
Educational Consultant
Berkeley, California

Albert Snow, Ed.D.
Director of Science Education
The Discovery Museum
Bridgeport, Connecticut

Multicultural Photo/Art Reviewers
Cynthia Cooksey
Marlene C. Davis
Cammie Harris
Marie Kitajima
Edna Ahgeak MacLean
Mattie McCloud
Renya Ramirez
June Tanamachi

Environmental
Linda Furuness, Ph.D.
School of Education
Indiana University
Indianapolis, Indiana

Science, Technology, and Society
Jon E. Pedersen, Ph.D.
Assistant Professor of Curriculum and
    Instruction–Science Education
University of Arkansas
Fayetteville, Arkansas

Urban
Doris Williams
Martin Luther King Junior
    High School
Oakland, California

Safety
Jay A. Young, Ph.D.
Chemical Safety and
    Health Consultant
Silver Springs, Maryland

ESL
Rosa Leon
Coordinator
Bronx School District
Bronx, New York

Cheryl McElvain
E.L.D. Educational Consultant
Morgan Hill, California

Irene Musman
Coordinator
Philadelphia School District
Philadelphia, Pennsylvania

Alice Parra
Hughey Elementary School
El Paso, Texas

Content Consultants

Kurt Brorson, Ph.D.
Division of Monoclonal Antibodies
Food and Drug Administration
Bethesda, Maryland

Brenda Bussard
Educational Consultant
Fremont, California

Geoff Chester
Albert Einstein Planetarium
Smithsonian Institution
Washington, DC

Eric Engles, Ph.D.
Education Consultant
Felton, California

Robert W. Hinds, Ph.D.
Department of Geology
Slippery Rock University
Slippery Rock, Pennsylvania

M. Frank Watt Ireton
American Geophysical Union
Washington, DC

Barry Lessow, Ed.D.
Assistant Professor of
   Teacher Education
Indiana University
Bloomington, Indiana

Chelcie Liu, Ph.D.
Physics Instructor
City College of San Francisco
San Francisco, California

Elizabeth Looney
Woodrow Wilson High School
San Francisco, California

Rosalind Philips
New Century High School
Olympia, Washington

Terry M. Phillips, D.Sc.
Professor of Medicine
George Washington University
   Medical Center
Washington, DC

Deborah Tippins, Ph.D.
Assistant Professor of
   Science Education
University of Georgia
Athens, Georgia

Reviewers

Don Collins
Science Coordinator
Flint Community Schools
Flint, Michigan

Ron Fairchild
Sierramot Middle School
San Jose, California

Shannon Hardwick
Blair Middle School
Norfolk, Virginia

Margo Lalchandani
Hillview Middle School
Menlo Park, California

Edward F. Moore
K–8 Science Curriculum Coordinator
Manchester Public Schools
Manchester, Connecticut

Nancy Rankin
Science Specialist
Oak Knoll Elementary School
Menlo Park, California

Gus Samaniego
Barnard White Middle School
Union City, California

Ruth Schloemer
Educational Consultant
Fort Mitchell, Kentucky

Bruce Schulert
K–12 Science Consultant
Lansing School District
Lansing, Michigan

Rosalie Shepherd
Jordan Middle School
Palo Alto, California

Hettie Teachey
Myrtle Grove Middle School
Wilmington, North Carolina

Field Test Teachers

Sarah Claire Dyer
Christian Life Academy
Baton Rouge, Louisiana

Larry Pickford
North Park Elementary School
Roy, Utah

Mike Sentz
Seymour Community Schools
Seymour, Indiana

Carol Van DeWalle
Alwood Elementary School
Alpha, Illinois

Gail Winter
Lamar Middle School
Lamar, Missouri

Christine Zerillo
St. Barnabas School
Louisville, Kentucky

Student Reviewers

Kevin Jeffery
Hillview Middle School
Menlo Park, California

Geoffery McCann
Hillview Middle School
Menlo Park, California

DESTINATIONS IN SCIENCE

Dear Travelers,

You are about to begin a fantastic journey to investigate science.

Your ticket to *Destinations in Science* will take you to real places to learn about science. You may travel to places such as Chesapeake Bay, where you'll investigate plant and animal classification systems. Or, you may learn about our evolving earth by studying earthquakes during a trip to the San Andreas fault.

Some destinations might be familiar to you, such as the amusement park where you'll learn about the thrills of motion and energy. Others, such as the Space Probe, explore galaxies, black holes, absolute silence, and the unknown. Imagine what you'll discover when you touch the future aboard the *Pathfinder*!

Destinations in Science is your passport to real-world science adventures! Welcome to an exciting way of thinking about science. You'll discover that science is *everywhere*—here and over the next horizon.

Bon voyage!

The Authors

The Authors

James, York, Piankatank,
and Patuxent, Nanticoke, Choptank
into me their waters vent.
I hold sail boats a-plenty,
full of boys and girls.
In the summers I get crabby,
but oysters are my pearls.
Toadfish, pipefish, waterbugs, and eel
swim through my reeds and grasses
lookin' for a meal.
The water in me is both salty and
fresh.
Who am I? What am I?
Can you guess?

MARYLAND

DELAWARE

Washington, DC

Chesapeake
Bay

VIRGINIA

Atlantic
Ocean

Chesapeake Bay

You put the field glasses to your eyes and gaze out over the cordgrass. Cattails and spartina grass wave in the wind. A blue heron stabs for food in the weedy shallows. A snapping turtle pokes its head out of the water to breathe. There are swarms of mosquitoes and deerflies.

You hike down a path toward the shore. You see tiny brown fiddler crabs, each waving one enormous claw. There are animals everywhere!

In the distance is Chesapeake Bay. It is alive with birds. Gulls swoop overhead or stand on the beach. A large bird with a big red beak wades among other birds that are busy scooping at the water with their bills. An osprey hits the water and snatches a fish with its sharp talons.

There is a greater variety of living things along Chesapeake Bay than you've ever seen.

■ How can you group living things to understand them better?

■ What are the characteristics that all invertebrates have in common?

■ How are vertebrates different from one another?

CLASSIFICATION

CHESAPEAKE BAY

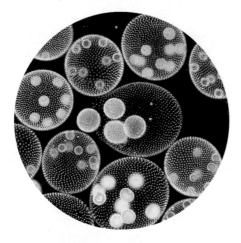

Activities

Features

Chapter 1

Living Things

Your observation that Chesapeake Bay has many kinds of living things is right. Chesapeake Bay has many estuaries (es´tyo̅o̅ er ēz), shallow areas where rivers meet the ocean. Here fresh water mixes with salt water. Food is carried into the estuary from both the rivers and the ocean. This makes the estuary and the surrounding areas a rich environment for many kinds of living things.

How might you describe the life of Chesapeake Bay? You could say there are "lots of animals," but that wouldn't tell very much. If you found a new bird at the beach, how could you tell someone what kind of bird you had found?

Bird-watchers, often called birders, look for characteristics such as color, size, and the shape of the bird's beak and feet. In this way, they can identify the exact kind of bird they have found.

Scientists have developed a system to classify, or group, living things. They classify organisms based on features. For example, animals that have wings and feathers are classified as birds.

The Chesapeake Bay is an excellent place to learn about classification because it has so many different kinds of organisms. Your visit to Chesapeake Bay will help you understand why classifying organisms is important and interesting. Some classification groups, such as birds, are familiar to you. Another familiar classification group is fish. In your Science Journal, list characteristics of fish.

An avocet is a shore-bird with a long, slender upturned bill.

We are sloshing in a tidal salt marsh. It has a grassy fringe along its edge.

A7

Explore Activity

How can you classify objects?

Process Skills

Observing, Collecting data, Classifying

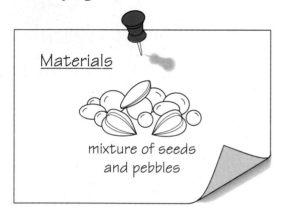

Materials

mixture of seeds and pebbles

Observe and Collect Data

1. Get a box of objects from your teacher and empty it onto a desk. Examine the objects. **Predict** ways that you think they will be alike and ways they will be different. Look at characteristics such as size, color, shape, and kind of material.

2. Determine what characteristic you will use to divide the objects into two major groups. In your Activity Journal, list this characteristic and label each group.

3. Decide on characteristics you can use to divide each group into two more groups. (You will have four groups.) List the characteristics you chose and label each group.

4. Divide the four groups into as many smaller groups as you can. List the characteristics and label each final group.

Share Your Results

1. Into how many groups did you sort your objects? Did other groups of students have the same number of groups?

2. How did your sorting, or classifying, method compare with those used by other groups of students?

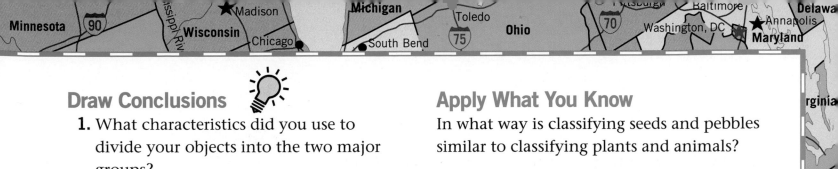

Draw Conclusions 💡

1. What characteristics did you use to divide your objects into the two major groups?
2. How were the characteristics you used for separating the first two groups different from characteristics you used to divide the objects into smaller and smaller groups?

Apply What You Know

In what way is classifying seeds and pebbles similar to classifying plants and animals?

Why do we classify organisms?

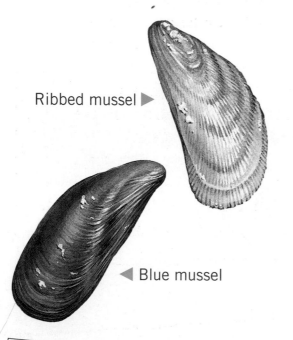

Ribbed mussel ▶

◀ Blue mussel

Your class is going to have a cookout on the shore, and it's your job to find mussels for dinner. One of your friends describes a mussel as a two-shelled animal that is "kind of like" a clam. Off you go on your search. When you get back your friend greets you with, "Oh, no! We can't eat these. They're ribbed mussels. We want some blue mussels."

Being able to identify and classify animals is important for more things than just dinner. For example, a new plant found in the rain forest helps cure a disease. Scientists need to know what plant it is so that they can learn how to use the medicine it contains. Or imagine that a newly discovered type of bacterium is causing a disease. Doctors need to know exactly what kind of bacterium it is in order to fight it. We also need to identify plants and animals that are endangered. By knowing how an organism is related to similar organisms, people can make plans to save it.

Organisms are grouped by the ways they are the same. The most obvious groups are plants and animals. Plants are grouped in one **kingdom,** and animals are grouped in another. A kingdom is the name given to the broadest category of organisms. All the organisms within a kingdom share basic characteristics. For example, trees, ferns, and grasses are in the plant kingdom. They all make their own food.

Examining mussels attached to some rocks. Their edges are sharp!

Aristotle's Classification System

Aristotle (ar´is tät´'l), a Greek philosopher who lived more than 2,000 years ago, was the first to classify organisms as plants or animals. He grouped organisms according to where they live. He put plants into one group and animals into another. Then he looked at where different organisms within each category live: in air, on land, underground, or in water. According to Aristotle's system of classifying animals, whales and sea turtles were grouped together because they both live in water. Some animals, like giraffes and tortoises, were grouped together because they live on land. Yet whales and giraffes are more closely related because they are both mammals. Tortoises and sea turtles are closely related reptiles, even though they live in very different environments.

Why do you think biologists don't use Aristotle's system today? Do you think it might have value for people in other occupations? Explain your answer.

Placing an organism into a kingdom is easy because kingdoms are such broad categories. After an organism is put into a kingdom, additional details help classify it into smaller and smaller groups. Scientists study the structure of an organism and its chemistry. They compare this organism with others like it. Then they place the organism in a group with others that are very similar to it. This small classification group is called a **species.**

Visit a grocery store in your neighborhood. Figure out how the items are organized. What groups of items are displayed together? For example, dairy foods may be placed in one part of the store and baking goods in another part. List all the different groups of items in your Science Journal. Think of new ways you might organize the items in the store and record your ideas.

BACK HOME

What are the kingdoms?

For more than 2,000 years, scientists divided living things into two groups—plants and animals. Anything that moved and needed to eat was classified as an animal. Anything that made its own food and did not move was classified as a plant. But it became difficult

▲ Monerans

Monerans (mə ner′ənz) are simple one-celled organisms. They are microscopic, and their cells have no special structures. This kingdom is made up of all the **bacteria,** most of which are decomposers. One kind of moneran is blue-green bacteria. Monerans are believed to be the first living things on the earth.

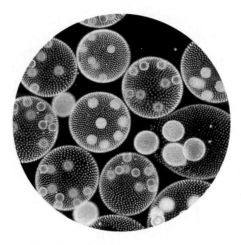

▲ Protists

Protists (prōt′ists) have a more complex cell structure than monerans. They have a nucleus. Some protists are one-celled, while others have many cells. Some, like protozoa, are animallike—they move around and take in food. Others, such as algae, are plantlike and make their own food.

▲ Fungi

Fungi (fun′ji) are many-celled organisms. Most cannot move. Most are plantlike organisms that cannot make their own food, but absorb food from other living things or once-living things. If you've eaten a mushroom, you've eaten a member of the fungi kingdom. Other kinds of fungi include molds, yeasts, and mildews.

to place some organisms into either category. For example, scientists wondered how to classify mushrooms. They are not animals, but they don't make their own food as plants do. Scientists also found other organisms that needed their own separate group. So today scientists divide all living things into five major kingdoms. The five major kingdoms include monerans, protists, fungi, plants, and animals.

▲ Plants

Plants are many-celled organisms that make their own food. Generally, plants cannot move from place to place. Some plants, such as mosses and liverworts, lack true roots, leaves, and stems. Some plants, such as ferns and trees, live on land. They have a vascular system, true roots, stems, and leaves.

◄ Animals

Animals are many-celled organisms that eat food. Most can move from place to place and react quickly to changes in their environment. Animals are divided into two major groups— those with backbones and those without backbones.

How are you doing?

1. Why is Chesapeake Bay a good place to study living things?
2. What are some reasons why it is helpful to classify living things?
3. **Think** Why is it helpful to group organisms into five kingdoms instead of only two?
4. **Think** There are many levels of classification between kingdoms and species. Would the organisms be more varied or more alike as the number of groups increases? Explain your answer.

What are some simple organisms?

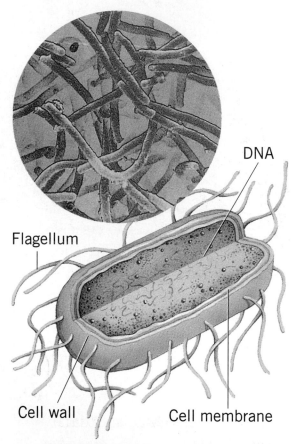

Flagellum

DNA

Cell wall

Cell membrane

▲ A bacterium cell is filled with strands of DNA, which is a set of directions that control the cell. In other types of cells, the DNA is inside a structure called the nucleus. The **nucleus** is the control center of the cell. These monerans, or bacteria, are different from other living things—bacteria cells do not have a nucleus or some other internal structures found in the cells of other organisms.

You and some classmates are going collecting. You've packed your lunch, first-aid kit, and several collection jars in your backpack. Your first stop is a freshwater pond near the bay. Here a friend fills a jar with pond water. She then leads you to the rocks at the edge of the bay. Here she busily scrapes something green from a rock and drops it into another jar. She asks you to collect a reddish-brown clump of stuff from the mud. By the time you're ready to go back to school, you've collected a shell with thin strands of brown hairlike material, a crinkled green pebble, and some limp, smelly sheets of green goo that were lying on the beach.

Back at school, you place a drop of the water on a glass slide and look at it through a microscope. Tiny specks are darting about, and there are some long green strands. Your friend tells you that the green strands are long chains of bacteria cells.

The drop of pond water holds more than monerans. Most of the specks darting from place to place in the water are protists. Some single-celled protists share characteristics with animals. They must get food and move from place to place. Others are similar to plants because they make their own food.

What else did you and your friends collect at the shore? You might also find different kinds of algae in the water of your collection jars. These many-celled algae, or seaweeds, take many forms. You may have collected broken-off parts of brown algae. Kelps are giant brown algae that can grow up to 65 meters long.

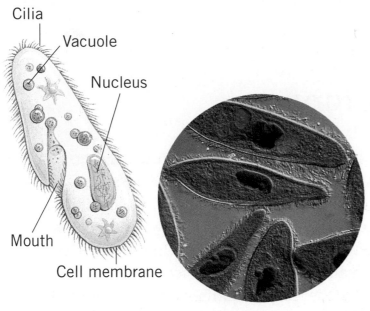

Cilia

Vacuole

Nucleus

Mouth

Cell membrane

▲ The structure of a single-celled protist is different from that of a moneran. Note the several structures within the cell, including a nucleus. This protist is called *Paramecium.*

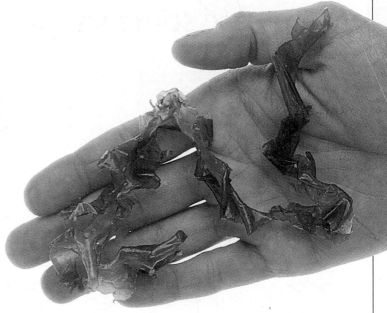

Sea lettuce is one kind of many-celled algae. It lives in salty ocean water and often washes up on beaches. ▼

Be a Scientist

HANDS-ON ACTIVITY

How would you classify *euglena*?

1. Use a microscope to observe a slide of *Euglena* (yōō glē´nə). When *Euglena* live in sunny ponds, they are green and make their own food. When they live in dark places, they lose their color and need to take in food. In light or dark, the *Euglena* uses its whiplike flagellum (flə jel´əm) to move.

2. **[ACTIVITY JOURNAL]** In your Activity Journal, list the characteristics of *Euglena*. Which are char-

acteristics of plants? Which are characteristics of animals?

3. How would you classify *Euglena*? Explain your answer.

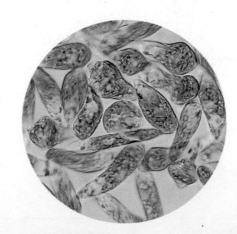

What are some kinds of fungi?

▲ A puffball is a round-shaped fungus. It releases its reproductive spores like puffs of smoke. Some puffballs produce more than 10 billion spores. These spores form new puffballs.

While you and your friends were collecting, you spotted something growing on a dead tree. This growth is a kind of fungus (singular form of *fungi*). Like plants, fungi do not move. They have cell walls. A major difference between fungi and plants is that fungi lack chlorophyll. This means that they cannot make their own food—they absorb nutrients from other organisms. They reproduce by special cells called **spores**. Some kinds of fungi you may have heard of are bread molds, yeasts, mushrooms, and lichens.

Many fungi are decomposers. They break down once-living things and release their materials back into the environment.

Fungi are used in medicine. Antibiotics (an´tī bī ät´iks) are used to fight illnesses caused by bacteria. The first antibiotic was penicillin, made from a fungus.

The mushroom that you see is only a part of the organism. The rest of it is a large mass of threadlike parts that grow underground and absorb nutrients. ▶

Cap

Gills

Spores

Stalk

▲ Some mushrooms and other fungi grow in warm, dark, moist places—like on a rotting log. Many bracket fungi look like shelves. They are soft and flexible when young, but become tough like leather when mature.

▲ Lichen is formed from some algae cells that live together with fungi. The fungi gather water and nutrients, and the algae use these substances to make food. This partnership helps each organism to live in harsh environments.

Be a Scientist

HANDS-ON ACTIVITY

What is a mushroom like?

1. 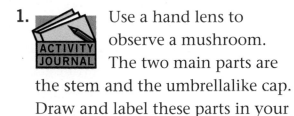 Use a hand lens to observe a mushroom. The two main parts are the stem and the umbrellalike cap. Draw and label these parts in your Activity Journal.

2. Look at the underside of the cap. Note the pattern of lines from the stem to the outer edge of the cap. Each of these lines is called a gill. The gills produce spores.

3. Feel the gills and look at them with a hand lens. Draw and label the gills.

Stale bread and old strawberries sometimes get a fuzzy substance growing on them. This kind of fungus is called mold. Mold needs warmth and moisture to grow well. ▶

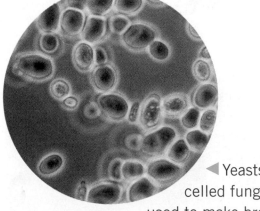

◀ Yeasts are single-celled fungi and are used to make bread rise. Yeast cells grow into colonies if they have food and are kept warm and moist.

What are some kinds of plants?

Today your class is going on a plant hunt. Your class hikes single file along a trail. Someone says, "Look, there's some moss." Your classmates gather around a decaying log near a pond. You stoop to examine the moss covering the log.

Moss is a very simple plant. It is green and makes its own food. It lacks features of more advanced plants. It does not have true roots, stems, or leaves. It doesn't produce flowers. Mosses and other simple plants do not have special structures to carry nutrients throughout the plant. Water and other materials move slowly from one cell to the next. As a result, these plants are only a few centimeters tall and live near water or in damp, shady places. One kind of moss that grows at Chesapeake Bay is sphagnum moss.

Near the pond is a wooded area. Trees filter the sun, keeping the woods moist, cool, and shady. Here plants with lacy, pointed leaves grow on the forest floor. These plants are ferns and are more complex than mosses and their relatives. Ferns have true roots, stems, and leaves. The stem grows underground, and the roots grow underneath the stem. New leaves grow from the stem. Inside these structures is a system of tubes that carry water and other materials throughout

Tall salt-marsh cordgrass along the shore of Chesapeake Bay

▲ Some seed plants are conifers, such as pine, fir, juniper, and redwood. Conifers are used by humans in many ways. Most wood products are made out of conifers.

the plant. These tubes make up the vascular tissue. Although ferns around Chesapeake Bay are small, tree ferns may grow to 30 meters high in the tropics.

Like mosses, ferns reproduce with spores. The spore cases are on the underside of the leaves. They look like small, rusty bumps.

Most of the plants you see around you are seed plants. Seed plants are more complex than mosses or ferns. Like spores, seeds grow into new plants. Seeds contain food for the young plant to live on before it can make its own food.

Seed plants are very important to people. Wheat, corn, and other grains are the seeds of flowering plants. These grains provide an important food source for people and other animals. In addition, the fruits and vegetables you eat are parts of seed plants.

How are you doing?

1. How does a cell of a moneran differ from a cell of any other kind of living thing?
2. In what ways are fungi useful to people?
3. **Think** How do mosses differ from other types of plants?
4. **Think** Explain why algae and fungi are not classified as plants.

Auks, Rocks and the Odd Dinosaur

Inside Stories from the
Smithsonian's Museum of Natural History
by Peggy Thompson

This is an excerpt from a book about the Smithsonian Institution. Spencer Baird began the museum's natural history collection in the 1800s.

. . . Baird sent out his own people, who enlisted still others—trappers and traders and missionaries, even lighthouse keepers, who provided him with whales. He had a whole network. One of his men said there was not a schoolboy with a talent for fishing or finding nests whom Baird didn't know and encourage.

Baird equipped his collectors from Washington. He sent them kegs of alcohol and ammunition, fish-collecting trunks, sieves, insect pins and advice: how to stitch extra pockets to jackets, how to pickle a skin and how to pack eggs in twists of paper, not in moss . . . .

He named new species after their faraway finders. And the finders named new species—some 40—for him, among them a Baird's tapir, a Baird's octopus, a Baird's dolphin and a Baird's sandpiper. Audubon gave the name to a Baird's sparrow.

Some of the young collectors Baird put to work in

Washington. They had a club called the Megatherium Club, which held oyster roasts and had special yells . . . . In snatches of time from other museum duties Baird wrote huge volumes on the birds, fishes, snakes and mammals of North America. When he wrote at home, he kept a small barrel of reptiles by his desk for his little daughter Lucy to play with.

In the Baird years the collections began their rapid growth—to 2 million things at the time of his death, to 68 million now. Collections grow as natural history collections have to grow. For one single animal does not tell the story of its species. Whether it's a rhinoceros or a shellfish the size of a speck of dust, examples are needed of male, female and young; from times past and present; from this locality, from that; collected in winter, in spring, in sickness, in health.

Collections also grow because scientists, who are everywhere, diving, digging, chipping, scanning, keep finding new and different things. Beyond the 26 million insects at hand, they net new and different insects in the canopies of trees. They scoop them from the dew in tire treads, pick them off snowfields and cactuses.

In similar ways vast numbers of new things are gathered up, not out of greediness, but from a need to fill in the gaps and chinks. In Baird's day the rush was on to collect everything. Now there's still a rush, for species go extinct. . . .

Think About Your Reading
1. What skills and interests are helpful for a collector like Baird? What types of things might you be interested in collecting?
2. List two or more causes why scientists collect plant and animal specimens.

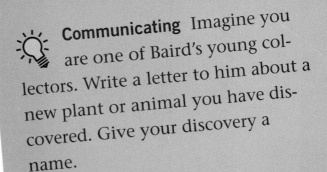 **Communicating** Imagine you are one of Baird's young collectors. Write a letter to him about a new plant or animal you have discovered. Give your discovery a name.

Where to Read More
Jean Craighead George, *The Talking Earth* (New York: Harper Collins, 1983)
A Seminole girl finds why it is important to know about the plants and animals in the Everglades.

Looking Back

Words and Concepts

Complete the following statements.

1. The five kingdoms of living things are
   ———— , ———— , ———— , ———— ,
   and ———— .

2. Bacteria cells do not have a(n) ————
   or other structures found in the cells of
   other types of living things.

3. The smallest classification group is a(n)
   ———— .

4. Algae are not classified as plants. Instead
   they are classified as ———— .

5. Unlike plants, fungi do not ———— .

6. Ferns and other complex plants have
   ———— , which carry materials through
   the plant.

7. Most of the plants you see around you
   are ———— plants.

Applied Thinking Skills

Answer the following questions. You can
use words, drawings, and diagrams in your
answers.

8. Why were classification systems in the
   past based on two kingdoms, plant
   and animal? Why are there now five
   kingdoms?

9. How would you classify an organism that
   lives in the water, makes its own food, is
   made up of a single cell, and has structures that it uses to move from place to
   place? Explain your answer.

10. **Your World** Where in your neighbor-
    hood would you expect to find mosses
    growing? Explain your answer.

This pancake-shaped sand dollar is
about 7 centimeters wide.

Show What You Know

How can you classify plants?

Observe and Collect Data

1. Get a set of pictures. Each picture shows a different plant. Study the characteristics of the plants.
2. Classify the plants by dividing them into groups based on their characteristics. Then name each group based on these characteristics. For example, you may have *plants with wide leaves* or *plants with needle leaves*.
3. Write the name of each plant group on an index card. Arrange the index cards on your desk and place the pictures in their group.

Draw Conclusions

1. Compare your plant groups to those plant groups of your classmates.

Process Skills:
Observing, Classifying, Hypothesizing

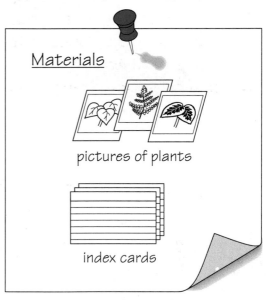

Materials

pictures of plants

index cards

2. What characteristics do all your plants have in common?
3. What characteristics have you read about that are difficult to identify in a picture?
4. **Predict** a general rule you can make about the size of a plant and its structure. What is your rule?

Chapter 2

Invertebrates

This is tideland. It is covered by water at high tides.

"Ouch!" Another mosquito bite! Mosquitoes are everywhere around wetlands. You wonder how mosquitoes are classified. You would put them in a group called "pests." But mosquitoes are classified in the same kingdom as people, lions, and frogs—they all are animals.

Animals share some basic characteristics. They are many-celled organisms. They capture and eat their food. They move from place to place during their lifetime. They react quickly to changes in their environment. And their bodies are made up of many cells and have complex structures.

There are more than 1 million species, or types, of animals. Most animals are **invertebrates**, animals without backbones. Some examples of invertebrates are sponges, worms, and beetles. Imagine how many ants you might find in a single anthill. A spoonful of good garden soil may hold more than a thousand animals. These animals, too small to be seen without a microscope, are all invertebrates.

So far scientists have identified many different kinds of invertebrates. But it is possible that millions of invertebrates have yet to be found and classified. Chesapeake Bay is home to many kinds of invertebrates.

 Animals that lack backbones don't have any other bones either. In your Science Journal, list ways that animals without bones would be different from animals that have bones.

Dragonflies have narrow, transparent wings. Their eyes are big!

Montana
Helena   Billings   Yellowstone   South Dakota
90   94
Orego
lumb
nento
Fresn
Los
annel
ands
California   Gila River   Arizona   New Mexico
Colo   Cos   20

Explore Activity

What are the characteristics of an earthworm?

HANDS-ON
ACTIVITY

Process Skills
Observing, Inferring, Classifying

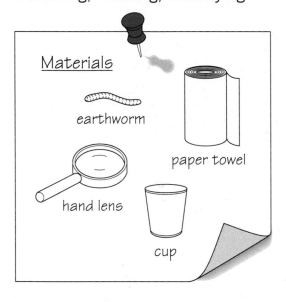

Materials

earthworm

paper towel

hand lens

cup

Observe and Collect Data

1. Get an earthworm from your teacher. Gently place it on a moist paper towel. Remember to handle all living things carefully.

2. Gently run your finger along the length of the earthworm's back, or topside. Don't press hard, but try to feel what is below the surface. Wash your hands after handling the worm.

3. Use the hand lens to find the hairlike structures on its underside. Watch the worm use these hairlike structures to move across the paper towel. In your Activity Journal, describe what you see.

ACTIVITY JOURNAL

4. **Predict** what will happen if you place a cup or another object in front of the earthworm. Then place an object in front of the worm. Note what happens when the worm touches the object.

Share Your Results
Compare your observations of the earthworm with those of another student. How were your observations similar? How were they different?

Draw Conclusions

1. Which of your observations indicate that the earthworm is an animal?
2. Which of your observations indicate that the earthworm is an invertebrate?

Apply What You Know

How does the body structure of an earthworm differ from that of a person?

What are the simplest animals?

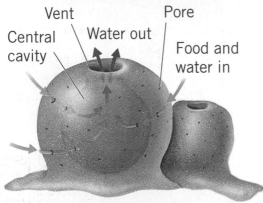

Vent   Pore

Central   Water out
cavity   Food and
water in

▲ A sponge gets food from the water.
Water is pulled through the sides
through tiny openings called pores.
While the water flows through the
central cavity of the sponge, bits of
food are removed and the water
flows out the vent.

"How would you like to find some simple animals?"
you ask your friends. "Follow me." Soon you and your
class are hopping from rock to rock along the shore of
Chesapeake Bay.

Clinging to some rocks are colorful, odd-shaped
lumps. They are sponges, animals whose bodies have a
simple structure. Sponges live in salt water or fresh
water. Sponges are many-celled organisms. Their bodies
are made up of two cell layers. You may have used a
"natural sponge" in the bath. This sponge is what
remained after the sponge died—a flexible network of
material that once supported the body of the sponge.

Drifting through the bay waters are more strange-
looking animals. They look like plastic bags with
dangling strings. They are jellyfish, and the "strings" are
their tentacles. Jellyfish and their relatives, the hydras
(hī´drəz), are simple animals that are more complex
than sponges. The cells in both hydras and jellyfish are
organized to work together, forming layers called
tissues.

A jellyfish can give a painful sting. The tentacles
have stinging cells, which the jellyfish uses to catch its
prey. The sting can stun and stop a fish from moving.

Two other animals related to hydras and jellyfish are
sea anemones (ə nem´ə nēz´) and corals. You may find
some of the colorful sea anemones near the Chesapeake
shore. Corals live in warm ocean waters and form hard
skeletons around their bodies. After many years, the
buildup from these skeletons forms coral reefs.

◄ A jellyfish is umbrella-shaped and its tentacles hang downward. The jellyfish and sea anemone have the same body plan. Their mouths are in the center of their hollow bodies and are surrounded by tentacles. The jellyfish's mouth faces downward as it swims. The sea anemone's mouth and tentacles face upward.

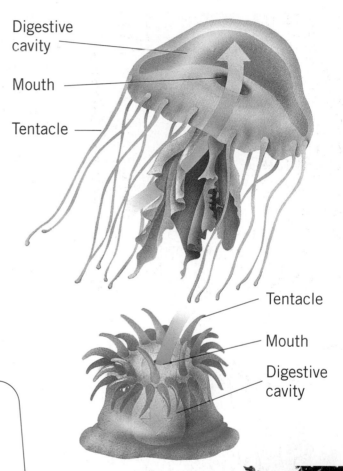

Digestive cavity

Mouth

Tentacle

Tentacle

Mouth

Digestive cavity

YOU CAN HELP

Wetlands, like estuaries and marshes, are important because so many organisms live there. You can help preserve these areas by taking care of them. Get permission from your parents to pick up litter from a wildlife area near your home.

Anus

What are some kinds of worms?

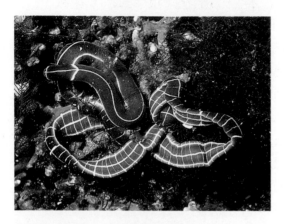

▲ Although ribbon worms live in the ocean or shore areas, some types of worms live in soil, fresh water, or the ocean.

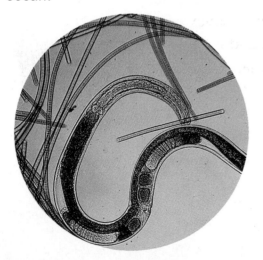

▲ Many roundworms are too small to be seen without a microscope but some can be more than 1 meter long. They live in fresh water, salt water, mud, or soil.

Early the next morning, everyone continues to hunt for more simple animals. You take a trail leading through the tidal mud flats, which appear deserted. One of your friends is digging into the mud. "There's a whole world beneath this mud," she says. After a few minutes, you see what she means.

She unearths a worm that is long, skinny, flat, and smooth. It's a red ribbon worm, related to a group of organisms called flatworms. These simple animals have flat bodies. Many flatworms are parasites. One of the parasitic flatworms that live inside animals is a tapeworm. It attaches to the intestinal walls by hooks and suckers. It absorbs digested food. People can get tapeworms by eating beef that has not been fully cooked.

Another group of worms is roundworms. These simple animals have long, tapered bodies. They are more complex than flatworms because they have a complete digestive tract. Some roundworms are parasites in animals or plants.

You find another worm. This one is made up of separate sections, or segments. Segmented worms are a third major group of worms. They have the most complex body plan of the worms. Most segmented worms live in the ocean, but the one you know best—the earthworm—lives underground. Bristles on each segment help the worm move through the soil. As it moves, the earthworm swallows soil, which passes through its body. The earthworm digests nutrients from the soil. Earthworms are a food source for other animals.

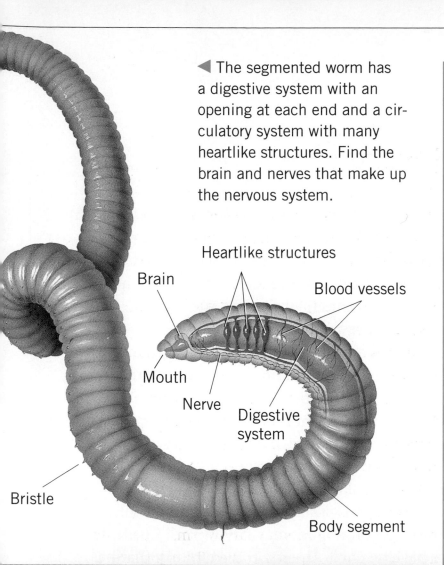

◀ The segmented worm has a digestive system with an opening at each end and a circulatory system with many heartlike structures. Find the brain and nerves that make up the nervous system.

Heartlike structures

Brain

Blood vessels

Mouth

Nerve

Digestive system

Bristle

Body segment

Be a Scientist

How do earthworms mix soil?

1. Put a 2-centimeter layer of dark soil in the bottom of each of two jars. On top of this put a 1-centimeter layer of light sand. Continue layering the soil and sand until the jars are almost full. As you layer, add enough water to slightly dampen each layer. Be careful not to add so much water that the soil or sand gets soaked.

2. **ACTIVITY JOURNAL** Carefully put two earthworms in one jar. Add some grated carrot. Wash your hands after handling the worms. Cover each jar loosely with a lid and tape dark paper around each jar. Write your name on two labels and stick one on each jar. Set the jars aside in a cool place. In your Activity Journal, write what you think will happen during the next three days.

3. After three days, unwrap the jars and examine the carrot, soil, and sand. What happened in each jar? Describe the differences you see. In which jar do you think a plant would grow best? Why?

What are mollusks and echinoderms?

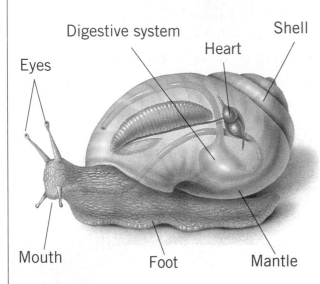

Digestive system

Shell

Heart

Eyes

Mouth

Foot

Mantle

▲ A mollusk has a digestive, circulatory, and nervous system. In most mollusks, a muscular foot is used for movement and to search for food.

▲ When necessary, this squid can move very quickly backward by squirting water out of its body.

The beaches along Chesapeake Bay are dotted with hundreds of shells. These shells are the remains of **mollusks** (mäl´əsks). A mollusk is a soft-bodied animal that has a protective covering, or tissue, called a mantle. The mantle sometimes makes a hard shell.

Some of the most common kinds of mollusks in Chesapeake Bay have two shells hinged together. You might find clams, mussels, and oysters around the bay. These kinds of mollusks live in salt water. They can open their shells and filter food from the water. Scallops are another kind of mollusk that lives in the ocean.

Snails also are mollusks. They each have a single shell. Although a slug has no shell, it is classified in this group because it is basically a snail without a shell.

A third kind of mollusk may have a shell inside its body or have no shell. The squid is a mollusk that has a remnant of a shell. The octopus has no shell. In the octopus, the foot is divided into eight arms. These arms are used to catch prey.

Another animal you can find in Chesapeake Bay's salty water is the starfish. This is a type of **echinoderm** (ē kī´nō dərm´), a complex invertebrate with spiny skin. Other kinds of echinoderms are brittle stars, sand dollars, and sea urchins.

To eat, the starfish wraps its arms around a clam. It attaches its tube feet to each shell of the clam and pulls the shells apart. Then the starfish pushes its stomach out through its mouth and between the clam shells. Here it digests the soft body of the clam.

Stomach

Arm

Water canal

Suction cup

Tube foot

▲ The internal body parts of all echinoderms are arranged in a circle. On the bottom of each of its arms are rows of tube feet. At the tip of each foot are suction cups. The starfish uses its tube feet to move and to get food.

Be a Scientist

What do snails eat?

1. Get a dish and a snail from your teacher. Cut celery leaves, spinach, and lettuce into pieces. Put them into your dish, then loosely cover and place the dish where it will not be disturbed.

2. In your Activity Journal, draw what you see and predict which food the snail will eat.

ACTIVITY JOURNAL

3. The next day, observe your snail and its food and draw what you see. What kind of food did your snail eat?

How are you doing?

1. How do sponges get their food?
2. What are the three main groups of worms? Which one is the most complex?
3. **Think** How is the octopus different from most other kinds of mollusks?
4. **Think** A starfish gets food by pulling apart the shells of mollusks. What do you think holds the mollusk shells together?

What are arthropods?

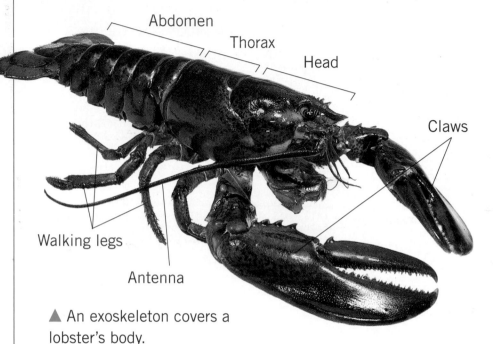

Abdomen

Thorax

Head

Claws

Walking legs

Antenna

▲ An exoskeleton covers a lobster's body.

▲ One type of crustacean that lives on land is the pill bug. You may have seen pill bugs curled up under a rock or in a pile of rotting leaves.

The next day, you notice an animal that looks like a small lobster swimming in the shallow waters of the Chesapeake Bay. With its huge front claws, it grabs the bait you dropped in the water. This armored animal is a crayfish, a relative of the lobster, which lives in the nearby Atlantic Ocean. Lobsters, crayfish, and crabs belong to the huge group of complex animals called **arthropods** (är´thrō pädz´). This name means "jointed leg." An arthropod has a body made up of segments, with jointed legs and a hard outer covering. This outer covering is called an **exoskeleton,** which is a skeleton on the outside of the body. The exoskeleton supports the arthropod's body, much as the skeleton within your body supports you. The exoskeleton also helps protect the animal from drying out or being eaten.

Unlike a person's skeleton, an exoskeleton cannot grow. When an arthropod grows, it sheds its skeleton and forms a new one. This process is called molting. After an arthropod has molted, the animal hides for protection while its new covering hardens.

Arthropods are the most successful group of animals in the world. There are more different kinds of arthropods than all other types of animals put together. They live almost everywhere. There are lice so tiny that they live on bees, and there are giant lobsters that live in the depths of the ocean.

Arthropods are classified into several large groups. Crayfish belong to the group known as **crustaceans** (krus tā´shənz). Animals in this group have four pairs of walking legs. The fifth pair of legs forms claws. There are antennae, which are used for touch, taste, and smell. Most crustaceans, including lobsters, crabs, and shrimp, live in salt water.

Another group of arthropods, the **arachnids** (ə rak´nidz), have four pairs of legs. Ticks, mites, and scorpions belong to this group, but the spider is the arachnid you probably know best. At Chesapeake Bay, the dune spider can be found hiding in its burrow in the sand. This spider makes a door for its burrow from sand and the silk strands that it makes.

Spiders are arachnids. Many spiders use their silk strands to make webs for trapping their prey. ▶

 Many people are afraid of spiders, but spiders are helpful animals. They eat insect pests, including many that eat crops. Survey your family, friends, and neighbors to find out how they feel about spiders. In your Science Journal, list the questions you ask people. Then write their answers. Compare your results with those of your classmates.

BACK HOME

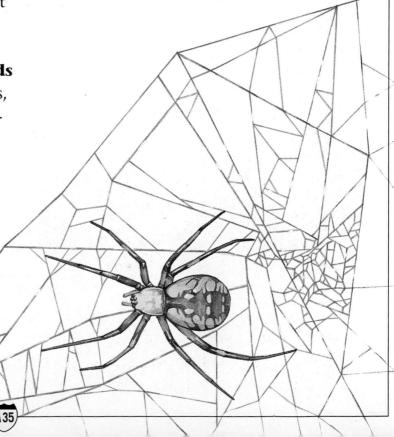

What are insects?

The largest group of arthropods are the insects. An insect has three pairs of legs and three main body parts. Adult insects are the only invertebrates that can fly. They may have one or two pairs of wings.

More than one million species of arthropods have been identified, and most are insects. You may see ants or hear chirping crickets at Chesapeake Bay. You may be lucky and not feel the bite of a mosquito or, worse, the sting of a sand wasp.

Some insects, like grasshoppers and crickets, have long back legs. These strong legs are used for jumping. Honeybees use their back legs to carry pollen back to the beehive.

An insect, like this bee, has one pair of antennae that are generally used for touching and smelling. Insects also have compound eyes. You can think of these eyes as a collection of tiny eyes. This type of eye is especially good at seeing movement. ▼

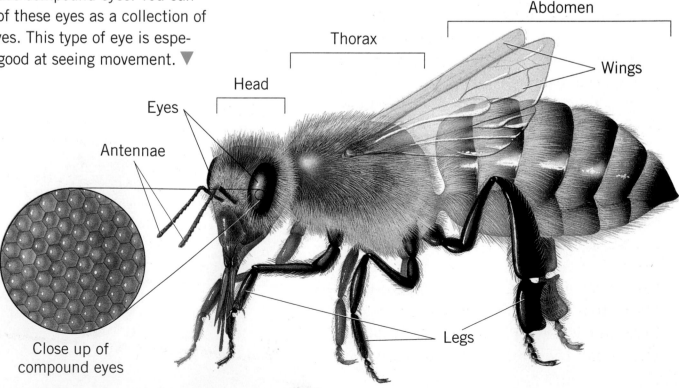

Close up of
compound eyes

Antennae

Eyes

Head

Thorax

Abdomen

Wings

Legs

▲ Centipedes and millipedes differ in their body shape. Centipedes have a flatter body, and millipedes are rounded and look more like worms.

Amazing!

Scientists study rain forests, looking for organisms that are still unidentified. A team of scientists found more than 100 new types of insects in a single tree!

Insects that eat leaves have sharp mouthparts that help them chew the leaves. Butterflies have tube-shaped mouthparts to drink nectar from flowers.

Two more groups of arthropods include centipedes (sen´tə pēdz´) and millipedes (mil´i pēdz´). Both of these arthropods live in dark places, such as under rocks and logs. These animals have a head attached to a chain of small body parts. In centipedes, one pair of jointed legs is attached to each segment. Two pairs of jointed legs are attached to each segment of a millipede. At the head of a centipede are poison claws, which it uses to capture insects and worms. The millipede mainly eats the remains of dead plants.

How are you doing?

1. What are the characteristics of arthropods?
2. Give some examples of crustaceans. Where are most crustaceans found?
3. **Think** Mosquitoes bite people to feed on their blood. What do you think a mosquito's mouthparts are like?
4. **Think** Why are centipedes and millipedes classified as arthropods, even though they are shaped like worms?

Using Mollusks

Clams, mussels, and squid are popular foods. Some people like to eat oysters and snails, too. The best-known way people use mollusks is for food, but people have found other uses for mollusks and their products. Some of these uses are very old.

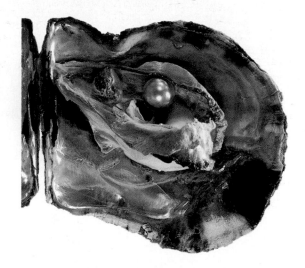

Pearls are produced by oysters. When a grain of sand gets inside an oyster's shell, the oyster's mantle produces layers of pearly material around the grain of sand. More than 700 years ago, the Chinese learned that a bead placed inside a live oyster's shell would result in a smooth, round pearl. The Japanese improved this technique about 100 years ago and are still the world's major source of these cultured pearls.

Nearly 3,000 years ago, the Phoenicians learned to make a purple dye from the murex snail. This dye was used to make wool and cotton cloth purple. The Greeks and Romans also used this dye. Because the snail was rare, the dye was expensive. Only wealthy people, such as royalty, could afford the purple cloth. As a result, the dye came to be called royal purple.

▲ This mosaic was made of tiny stones around A.D. 527 in Ravenna, Italy. It shows the Roman emperor Justinian wearing a royal purple robe.

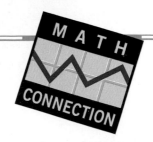

What kinds of invertebrates do you see?

Observe and Collect Data

1.  In your Activity Journal, keep a record of all the invertebrate animals you see in one week. Write the name of each animal if you know it. If you don't, write a description of it or draw a picture that shows its characteristics.

2. Next to the name or picture of each animal, write the name of the group it belongs to. For example, if you see an ant, write *insect, arthropod*. To decide on the correct group, or classification, carefully observe the characteristics of each animal.

3. At the end of the week, list all the groups of invertebrates you observed. Then count the number of animals you saw in each group. Share the data with your class.

4. Create a class bar graph using the data from everyone in the class.

Draw Conclusions

1. Which classification of animal did you see most often?

2. Which classification group did you observe least often?

3. You may have studied some types of invertebrates that you did not find this week. If so, explain why.

4. How did the number of insects you found compare with the number of other invertebrates?

Looking Back

Words and Concepts

Complete the following statements.

1. _____ are simple animals that have only two layers of cells.
2. The mouths of a jellyfish and a sea anemone are surrounded by _____ .
3. The most complex kind of worm is a(n) _____ worm.
4. Clams, snails, and octopuses are examples of _____ .

5. Three characteristics of arthropods are _____ , _____ , and _____ .
6. Arachnids are a group of arthropods that have _____ pairs of legs.
7. The largest group of arthropods are the _____ .

Applied Thinking Skills

Answer the following questions. You can use words, drawings, and diagrams in your answers.

8. How is the way a sponge feeds different from the way a jellyfish feeds?
9. You could think of a clam's outer covering, or shell, as its house, which the clam carries wherever it goes. What could you compare a crab's outer covering to?
10. **Your World** Crabs from Chesapeake Bay are sometimes eaten as soft-shell crabs. Would you eat a crab with the exoskeleton on it? Under what conditions could you do this?

Blue crabs caught in Chesapeake Bay

Show What You Know

Can you create your own invertebrate?

Observe and Collect Data

1. 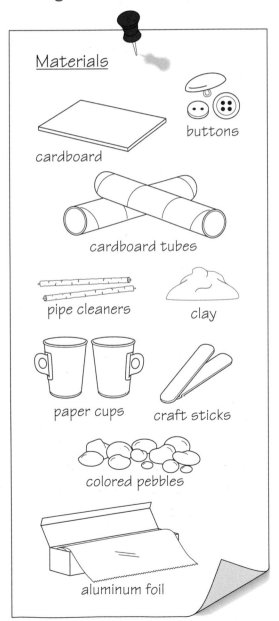 How might the earth's environment change? Think about some possible changes and the characteristics that might help an animal survive in the new environment. In your Activity Journal, describe these changes and characteristics.

2. Design an invertebrate with characteristics that will help it survive in the future. You may draw a picture in your Activity Journal.

3. Use art materials and any other materials you need to build your new animal.

Draw Conclusions

1. Does your new animal belong to a group you have studied? Why or why not? If it does not fit into a group, list the characteristics of the new group your animal would belong to.

2. Show your animal to your classmates and explain how its characteristics would help it survive in a new environment.

3. Ask your classmates to classify your animal based on the characteristics they can observe.

Process Skills
Predicting, Hypothesizing, Making models

Materials

buttons

cardboard

cardboard tubes

pipe cleaners   clay

paper cups   craft sticks

colored pebbles

aluminum foil

Chapter 3

Vertebrates

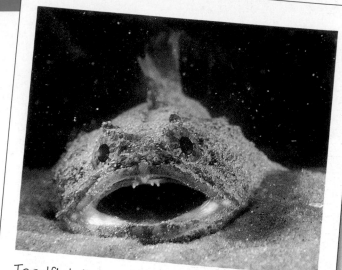

Toadfish have thick heads and wide mouths. They feed along the shoreline.

A friend asks if you'd like to go snorkling. You grab your face mask, swim fins, and snorkel, put on your swimming suit, and the two of you are on your way.

The water seems alive with fish. There are tiny killifish, catfish with long whiskers, and flat flounders. Chesapeake Bay and the nearby ocean are habitats for many vertebrate animals, especially fish. On the shore, there are other vertebrates, like birds and horses.

Vertebrates are animals with backbones. Their skeletons are inside their bodies. Their backbones look like chains of small bones that cover and protect their spinal cords. The spinal cord is a bundle of nerves that runs down an animal's back through the middle of each small bone. The spinal cord connects the brain to nerves in the body. Because the backbone is made up of small separate bones, the animal can bend its back.

All vertebrates have well-developed body systems, such as circulatory, nervous, and digestive systems. They also have specialized sense organs, such as eyes.

There are five major groups of vertebrates. They are fish, amphibians, reptiles, birds, and mammals. Members of each of these groups can be found around Chesapeake Bay and the nearby ocean.

SCIENCE JOURNAL Try twisting and bending your body. In your Science Journal, describe the ways your backbone can bend. How would you move if your body were one long, solid bone?

The Canada goose is the largest wild goose in North America.

Explore Activity

How can you identify birds?

Process Skills
Observing, Classifying

When scientists see an organism they cannot identify, they use a "key" to help them. By closely observing the characteristics of the organism and then following the instructions in the key, scientists can determine the organism's species.

Observe and Collect Data

1. Observe the key for birds at the bottom of this page. To use the key, look at the birds shown on the next page and decide which of the paired statements describes the birds. Does the bird have webbed feet? It does, so look at the descriptions that follow statement 1.

2. The next two statements describe the bird's bill. Is it broad and flat, or is it thick? The bill is thick, so look at the descriptions that follow statement B.

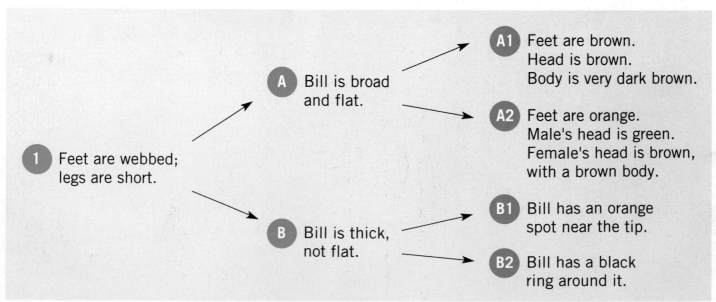

1 Feet are webbed; legs are short.

A Bill is broad and flat.

A1 Feet are brown. Head is brown. Body is very dark brown.

A2 Feet are orange. Male's head is green. Female's head is brown, with a brown body.

B Bill is thick, not flat.

B1 Bill has an orange spot near the tip.

B2 Bill has a black ring around it.

3. Look closely at the bird's bill and read statements B1 and B2. The bird has an orange spot near the tip of its bill, so it is a herring gull.

4. Use the key to identify the other birds.

Share Your Results

Compare your results with those of your classmates. Did you agree on the identities of the birds? If your results do not agree, work together and check your answers.

Draw Conclusions

1. What kind of birds did you identify using this key?

2. Does a key give a complete description of each bird? If not, why does it work?

Apply What You Know

There are several kinds of gulls that have an orange spot on their bills. What other details might you use to tell a herring gull from another similar kind of gull?

Black duck

Ring-billed gull

Mallard

Herring gull

What are fish?

Fish are vertebrates that spend their entire lives in water. They are the major vertebrates living in bodies of water. Although they can be as tiny as a killifish or as large as a shark, fish have many characteristics in common. Fish are cold-blooded, which means that their body temperature changes with the temperature of the water around them. The bodies of most fish are streamlined and covered and protected by hard, flat scales. Fish have several fins that help them move through the water.

When fish breathe, they take in oxygen and give off carbon dioxide, as humans do.

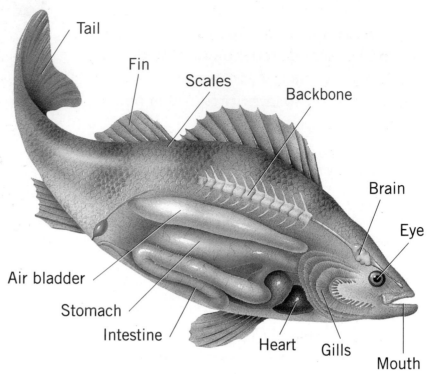

Tail
Fin
Scales
Backbone
Brain
Eye
Air bladder
Stomach
Intestine
Heart
Gills
Mouth

The difference is that in fish the gases are exchanged in structures called gills. When water flows over the gills, oxygen moves from the water to the blood inside the gills.

▲ Many kinds of fish, like these killifish in Chesapeake Bay, swim in groups called schools.

▲ A skate is a cartilage fish that has a broad, flat body and jaws.

Wetlands Naturalist

A wetlands naturalist helps people explore and learn about the ecology of wetlands. To do this, the wetlands naturalist leads field trips, gives talks, produces brochures, and develops exhibits.

66 My name is Steve Cochrane and I'm a wetlands naturalist. I teach about plants and animals that live in or near both fresh and salt water. One of my responsibilities is to take students on walks to discover how plants and animals are adapted to live in wet or salty areas. One way I do this is by having students observe how plants are able to tolerate salt. We look for salt crystals on the leaves of grass and taste the stems of pickleweed.

"In college I studied biology and chemistry. I learned about the relationships among organisms and between organisms and their environments. I also learned how our growing human population puts a great stress on the environment by using so many natural resources.

"What I like best about my job is working with people to preserve biological diversity for future generations.**99**

Carbon dioxide moves from the blood into the water as it goes out.

There are three groups of fish. One class has a skeleton made of bone. Most of the fish you find in Chesapeake Bay are bony fish. Some of these fish are trout, cod, and perch. Their skeletons are made of bones. An adaptation that helps bony fish swim more easily is an air bladder. Like a little balloon, the air bladder inside the body of the fish can fill with air as the fish breathes. When it's filled, the fish rises in the water. When air is let out, the fish sinks.

The other two groups of fish have skeletons made of cartilage. Your ears and the tip of your nose are made of cartilage. Cartilage is firm but flexible, not hard and stiff like a bone. The first group, which includes sharks, skates, and rays, have jaws that open and close, so they can catch and hold prey.

The other class of cartilage fish has no jaws. These jawless fish have circular mouths surrounded by small teeth. They attach themselves to animals with their mouths and suck body fluids from their prey. Some jawless fish are lamprey and hagfish.

What are amphibians?

Some nights at Chesapeake Bay you can hear a faint chirping. It's a chorus of tree frogs, peeping and grunting from the uplands past the marshes. Frogs are a kind of amphibian. The word *amphibian* means "double life," which is a good description for how these animals live. **Amphibians** are cold-blooded vertebrates that live part of their lives in water and part on land.

Being cold-blooded, amphibians cannot control their body temperatures. Their environments control their body temperatures. During cold winters, amphibians become inactive as their body processes slow down. While the weather is cold, amphibians might dig into a lake bottom and hibernate. They remain inactive until the environment warms in the spring.

Frogs and toads make up one group of amphibians— those without tails. Young frogs live in water and breathe through gills as fish do. In time, the tadpoles grow legs. Then lungs develop, the gills disappear, and the tail shrinks.

As adults, most frogs have thin, moist skin and live near water. They breathe through their skin as well as through their lungs. The adults return to water to mate and lay their eggs.

Amphibian eggs do not have a protective, waterproof shell. Because their eggs can easily dry out, amphibians lay their eggs in ponds, swamps, streams, and even in irrigation ditches. Some toads have adapted to desert

▲ Frogs have well-developed hind legs, which are used for swimming and jumping.

▲ Toads have thicker, rougher, and drier skin than frogs.

▲ Salamanders, like this red-backed salamander, walk on land with a bending back-and-forth motion of their bodies. They eat insects and worms.

life. Because water is scarce, some toads lay their eggs in a moist foam that they produce so that the eggs won't dry out. Other desert toads depend on rainstorms to provide enough water for the tadpoles to develop.

Another group of amphibians has tails. Two members of this group are salamanders (sal´ə man´dərz) and newts (no͞ots). Like frogs, most salamanders can breathe through their skin and live near water. They have moist skin, four legs, and long tails. One type of salamander, the mud puppy, spends its whole life in water and breathes through external gills—gills on the outside of its body. Some newts can live either in water or on land when they are adults.

DILEMMA

Taking Care of the Bay

Rivers that flow through a very large area drain into the Chesapeake Bay region. Industries along these waterways give off wastes that end up in the bay and might poison the fish and other animals. Farms from many miles away also add to the pollution. Some of the chemicals used on crops and some farm animal droppings wash into nearby streams and then into the bay.

People need the products of the industries. They need the food that the farms grow. How can people keep pollution out of the bay and still have the jobs and products they need?

Think About It Get together with your classmates to find the best way to protect Chesapeake Bay from pollution. But don't forget the needs and problems of the people living near the bay or the rivers that feed into the bay. Divide up the class and pretend to be fishers, farmers, townspeople, and businesspeople. Explain your problems and work out a plan that everyone can accept.

What are reptiles?

▲ Snakes do not have legs. Most snakes move by curving their bodies into S-shaped patterns and then pushing against the ground.

Snakes are one type of reptile, a group of cold-blooded vertebrates that generally live on land. There are three major groups of reptiles: snakes and lizards, crocodiles, and turtles. The crocodile group includes alligators and the turtle group includes tortoises.

A reptile's body has a layer of skin that is covered with scales. This scaly skin helps the animal retain moisture even in hot, dry climates. Reptiles have lungs and breathe air. Except for snakes, most reptiles have four legs.

Snakes can move very quickly to attack their prey. Some coil their bodies and then suddenly strike. If the prey is larger than the snake's mouth, the snake can unhinge its jaws to swallow the prey whole.

Both snakes and lizards smell and detect body heat with sense organs on their tongues. They flick their tongues to detect body heat or scent. This way they can locate their prey.

Turtles generally live in water and tortoises on land. Both are toothless. Tortoises can grow to a large size and live for as long as 150 years. Giant sea turtles live their whole lives in the ocean. They come onshore only to lay their eggs in the sand. As soon as the eggs hatch, the tiny baby turtles race down the beach to the ocean water.

◄ Most reptiles, like this lizard, lay eggs. Their eggs have a tough covering, which helps keep them from drying out.

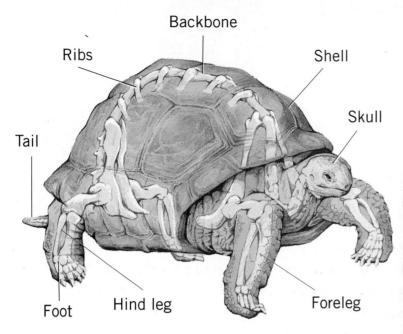

Backbone

Ribs

Shell

Skull

Tail

Foot

Hind leg

Foreleg

◀ If someone says "turtle," what do you think of? It's probably the shell. Turtles and tortoises are the only vertebrates with shells. Unlike the shells of crabs or other arthropods, the shell of the turtle is not its skeleton. Tucked inside the shell is a complete animal with a backbone.

▲ Crocodiles and alligators are closely related. In Florida you can find both, and unless you're looking at both of them at the same time, they're hard to tell apart. The crocodile's snout is more pointed than the alligator's snout.

Be a Scientist

MINDS-ON ACTIVITY

Can you predict an alligator's sex?

Some scientists believe temperature determines an alligator's sex. They think the sex depends on how warm the alligator egg is during incubation. Cooler temperatures (26°C–32°C) seem to produce relatively more females, while higher temperatures (33°C–36°C) produce relatively more males.

Pretend that the earth's temperature becomes warmer than it is now. If the average temperature became 35°C, predict what would happen to the earth's alligator population. Could this warming trend have any effect on other animal or plant populations?

How are you doing?

1. What are four traits of fish?
2. What does the word amphibian mean? How does this relate to this group of animals?
3. **Think** How is a reptile's egg different from that of an amphibian's? How does the difference help reptiles survive on land?
4. **Think** On a cool day a lizard may sit on a sunny rock. On a hot day it might hide under the rock. Explain why.

What are some characteristics of birds?

Birds are vertebrates that have two legs, two wings, and a body covered by feathers. They have beaks, but no teeth.

Birds are considered warm-blooded. Warm-blooded animals have a constant body temperature, even when the temperature around them changes.

Most birds lay from two to six eggs at a time. The eggs are large and well-protected by their hard shells. Once the eggs are laid, one or both parents take care of the eggs.

YOU CAN HELP

The piping plovers of Chesapeake Bay are endangered, so areas of some beaches are set aside to protect these birds. You can help by keeping out of protected areas. If you take your dog to a beach, keep it on a leash so that it will not stray into nesting areas.

SIDE TRIP

Adaptations in the Galápagos

The Galápagos (gə lä´pə gos´) are a group of islands in the Pacific Ocean along the equator and west of South America. Birds called Galápagos finches live there. These finches differ from island to island.

On each island, the finches have different adaptations and eat different foods. Birds that feed on small seeds have small beaks. Birds that feed on large seeds have larger, stronger beaks for cracking the seeds. The woodpecker finch has a narrow beak and eats insects,

which it digs from the bark of trees. The woodpecker finch uses a spine from a cactus as a tool to get at the insects. A true woodpecker uses its long, strong beak to remove insects from the bark.

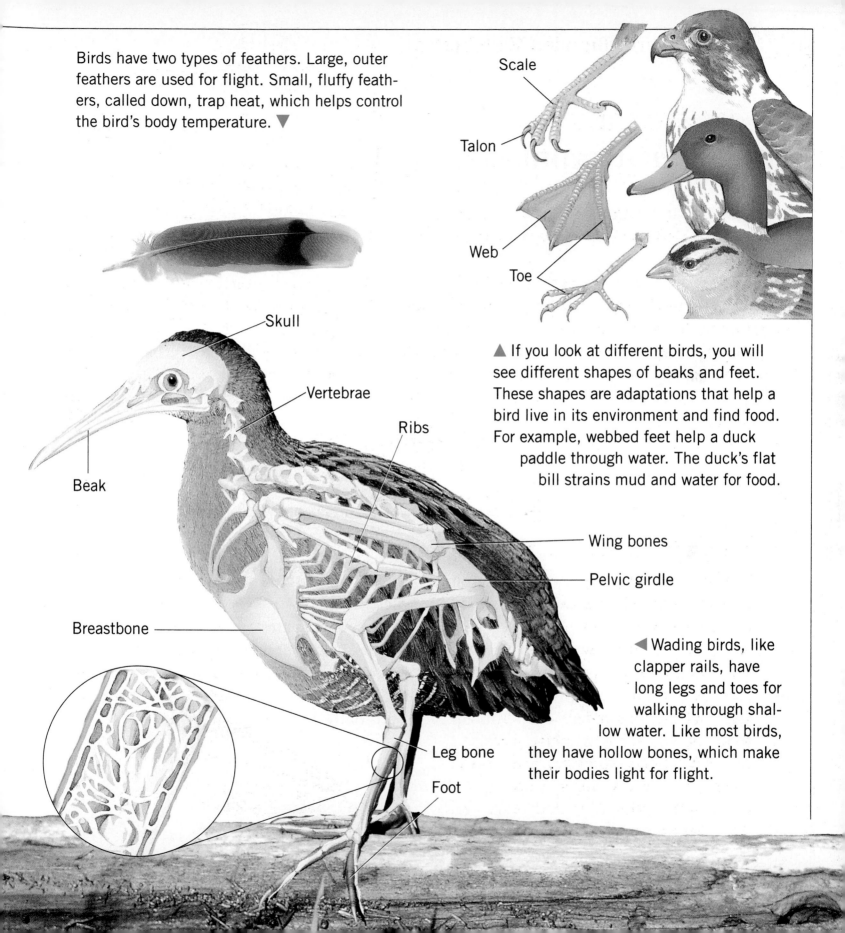

Birds have two types of feathers. Large, outer feathers are used for flight. Small, fluffy feathers, called down, trap heat, which helps control the bird's body temperature. ▼

Scale

Talon

Web

Toe

Skull

Vertebrae

Ribs

Beak

Wing bones

Pelvic girdle

Breastbone

▲ If you look at different birds, you will see different shapes of beaks and feet. These shapes are adaptations that help a bird live in its environment and find food. For example, webbed feet help a duck paddle through water. The duck's flat bill strains mud and water for food.

◄ Wading birds, like clapper rails, have long legs and toes for walking through shallow water. Like most birds, they have hollow bones, which make their bodies light for flight.

Leg bone

Foot

What are mammals?

▲ Mammals are the only animals that have milk glands and nurse their young.

▲ Mammals are the only animals that have hair or fur.

The Chesapeake Bay area is home to muskrats, mink, deer, and people. All these animals are mammals, and they have several characteristics in common. Mammals are warm-blooded and have hair or fur on their bodies. The hair helps keep in body heat.

All mammals have eggs that are fertilized inside the female's body. Here the young grow and develop before they are born. The young are usually very well developed before they are born. This extra time for development helps each baby survive. This is important, because mammals have only one baby or a few babies at a time.

Mammals are the only animals that have milk glands, which they use to nurse their young. Unlike some other kinds of animals, most mammals spend a long time feeding and caring for their young. And mammals often live in family groups to share the work of protecting the young.

Mammals have well-developed circulatory and nervous systems. The heart pumps oxygen-rich blood to all parts of the body. The blood picks up oxygen and gives off carbon dioxide in the lungs. The brain directs the action of the body. And nerves carry messages from the brain to all parts of the body.

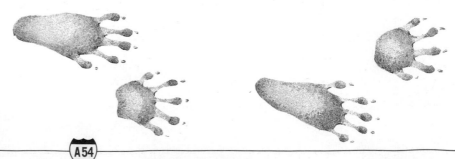

◀ Humans are mammals. Like other mammals, humans take care of the young until the young are adults. Humans have complex behavior patterns and interact with each other in many ways.

 ▲ Mammals move from place to place to find food or escape enemies. Many run on land using all four limbs.

What are some examples of mammals?

Mammals are classified into three groups, based on the way they produce their young. Most mammals are **placental** (plə sen´təl) **mammals.** Until they are ready to be born, these animals develop inside the mother's body. There they get food and oxygen through a structure called the placenta.

Another group of mammals are the **marsupials** (mär soo´pē əlz). Their young are born before they are fully developed. After they are born, the young move to a pouch on the mother's body. Here they get milk from the mother's milk glands.

The third group of mammals lay eggs. The duck-billed platypus and the spiny anteater are the only species of egg-laying mammals.

▲ This opossum is a marsupial that lives in North America. Most kinds of marsupials, such as kangaroos and koalas, are found in Australia.

Be a Scientist

MINDS-ON ACTIVITY

How do mammals keep cool?

You know that you sweat when you are warm. Most mammals sweat to keep cool. Sweat makes the skin wet. How do you think this affects body temperature? Design an experiment to test the effect of moisture on your skin. What does the moisture do that cools you?

Many mammals have sweat glands on only a few parts of their bodies. For example, cats and dogs sweat only on their paws. What else do cats and dogs do when they're warm? How is this related to sweating?

◀ River otters have short, thick fur. They have webbed feet for swimming. Their tails are long and a little flattened. They are fast swimmers, which helps them catch prey.

◀ The bat is a placental mammal that can fly. Its front limbs are used as wings. Bats are active at night. Most feed on insects, although some feed on fruit nectar.

Whales and dolphins are placental mammals that live in the water. Their limbs are fins or flippers that help the animal move through the water. Although they spend their entire lives in the water, they must come to the surface to breathe air. ▼

▲ This furry animal lays eggs, has webbed feet, a flat tail, and a bill like a duck's. It's a duck-billed platypus, an egg-laying mammal.

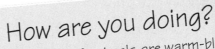

How are you doing?

1. What kind of animals are warm-blooded, and what does that mean?
2. What characteristics of birds help them fly?
3. **Think** The layer of fur on a mammal's body keeps the animal warm, especially when the hairs "stand on end," making the fur thick and fluffy. How else might having the hairs "stand on end" help a mammal survive?
4. **Think** What advantages do the young of placental mammals have over the young of marsupial mammals?

Looking Back

Words and Concepts

Match the description in Column A with the vertebrate group in Column B.

Column A

1. Produce milk, lay eggs
2. Cold-blooded, live on land, have scales
3. Cold-blooded, have fins and streamlined body
4. Young finish developing in mother's pouch
5. Live in water, then on land
6. Warm-blooded, lay eggs, have feathers
7. Warm-blooded, young develop inside mother's body

Column B

a. Fish
b. Amphibians
c. Reptiles
d. Birds
e. Egg-laying mammals
f. Marsupials
g. Placental mammals

Applied Thinking Skills

Answer the following questions. You can use words, drawings, and diagrams in your answer.

8. Both fish and mammals take in oxygen. How is the process different in the two groups of animals?
9. A bat has wings and flies, yet it is classified as a mammal. A penguin cannot fly, yet it is classified as a bird. Explain the reasons for the classifications of these animals.
10. **Your World** Is the climate where you live warm or cold? Would you expect mammals that live in your area to have lots of fur? Explain your answer.

Show What You Know

How are cats and dogs classified?

Observe and Collect Data

1. If you have a pet cat and dog, study the animal's characteristics for this activity. If you do not, get permission from your parents to visit a friend or neighbor to observe their pets. Ask the pet owner before touching or getting close to an animal that does not know you. Some animals may be frightened and might scratch or bite.

2. Observe a dog and a cat. How can you tell they are vertebrates? What else do you know about them? Record your answers in your Activity Journal.

3. Carefully observe a dog and list its characteristics. Look for details. Look at the nails on its paws. Describe its fur. Record the shape of the dog's eyes and ears. If you can do it safely, observe the animal's teeth. Draw a picture of the dog.

4. Next observe the dog's behavior. Does it run and jump? What noises does it make? What type of food does it eat?

5. Repeat steps 3 and 4 with a cat.

Share Your Results

1. What characteristics do cats and dogs share?
2. How can you tell that both cats and dogs are mammals?
3. In what ways do cats and dogs differ?

Process Skills

Observing, Classifying, Interpreting data

Materials

cat

dog

Classification

Show what you have learned about classification, animals, and the other four kingdoms. Work by yourself, with a partner, or in a group. Select one activity.

Writer Write a story about living in the Chesapeake Bay wetlands. Describe the kinds of living things you would see and classify each into its kingdom. Further classify the animals as invertebrates or vertebrates.

Songwriter Write a song about one or more of the living things found in the Chesapeake Bay wetlands. You might wish to write the song as if the organism were singing about itself and its classification group.

Artist Make a drawing or a model of an organism from each of the five kingdoms. Display your drawings or models for the class.

Mime Act out the characteristics and behavior of one or more animals. Ask your classmates to identify the animal you are imitating.

Classification Expert Make a classification key, such as the one you used in the Explore Activity. Choose any group of organisms and design your key to be used for identifying different organisms within this group. For example, your key might be used to sort organisms into the five kingdoms, or it might be used to sort vertebrates into their five groups.

Zoo Planner Your city or town wants to build a new zoo, and you're in charge. Make a plan or a map of your zoo. Think about how many displays you would have. How many different kinds of animals would you show? How would you group the animals into separate areas?

Glossary

amphibian (am fib´ē ən) A cold-blooded vertebrate that lives part of its life in water and part on land. (page A48)

arachnid (ə rak´nid) An arthropod with four pairs of legs. Spiders, ticks, and mites are arachnids. (page A35)

arthropod (är´thrō päd´) An invertebrate that has an exoskeleton and jointed legs. Insects, spiders, lobsters, and crabs are arthropods. (page A34)

bacterium (bak tir´ē əm) A simple one-celled organism that belongs to the moneran kingdom.(page A12)

crustacean (krus tā´shən) An arthropod with five pairs of legs. Lobsters, crabs, and shrimp are crustaceans. (page A35)

echinoderm (ē ki´nō dərm´) An inverte-brate that has spiny skin. Starfish are echinoderms. (page A32)

exoskeleton (eks´ō skel´ə tən) A skeleton on the outside of the body. The "shell" of a lobster is its exoskeleton. (page A34)

fungus (fun´gəs) A many-celled organism that is a decomposer, cannot make its own food, and cannot move. Mushrooms, molds, and yeasts are fungi. (page A12)

invertebrate (in vər´tə brit) An animal that does not have a backbone. (page A24)

kingdom (kiŋ´dəm) The broadest category of organisms. Scientists classify all living things into five kingdoms. (page A10)

marsupial (mär soo´pē əl) A mammal whose young are born before they are completely developed. The young finish developing in the mother's pouch. (page A56)

mollusk (mäl´əsk) An invertebrate with a soft body covered by a mantle. (page A32)

moneran (mə ner´ən) The simplest one-celled organism. (page A12)

nucleus (noo´klē əs) The control center of a cell, containing DNA. (page A14)

placental mammal (plə sen´təl mam´əl) A mammal whose young develop inside the mother's body. (page A56)

protist (prōt´ist) An organism that has a more complex cell structure than moner-ans and is often one-celled. (page A12)

species (spē´shēz) The smallest classification group. (page A11)

spore (spōr) A special cell that fungi use to reproduce. (page A16)

vertebrate (vər´tə brit) An animal that has a backbone. (page A42)

Unit A Index

Boldface numerals denote glossary terms. Italic numerals denote illustrations.

Credits

Photographs

1 Paul von Stroheim/Westlight; 2–3 Bob Burch/Bruce Coleman Inc.; 3B Guy Powers/Envision; 4BR Stephen J. Krasemann/DRK Photo; 4L Kim Taylor/Bruce Coleman Inc.; 4TR David Ulmer/Stock, Boston; 5 Ken Karp*; 6B Stephen Frisch*; 6T Barbara von Hoffmann/Tom Stack & Associates; 7 Carr Clifton/AllStock; 9 Elliott Smith*; 10 Stephen Frisch*; 12C Eric Grave/Photo Researchers; 12L Manfred Kage/Peter Arnold, Inc.; 12R Stephen P. Parker/Photo Researchers; 13L E. R. Degginger/Earth Scenes; 13R Bob & Clara Calhoun/Bruce Coleman Inc.; 14 David Phillips/Photo Researchers; 15B Dwight R. Kuhn/DRK Photo; 15TL Michael Abbey/Photo Researchers; 15TR Tim Davis*; 16 A. Davies/Bruce Coleman Inc.; 17B Manfred Kage/Peter Arnold, Inc.; 17C Kevin Schafer/Tom Stack & Associates; 17TL Michael P. Gadomski/Photo Researchers; 17TR Darrell Gulin/AllStock; 18 Charles Krebs/AllStock; 19 E. R. Degginger/Bruce Coleman Inc.; 22 Stephen Frisch*; 23 Elliott Smith*; 24B GHP Studio*; 24C Stephen Frisch*; 24T GHP Studio*; 25 David Muench; 25 (inset) John Gerlach/DRK Photo; 27 Elliott Smith*; 28 David Sailors/The Stock Market; 29BR Fred Bavendam/Peter Arnold, Inc.; 29BL Ken Karp*; 29T William Amos/Bruce Coleman Inc.; 30B Tom E. Adams/Peter Arnold, Inc.; 30T Kathie Atkinson/Oxford Scientific Films/Animals, Animals; 31 Stephen Frisch*; 32–33T David Muench; 32B Mike Severns/Tom Stack & Associates; 34B Ed

Reschke/Peter Arnold, Inc.; 34T Brent Petersen/The Stock Market; 37B Donald Specker/Animals, Animals; 37TL J. & L. Waldman/Bruce Coleman Inc.; 37TR Jack Dermid/Bruce Coleman Inc.; 38B Runk-Schoenberger/Grant Heilman Photography; 38TC Ken Karp*; 38BL Scala/Art Resource; 39B Hans Pfletschinger/Peter Arnold, Inc.; 39T Jeff Rotman; 40 J.T. Miller/The Stock Market; 42B Stephen Frisch*; 42T Runk-Schoenberger/Grant Heilman Photography; 43B Stephen Frisch*; 43R Jack A. Barrie/Bruce Coleman Inc.; 43T David Muench; 45BC S. Neilsen/DRK Photo; 45BL John Gerlach/DRK Photo; 45BR Daniel J. Cox/AllStock; 45T Wayne Lankinen/DRK Photo; 46BL Joe McDonald/Bruce Coleman Inc.; 46BR Tom McHugh/AllStock; 47 Anne Dowie*; 48B Michael P. Gadomski/Photo Researchers; 48T Stephen Dalton/Photo Researchers; 49 John Burnley/Bruce Coleman Inc.; 50B E. R. Degginger/Animals, Animals; 50T Zig Leszczynski/Animals, Animals; 51 M. H. Sharp/Photo Researchers; 52B Tim Davis/Photo Researchers; 52T Ken Karp*; 53B Keith H. Murakami/Tom Stack & Associates; 53TL GHP Studio*; 54B Diana L. Stratton/Tom Stack & Associates; 54T William H. Mullins/Photo Researchers; 55B Thomas Kitchin/Tom Stack & Associates; 55T David Ulmer/Stock, Boston; 56B Edward R. Degginger/Bruce Coleman Inc.; 56T Stephen J. Krasemann/DRK Photo; 57B Brian Parker/ Tom Stack & Associates; 57TR Dave Watts/Tom Stack & Associates; 57TL Stephen Dalton/Photo Researchers; 58 Renee Lynn; 59 Ken Lax*

Special thanks to Malcolm X Elementary School, Berkeley, California; Franklin Year-Round School, Oakland, California; Carl B. Munck Elementary School, Oakland, California; Hintil Ku Ka Child Care Center, Oakland, California.

*Photographed expressly for Addison-Wesley Publishing Company, Inc.

Illustrations

Molly Babich 4, 6, 13, 28, 29, 30–31, 32, 33, 36, 46
Nea Bisek 8, 23, 26, 41, 59
Jane McCreary 8, 26, 37, 44
Larry Pearson 20–21
Rolin Graphics 2
Randy Vergoustraete 60–61
Cyndie Wooley 10, 14, 15, 16, 35, 51, 53, 54–55

Text

20–21 Peggy Thomson, *Auks, Rocks and the Odd Dinosaur* (New York: Thomas Y. Crowell Junior Books, 1985). Copyright © 1985 by Peggy Thomson. Reprinted by permission of HarperCollins Publishers.

Urban Garden

You don't have to live in a rural or suburban area to experience one of the great joys of nature—gardening. City dwellers know that with some hard work and tender loving care, a small plot of land can become a place of beauty like the one shown on these pages.

You can learn a great deal about living things by cultivating a garden. You can observe the changes that take place as tiny seeds mature and become full-grown plants. You can discover that different kinds of seeds produce different kinds of plants, some with flowers, others bearing fruit or vegetables for your table. You can also observe the interactions of the plants with insects and other living things around them. But one thing you are not able to observe are the cells that make up each of these living things. If you could see them, what do you think they would look like?

- What cell parts do all living things have in common?

- How do cells reproduce?

- How are traits passed from parents to offspring?

CELLS & HEREDITY

URBAN
GARDEN

Activities

Features

Urban spaces turned into garden places

Chapter 1

Cells

Look at the living things shown here. You can see they are different. You can certainly distinguish plants from animals, and yellow cucumbers from butterflies. However, suppose you were to look at a tiny part of some living thing through a microscope. You would see cells. **Cells** are the basic units of all living things.

Cells are the "building blocks" of which all living things are made. Some living things, such as the plants and

animals shown here, are made up of many cells. Other living things are made of a single cell.

Your body is made up of millions of cells. These cells make you the living, breathing human being that you are. There are blood cells, muscle cells, and many other kinds of cells. Each kind of cell has a specific job, or function. Some carry oxygen and others help you run and jump. Still others help you to think, see, and smell.

The plants in your garden also are made up of many different kinds of cells, such as root cells, stem cells, and leaf cells. These cells work together to make any organism the specific kind of living thing that it is.

Think of something that is constructed of smaller units. In your Science Journal, describe how this object is like a human body made of cells.

Round, yellow cucumbers that look like lemons

NET WT. 20G

CORN, SWEET

Golden Cross Bantam T.51
(Hybrid)

Late-season; Yellow

Explore Activity

How do plant and animal cells compare?

Process Skills

Observing, Comparing, Inferring

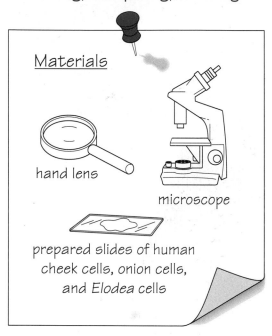

Materials

hand lens

microscope

prepared slides of human
cheek cells, onion cells,
and Elodea cells

Observe and Collect Data

1. Use a hand lens to observe and study the slides of plant and animal cells.
2. Place the slide of the cheek cells on the stage of a microscope. Use each power of the microscope to study the cells. In your Activity Journal, draw what you see.
3. Repeat step 2 with the slide of the onion cells.
4. Repeat step 2 with the slide of the *Elodea* cells.

Share Your Results

Compare your drawings of the cells with those of some of your classmates. Did you observe the same things?

Draw Conclusions

1. What do plant and animal cells have in common?
2. How are plant cells and animal cells different?

Apply What You Know

Which can help you learn more about plant and animal cells, a hand lens or a microscope? Explain your answer.

Cheek cells

Onion cells

Elodea cells

What makes a cell?

Cells contain tiny structures called **organelles** (ôr´gə nelz´). These structures work together to help the cell function, much as the organs of your body work together to help it function.

You have observed that all cells are not the same. However, they do have certain organelles in common. These are shown in the drawing on these pages. Some of these organelles can be seen with an ordinary microscope. Others can be seen only with a more powerful kind of microscope.

Mitochondria (mīt´ō kän´drē ə) produce energy in the cell. They use oxygen to change nutrients into energy. One cell may have as many as 2,000 of these organelles.

Vacuoles (vak´yōō ōlz´) store water, food, and wastes in the cell. Some vacuoles surround waste products and deposit them outside the cell membrane. Others help to transport food through the cell. The vacuoles of most animal cells are very small. Plant cells have much larger vacuoles for food storage.

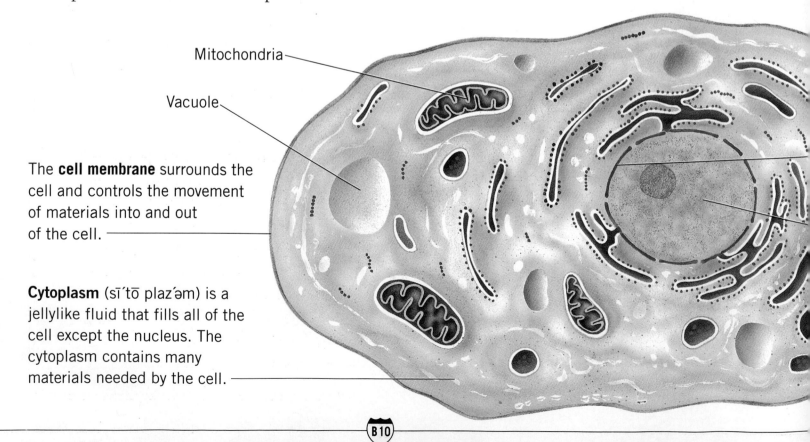

Mitochondria

Vacuole

The **cell membrane** surrounds the cell and controls the movement of materials into and out of the cell.

Cytoplasm (sī´tō plaz´əm) is a jellylike fluid that fills all of the cell except the nucleus. The cytoplasm contains many materials needed by the cell.

Ribosomes (rī´bə sōmz´) help the cell to make proteins. All parts of your body, including your muscles, skin, and hair, have many different types of proteins. Your blood contains proteins that help it to clot and other proteins that protect you against infections.

Cilia (sil´ē ə) are tiny hairs attached to the cell membranes of certain types of cells. Some kinds of single-celled organisms use cilia to help them move. Some cells in your body have cilia. Cilia on the cells lining your windpipe help remove any dust you inhale.

Ribosome

The **nuclear membrane** surrounds the nucleus and keeps it separate from the rest of the cell. This membrane also controls the flow of materials into and out of the nucleus.

The **nucleus** (nōō´klē əs) is the control center for the cell's activity. It interacts with other parts of the cell to help the cell use nutrients, dispose of wastes, reproduce, and carry out its special role.

Cell Theory

Most cells are too small to be seen with the unaided eye. For this reason, the nature and structure of individual cells were unknown until the microscope was invented.

In the 1660s, Robert Hooke, an English physicist and biologist, used his newly developed compound microscope to study a thin slice of cork from the bark of a tree. He found that the cork was made up of a series of small, boxlike spaces. These spaces, which Hooke called cells, were the outer walls of dead cells that had once been part of a living plant.

At about the same time, other scientists observed living cells in such materials as blood and scrapings of skin. Organisms consisting of single cells were observed in samples of pond water.

Since the mid-1600s, improvements in microscopes have made it possible for scientists to identify cell parts and their functions. These discoveries have led to the development and acceptance of the cell theory, which states that all living things are made of cells, cells are basic units of structure, and all cells come from other living cells.

How is a plant cell different from an animal cell?

Plants are very different from animals. Most plants in your garden have roots, stems, and leaves and can produce their own food. Many of the tasks carried out by plant cells are different from those performed by animal cells. Plant cells and animal cells are not exactly alike. These drawings show a comparison of a plant cell and an animal cell.

A Visit to a Pond

People might observe various kinds of wildlife and plants that are found in and near a pond. But many organisms found in a pond are not visible to the unaided eye. Most ponds of water are alive with varieties of single-celled organisms.

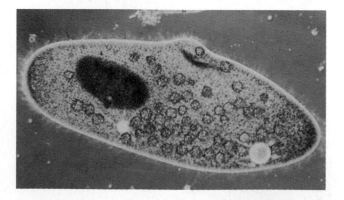

One organism found in pond water is the paramecium (par´ə mē´sē əm). The organelles of its single cell do the jobs of mouth, stomach, feet, and hands. The cilia that surround the cell membrane move the paramecium through the water and push food towards its mouth.

The food vacuole absorbs and digests food, transports nutrients, and then deposits wastes outside the cell.

A paramecium also has a nucleus. This organelle serves as a control center for the organism, directing all cell functions, including reproduction.

Chloroplasts (klôr´ə plasts) are the organelles that enable plants to make food. They contain chlorophyll, which gives plants their green color. Chlorophyll traps the sun's energy, which plants use to make the nutrients they need to live and grow. These nutrients also provide food for animals that eat the plants. Some leaf cells have as many as 100 chloroplasts.

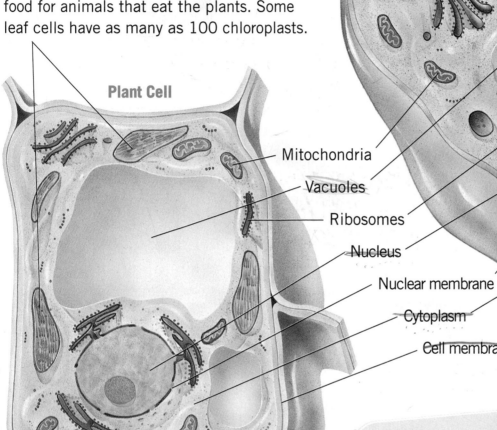

Plant Cell

Animal Cell

Mitochondria

Vacuoles

Ribosomes

Nucleus

Nuclear membrane

Cytoplasm

Cell membrane

A plant cell has a **cell wall** in addition to a cell membrane. This wall protects the plant cell and gives the plant its rigid shape. Cell walls also contain channels that allow fluids to circulate throughout the plant.

How are you doing?

1. Why are cells called the building blocks of life?
2. What are mitochondria, and what is their function?
3. **Think** Why are chloroplasts important to animals, even though they are found only in plant cells?
4. **Think** How are plant and animal cells similar? How are they different?

What are some kinds of animal cells?

Recall that your body is made up of millions of cells, and every one of those cells has its own job. So, too, does every cell in a dog, a sunflower, or a bee.

A cell that makes up a one-celled organism carries out all of the tasks necessary for the organism to live. This is not true of the cells in many-celled organisms. Most many-celled organisms have cells that are specialized. For example, in the human body, bone cells have a different role from that of skin cells. Therefore, each kind of cell is different.

Sometimes a cell's appearance and shape is a clue to its role. For instance, some nerve cells are more than 2 meters long and are thinner than a wire. These cells help to transfer messages between the brain and spinal cord and all other parts of the body. Most kinds of animal cells have very small vacuoles, but fat cells can be recognized by their large vacuoles.

In a complex organism such as a human, cells do not function individually. They are organized into different types of tissues. A tissue is a group of specialized cells that perform the same function.

There are many types of tissue in the human body, including skin, bone, fat, muscle, blood, and nerve. Skin tissue forms skin and lining of body parts. Bone tissue supports and protects body parts. Fat is stored as a reserve fuel in fat tissues. Muscle tissue helps body parts move. Food, water, and oxygen are carried in blood tissue. Nerve tissue sends messages to and from the brain and spinal cord.

Be a Scientist

HANDS-ON ACTIVITY

How do animal cells vary?

1. Use a microscope to observe the prepared slides of skin cells and blood cells.

2. 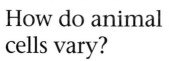 In your Activity Journal, draw a skin cell and a blood cell and label any parts that you can identify.

3. How does the rounded shape of the blood cells help them move through the blood vessels? How does the shape of skin cells help them cover the body?

▲ Nerve cells are the longest cells in the body. These cells carry messages throughout the body.

▲ Skin cells combine to form a thin, protective layer over the entire surface of the body.

▲ There are three different kinds of muscle cells in the human body. They are cardiac, smooth, and skeletal muscle cells. The above skeletal muscle cells make up tissues that move the bones.

▲ The large vacuoles in fat cells are used for the storage of fat.

▲ The disk-shaped red blood cells transport oxygen throughout the body.

What are some kinds of plant cells?

Like animals, the plants in your garden come in many sizes and shapes. Some plants and plantlike organisms have simple structures. Others are more complex and are made up of millions of cells.

The plant shown here is a flowering plant. The flower contains the reproductive organs of the plant. Many kinds of plants, such as evergreen trees, do not produce flowers. However, all complex plants have the same basic structures—roots, stems, leaves, and reproductive organs. Roots anchor the plant in the ground and absorb water and minerals from the soil. Stems support the leaves and reproductive organs and transport water, minerals, and nutrients throughout the plant. Leaves contain the materials that the plant uses to make food. These photographs show some of the kinds of plant cells that carry out these functions.

Be a Scientist

HANDS-ON
ACTIVITY

How do plant cells vary?

1. Use a microscope to observe a prepared slide of a leaf cross section.
2. In your Activity Journal, draw part of the leaf and label any cell parts that you can identify.
3. What structures can you find in the middle layer of cells, but not in the upper and lower layers? What is the function of the middle layers of cells in a leaf?

▲ **Reproductive cells**
Structures within the flower contain the reproductive cells of the plant. The pollen grains shown here contain the male reproductive cells.

Don't damage the leaves of plants. Without their leaves, plants can't use the sun's energy to make food.

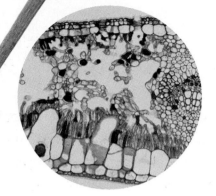

▲ Leaf cells

The surface tissue of a leaf is made up of epidermis (ep´əder´mis) cells. This tissue forms the leaf's outer protective layers. Cells in the two inner layers of the leaf are food-producing cells. These cells contain most of the chloroplasts. As in the stem, xylem and phloem cells of the leaf vein transport water, minerals, and nutrients. Guard cells help control the movement of carbon dioxide, oxygen, and water into and out of the leaf.

▲ Stem cells

The cells in the outer layers of stems form surface tissues that support the plant and protect the stem. Beneath the surface tissues are two kinds of transport tissues in a plant stem. These tissues are made of xylem (zī´ləm) cells and phloem (flō´əm´) cells. Xylem tissue transports water and minerals from the roots to the leaves. Phloem tissue transports nutrients that are made in the leaves to all parts of the plant.

How are you doing?

1. In the human body, why are the vacuoles in fat cells larger than those in other types of cells?
2. Name six types of tissue in the human body and tell what each does.
3. **Think** Why are all the cells that make up a type of tissue similar to one another?
4. **Think** Why is the cell that makes up a single-celled organism less specialized than the cells that make up a many-celled organism?

Taking a Closer Look

What do you see when you look at an object such as a building or a tree? It all depends on your point of view. Look at the wall of the building in the top photograph. This building is located at the National Autonomous University of Mexico.

From the distance the top photograph was taken, you can tell that many of the walls are covered with colorful and complex designs. If you were to move closer, you would be able to see more detail and perhaps identify different parts of the design.

What would you see if you got very close to one of the walls, as in the bottom photograph? You might not be able to see much of the overall design. However, you would discover that the design is a mosaic (mō zā´ik) made up of thousands of individual colored tiles.

Which viewpoint of the building do you prefer? Now think about that tree. How does what you see when you look at a tree change as you move closer to it? What viewpoint would be similar to the one in which you see the individual tiles of the mosaic?

Data Collection and Analysis

Can you calculate the number of cells?

Observe and Collect Data

1. Suppose a cell divided every hour. How many cells would you have after 12 hours? For this experiment, assume that no cells die during the 12-hour period.

2. 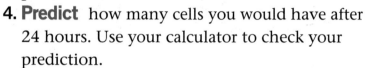 Use a calculator or pencil and paper to calculate the number of cells produced each hour and record this information in your Activity Journal.

3. In your Activity Journal, make a graph to show your findings. Along the horizontal axis put the number of cells produced every hour. Along the vertical axis put a mark for each of the 12 hours.

4. **Predict** how many cells you would have after 24 hours. Use your calculator to check your prediction.

Draw Conclusions

How many cells were produced after 12 hours? Bacteria divide much faster than this experimental cell. Some bacteria can divide every 30 minutes. If bacteria can divide this fast, why isn't the earth overrun with bacteria?

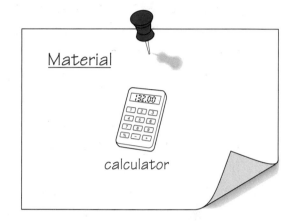

Material

calculator

Looking Back

Words and Concepts

Match the description in Column A with the correct term in Column B.

Column A
1. Something all living things are made up of
2. The longest cells in the human body
3. A group of similar cells working together
4. The organelle that controls the cell
5. An organelle that is usually much larger in plant cells than in animal cells
6. The plant organelle that contains chlorophyll

Column B
a. Vacuole
b. Chloroplast
c. Nerve
d. Tissue
e. Nucleus
f. Cells

Applied Thinking Skills

Answer the following questions. You can use words, drawings, and diagrams in your answers.

7. The photograph shows plant cells that have organelles that contain starch. What is the function of these cells?

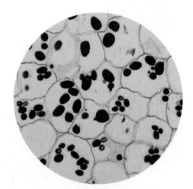

8. Why are the cells that make up a complex organism more specialized than those of a simple organism?

9. A paramecium is a single-celled organism with organelles that function as hands, feet, mouth, stomach, and waste disposal system. Draw a picture of a make-believe organism that can do everything with only one cell. You may only use the following organelles: cell membrane, nucleus, vacuoles, mitochondria, chloroplasts, and cilia. What is the role of each of these organelles?

10. **Your World** Compare the structure and function of cells that make up surface tissues in plants and animals.

Show What You Know

Can you make a cell?

Observe and Collect Data

1. Use what you have learned in this chapter to draw an animal cell and a plant cell on index cards.
2. On the back of each card, identify the kind of cell you drew.
3. Look at the drawings made by your classmates. Sort the drawings into two groups—plant cells and animal cells.

Draw Conclusions

1. Did all students sort the drawings in the same way?
2. How are the plant and animal cells different? How are they alike?
3. Why are chloroplasts found in plant cells? Why are chloroplasts not in animal cells?

Process Skills

Observing, Making models, Classifying

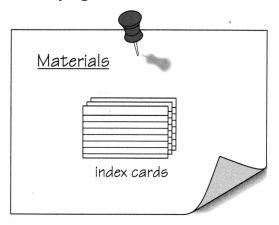

Materials

index cards

Chapter 2

How Cells Reproduce

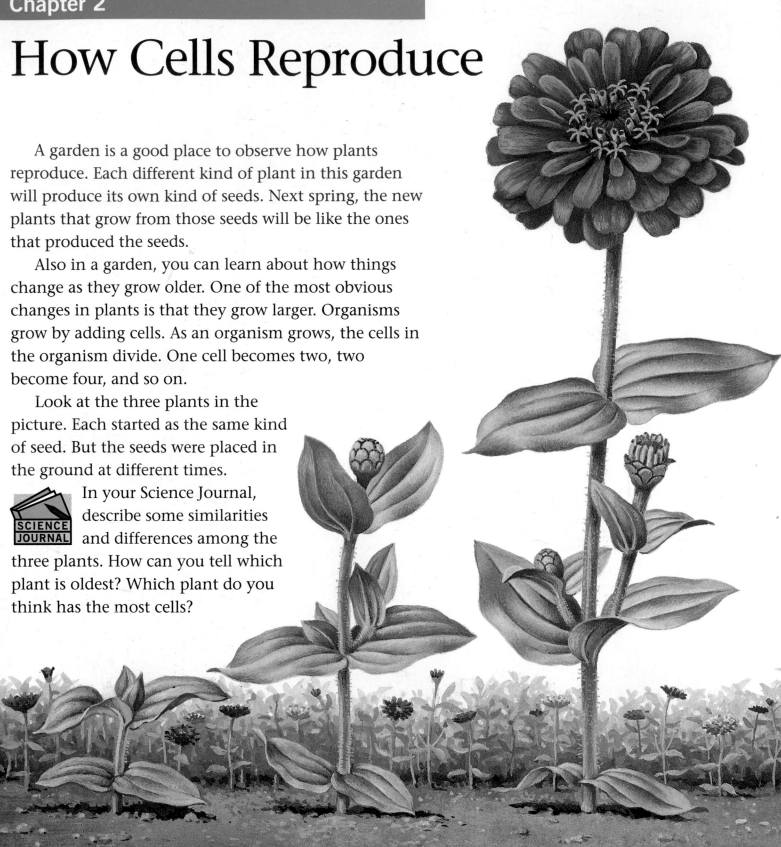

A garden is a good place to observe how plants reproduce. Each different kind of plant in this garden will produce its own kind of seeds. Next spring, the new plants that grow from those seeds will be like the ones that produced the seeds.

Also in a garden, you can learn about how things change as they grow older. One of the most obvious changes in plants is that they grow larger. Organisms grow by adding cells. As an organism grows, the cells in the organism divide. One cell becomes two, two become four, and so on.

Look at the three plants in the picture. Each started as the same kind of seed. But the seeds were placed in the ground at different times.

SCIENCE JOURNAL In your Science Journal, describe some similarities and differences among the three plants. How can you tell which plant is oldest? Which plant do you think has the most cells?

You can have your own mini-garden on a patio, deck, or balcony.

Explore Activity

What can you learn about cell division?

Process Skills

Inferring, Communicating, Hypothesizing

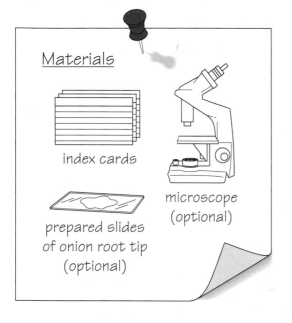

Materials

index cards

microscope (optional)

prepared slides of onion root tip (optional)

Observe and Collect Data

1. Use a microscope to observe a prepared slide of an onion root tip. Compare what you see through the microscope with the photograph on page B25.

2. Now study the photograph carefully. Observe the cells in different parts of the root tip. Try to identify cells that seem to be dividing.

3. On several index cards, draw what you think might be cells dividing. Describe what you drew on the back of each card.

4. Arrange your cards in order to show different stages of cell division.

Share Your Results

How did your arrangement of drawings compare with that of other students or groups?

Draw Conclusions

1. Where does most of the cell division seem to be taking place in the onion root? How do you know?

2. Why do you think cells divide fastest in this part of the plant?

Apply What You Know

One part of the onion plant that you might eat—the bulb—stores food and water for the rest of the plant. Knowing this, how do you think cells in this part of the onion plant might look?

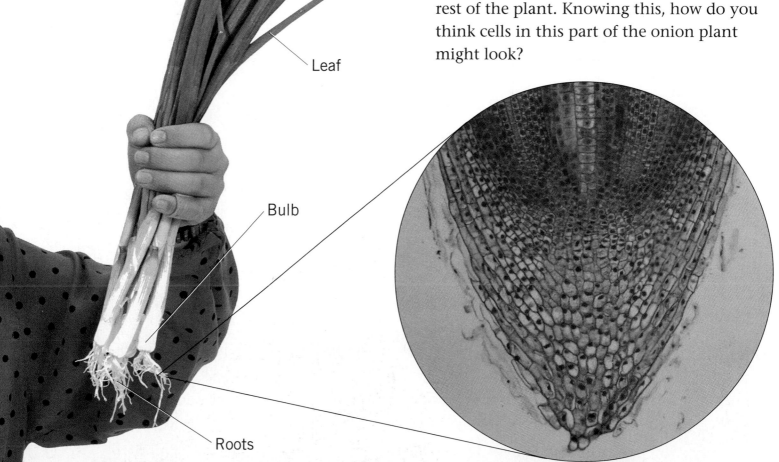

Leaf

Bulb

Roots

What is mitosis?

Sometimes while gardening, you may cut or scrape yourself. Have you ever had a scab form over a cut or scrape? The scab is a protective covering. Under the scab, the skin is repairing itself. Skin cells around the injured area are dividing to make new skin cells.

Cells divide for many reasons. In the example above, skin cells divide to produce new skin cells. Another reason cells divide is to help an organism grow. The process by which most types of cells divide is called **mitosis** (mī tō´sis).

Mitosis involves structures called **chromosomes** (krō´mə sōmz´). Chromosomes are in the cell nucleus and contain all of the instructions for cell activities. They tell

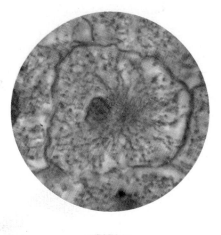

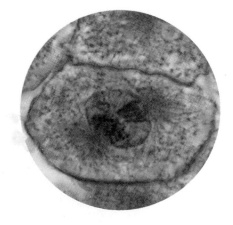

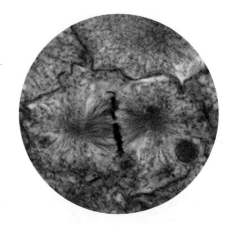

▲ Before cell division starts, the cell's chromosomes are copied.

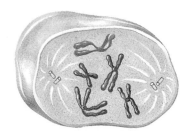

▲ The nuclear membrane disappears, and the chromosomes thicken.

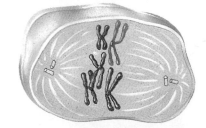

▲ Chromosomes continue to thicken as they line up across the middle of the cell.

the cell how to carry out its functions. The pictures on these pages show a cell dividing. Although mitosis is continual, the process is often described in stages, or phases, to make it easier to understand.

BACK HOME

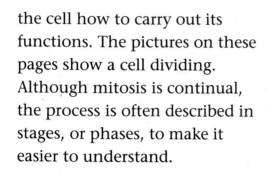

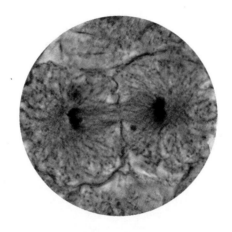

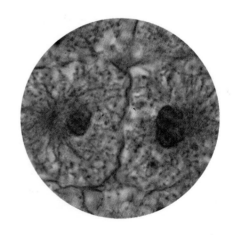

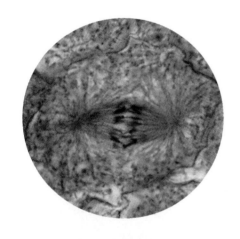

▲ The chromosomes separate into two identical sets and begin to move toward opposite sides of the cell.

▲ Chromosomes are at opposite sides of the cell. A nuclear membrane forms around each set of chromosomes.

▲ The cell membrane pinches off between the two new nuclei, forming two new cells.

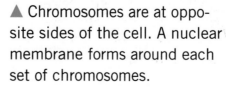

What is meiosis?

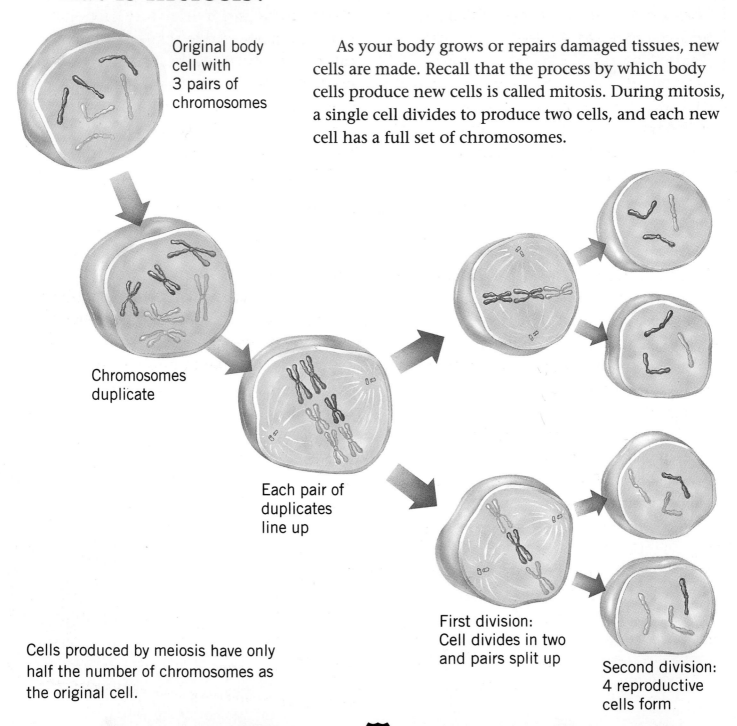

Original body cell with 3 pairs of chromosomes

As your body grows or repairs damaged tissues, new cells are made. Recall that the process by which body cells produce new cells is called mitosis. During mitosis, a single cell divides to produce two cells, and each new cell has a full set of chromosomes.

Chromosomes duplicate

Each pair of duplicates line up

First division: Cell divides in two and pairs split up

Second division: 4 reproductive cells form

Cells produced by meiosis have only half the number of chromosomes as the original cell.

Seed Bank

Germ plasm is a name for seeds and plant parts such as stem cuttings, which are stored in seed banks. Seed banks were started when scientists realized how important it was to preserve as many different kinds of plants as possible.

Germ plasm is valued because a plant's genetic diversity can be preserved and used when needed. If a crop is being threatened by a new pest, then germ plasm can be used to introduce new genes to fight the pest. For example, a disease called wheat bunt nearly destroyed wheat production in the Northwest. A variety of wheat in a seed bank was found to be resistant to bunt. The genes from this plant are now in the Northwest wheat and there is no bunt disease.

In complex organisms, cells used in reproducing offspring are made by a different division process. The process by which sex cells are produced is called **meiosis** (mī ō′sis). Cells produced by meiosis have only half the number of chromosomes as the original cell. This is why meiosis is sometimes called reduction division.

Except for sex cells, every cell in the human body has 23 pairs of chromosomes in the nucleus. Special body cells undergo meiosis to produce sex cells. Look at the original body cell shown in the drawing on page B28. It contains three pairs of chromosomes, or a total of six chromosomes. At the start of meiosis, each chromosome is doubled.

During the first division, two cells are formed. Each receives one doubled chromosome from each pair. After the first division, each new cell has two doubled chromosomes. These chromosomes are not a pair. Rather, there is one from each pair.

During the second division, the doubled chromosomes in the two new cells separate. These cells divide and produce four sex cells, each having two single, unpaired chromosomes, half the number found in the original body cell.

How are you doing?

1. What are three reasons that cell division is needed by living things?
2. Why is meiosis sometimes called reduction division?
3. **Think** If a cell had four chromosomes before dividing, how many chromosomes would each new cell have after mitosis?
4. **Think** Why is it important for the nucleus of a cell to make a copy of itself before mitosis takes place?

What is asexual reproduction?

You have learned that cells divide for different reasons. One reason is to produce other organisms. Reproduction by cell division requires only one parent and is called **asexual reproduction.** The soil in your garden is filled with bacteria that reproduce asexually. The mushrooms growing in the shade of an apple tree also reproduce asexually. The pictures on these pages show examples of some different kinds of asexual reproduction.

▲ Fragmentation
Some organisms can grow from a separate piece of a parent organism. For example, a new starfish can grow by the division of cells in a part of an arm and part of the center of a parent starfish.

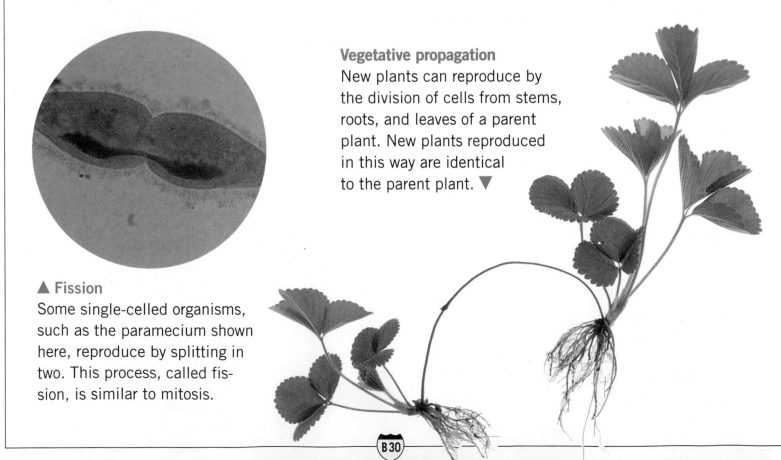

Vegetative propagation
New plants can reproduce by the division of cells from stems, roots, and leaves of a parent plant. New plants reproduced in this way are identical to the parent plant. ▼

▲ Fission
Some single-celled organisms, such as the paramecium shown here, reproduce by splitting in two. This process, called fission, is similar to mitosis.

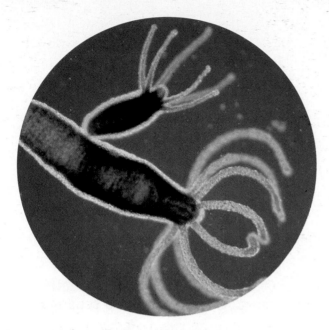

▲ Budding

The hydra is a simple animal that lives in water and reproduces by budding. Cell division forms a bud like the one shown. As the bud grows, it forms an identical copy of its parent and then separates from the parent and becomes independent.

▲ Spore formation

A mushroom can reproduce both sexually and asexually by making spores. Spores are similar to seeds, but are produced by cell division in only one parent. A spore grows into an organism identical to its parent.

Be a Scientist

HANDS-ON ACTIVITY

Can you make plants reproduce?

1. To understand how just one parent can produce an offspring, try growing a new plant without seeds. Cut a small stem from a coleus plant. Your cutting should be about 10 cm long.

2. Put the cut end in water and place it in good sunlight. In a few days, you will notice roots beginning to grow. Once you have a fair amount of roots, plant the cutting in soil. Make sure that your plant gets enough water and sunlight.

3. Your plant is a product of asexual reproduction. How is your new plant similar to the parent? Is it different in any way other than size?

What is sexual reproduction?

Most plants and animals are produced from cells from two parents. Many plants in your garden have two parent plants. Reproduction that involves two parents—a male and a female—is called **sexual reproduction.**

For sexual reproduction to occur, a female sex cell, called an egg, must join with a male sex cell, called a sperm. The joining of an egg and a sperm is called fertilization. The new cell that results from fertilization is called a **zygote** (zī′gōt).

1 Each pollen grain that sticks to the top of the pistil grows a pollen tube. This tube grows toward the ovary.

2 Sperm cells move through pollen tubes to the ovary.

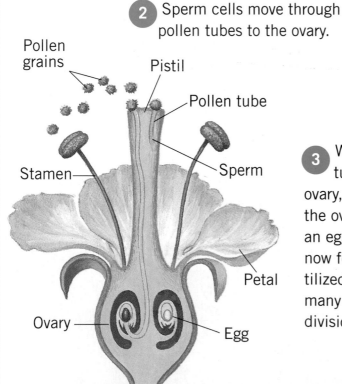

Pollen grains

Pistil

Pollen tube

Sperm

Stamen

Petal

Ovary

Egg

3 When a pollen tube reaches the ovary, the sperm enters the ovary and joins with an egg cell. The cell is now fertilized. The fertilized egg cell divides many times. After many divisions, a seed forms.

Seed

Fruit

4 As the seed forms, the ovary gets larger. It may change to a fruit or hard shell that protects the seeds inside.

Recall that sex cells, which are produced by meiosis, contain only half as many chromosomes as other cells. So when an egg cell and a sperm cell join, the zygote has twice as many chromosomes as either sex cell. Half of the chromosomes come from the mother, and half come from the father.

Most flowering plants reproduce sexually. As the drawing shows, the ovary, which produces the eggs, is contained in a structure near the base of the flower. Pollen grains are protective covers for sperm cells, which are found near the top of the flower.

Pollination is the process by which a pollen grain reaches the pistil. Insects or wind often carry pollen from one flower to another. After pollination occurs, sperm and egg cells can unite to produce a zygote. The zygote begins to divide and grow. The drawings on page B32 shows how a seed develops.

With animals, fertilization may take place inside or outside the female's body. The joining of sperm and egg outside the body is called external fertilization. The joining of sperm and egg inside the body is called internal fertilization. Frogs, toads, and most fish reproduce by external fertilization. Birds and mammals reproduce by internal fertilization.

Garden spider and web

Be a Scientist

What are a plant's reproductive parts?

1. Shake a flower over a piece of paper. Examine the pollen that falls onto the paper with a hand lens. Describe it in your Activity Journal.
2. Dissect the flower. Make a drawing that shows the parts of the flower.
3. Cut the piece of fruit in half. Make a drawing to show the location of the seeds.
4. Compare your observations with other groups' observations.

How do human sperm and egg make an offspring?

Fertilization occurs when an egg and a sperm join inside the female's body. The nuclei of the two cells combine to form a single nucleus. Almost immediately, this new cell begins to divide and continues dividing again and again. ▼

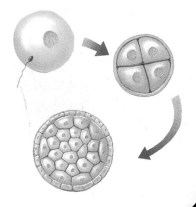

When a baby girl is born, her reproductive system already holds all of the eggs she will need to produce her own babies. When she reaches puberty—usually between the ages of 11 and 15—she will begin to release one egg a month.

A human male starts producing sperm cells when he reaches puberty. In his lifetime, he will produce billions of sperm cells. Any one of these sperm may join with an egg to produce a fertilized egg. The drawings and photo-graphs on these pages show what happens to that cell.

The fertilized egg attaches itself to the wall of the mother's uterus, or womb. Here it begins to develop into an embryo, the early stages of the new individual. The embryo has a head, buds where the arms and legs will form, and a heart. The embryo is about 1 cm long. ▲

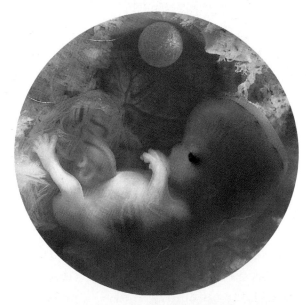

▲ After the second month, the developing embryo is called a fetus (fē´təs). The individual is now human-shaped and has a beating heart, and its eyes and brain are developing. The fetus is about 5 cm long.

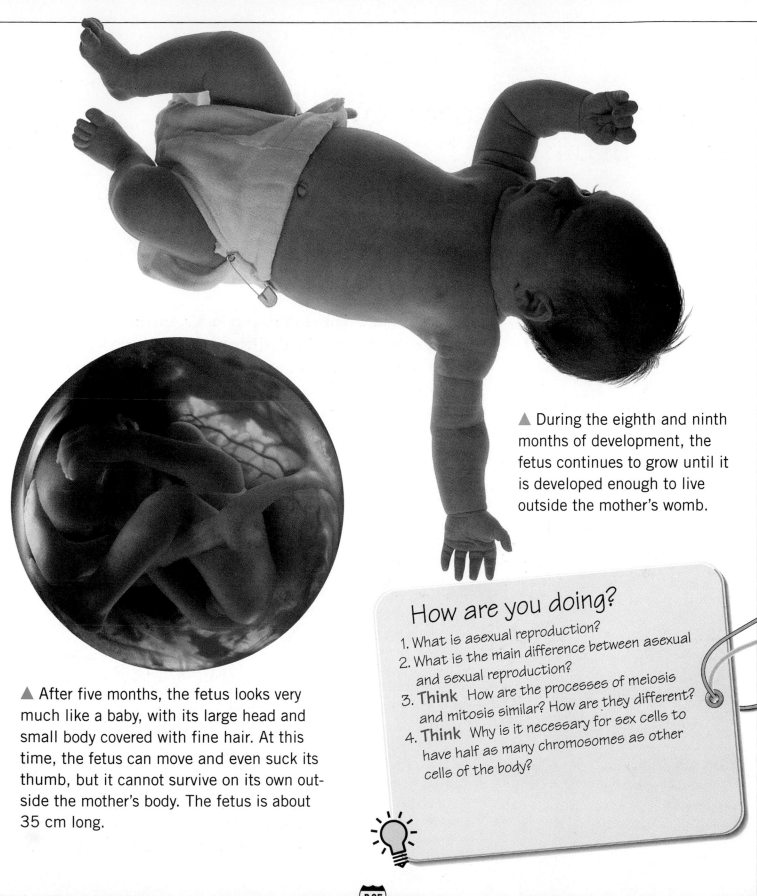

▲ During the eighth and ninth months of development, the fetus continues to grow until it is developed enough to live outside the mother's womb.

▲ After five months, the fetus looks very much like a baby, with its large head and small body covered with fine hair. At this time, the fetus can move and even suck its thumb, but it cannot survive on its own outside the mother's body. The fetus is about 35 cm long.

How are you doing?

1. What is asexual reproduction?
2. What is the main difference between asexual and sexual reproduction?
3. **Think** How are the processes of meiosis and mitosis similar? How are they different?
4. **Think** Why is it necessary for sex cells to have half as many chromosomes as other cells of the body?

SEA GLASS

by Laurence Yep

In this excerpt, you will find out why Craig's father has been captivated by gardens ever since he was a young boy.

"What's there to like about myself?" I sat down and bent my knees so I could wrap my arms around my legs and lean my chest against my thighs. "I'm lousy at swimming. I'm lousy at all the *Westerners'* games. I'm lousy at making friends. I'm even lousy at being Chinese. I'm not like anything Dad wants."

Uncle raised one eyebrow. "Is that all you think your father wants? Play games all the time?"

I hugged my legs tighter against my chest. "That's all we ever do."

"Your father, he want other things too." Uncle ran a finger lightly over a scab on his thumb. "At least he used to. I remember when he was a small boy—smaller than you, maybe only ten or eleven. It was only talk from a small boy, but it was GOOD talk. He tell me, 'Uncle, I'm going to know everything about plants. You want to know something about them, you come to me.'" Uncle cocked his head to one side. "Your father always have some book about plants. Always so he can read from it when he have nothing else to do."

It was funny hearing about Dad when he was a small boy; but what Uncle told me helped explain why Dad had been so hot to start a garden on our very first day here. "I guess he still likes plants," I said.

Uncle, though, was too busy reminiscing to hear me. "And your father, when he wasn't reading or talking about plants, he was drawing them."

"That's a little hard to swallow," I said. I couldn't associate anything artistic with my dad—not even something like drawing wavy lines on a notepad while he was talking on the phone.

Uncle stiffened and he thrust out his chin. "I'm no liar. I got eyes. I saw them. Maybe the pictures aren't so good, but he say drawing the pictures teach him more than just reading about the plants."

"It's just that I never heard Dad say anything about drawing." I set my chin on top of my knees.

"Your father, he want to grow all kinds of plants and flowers." Uncle pounded his fist against the rock he was sitting on. His fist made a flat, slapping sound. "But your grandfather, he say no. He say it's a waste of money to buy flower seeds. Waste of time to grow them. Your grandfather only let your father grow some vegetables. And your grandfather, he get mad when he find all the drawings. Your grandfather say not to waste good paper that cost so much."

Uncle put his hands down on either side of him and leaned back. "And I watch what happen. Your father was a good boy. It was just like he close a door inside himself. No more books about plants. No more drawing. And," Uncle added sadly, "no more talk about knowing everything about plants. He even tell me he not care about that stuff. But I got eyes. I saw."

I bit my lip for a moment and stared at the sea. It was a sad-enough sounding story—whether it was true or not. I guess I could believe some of what Uncle had said—at least the part about Dad's once wanting to grow some flowers, because it would help explain why he had already been planning a garden on our very first day at the store.

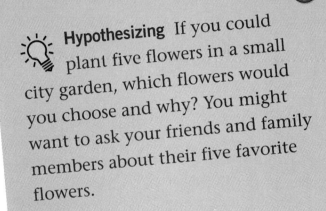

Think About Your Reading
1. Why didn't Craig's grandfather want his father to draw and plant flowers?
2. Reread the part about Craig's father drawing plants. Why do you think drawing plants might teach someone more than reading about them?

Hypothesizing If you could plant five flowers in a small city garden, which flowers would you choose and why? You might want to ask your friends and family members about their five favorite flowers.

Where to Read More
Anne Ophelia Dowden, *The Clover and the Bee: A Book of Pollination* (Thomas Y. Crowell, 1990) This book describes different tricks and traps flowers have evolved to be sure they are pollinated.

Looking Back

Words and Concepts

Match the description in Column A with the term in Column B.

Column A

1. The process by which most cells divide
2. Reproduction that requires only one parent
3. The joining of sex cells
4. Male sex cell
5. Structures that carry all instructions for a cell
6. The cell formed when a sperm and an egg join
7. Process by which sex cells are produced

Column B

a. Asexual
b. Chromosomes
c. Fertilization
d. Meiosis
e. Mitosis
f. Sperm
g. Zygote

Applied Thinking Skills

Answer the following questions. You can use words, drawings, and diagrams in your answers.

8. Describe and illustrate the process of meiosis.
9. Human body cells contain 23 pairs of chromosomes. How many chromosomes are in sperm and egg cells? How do you know?
10. **Your World** Does cell division take place at the same rate throughout a person's life? Explain your answer.

Show What You Know

What happens during cell division?

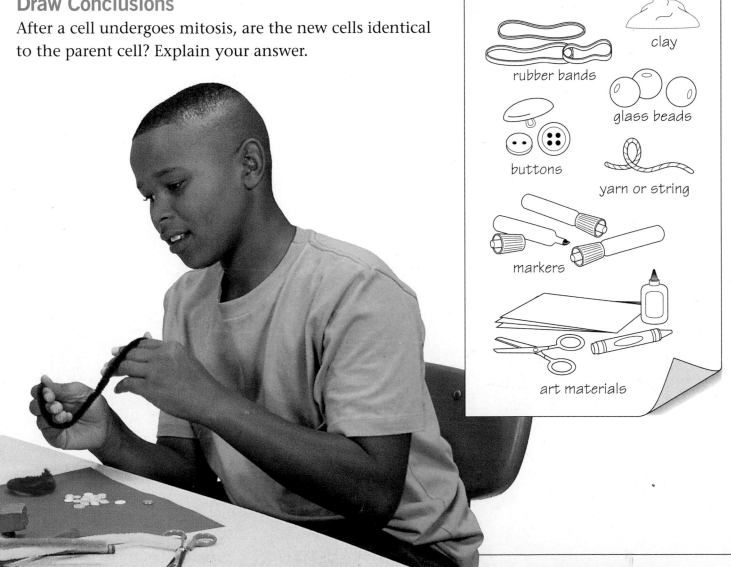

Observe and Collect Data

1. Using the materials, make a model of the different steps of mitosis.
2. Make a key to your model or label the parts shown on your model.

Draw Conclusions

After a cell undergoes mitosis, are the new cells identical to the parent cell? Explain your answer.

Process Skills

Making models, Observing, Interpreting data

HANDS-ON ASSESSMENT

Materials

rubber bands

clay

glass beads

buttons

yarn or string

markers

art materials

Chapter 3

Heredity

Look in the basket at some of the vegetables harvested from a garden. Can you tell what they are? They are all peppers. Even though they come in a variety of colors, sizes, and shapes, each has certain features, or characteristics, that make it a pepper.

Now look at the two snails. You wouldn't mistake them for peppers or peas or any other kind of living thing shown on the page. These organisms have certain characteristics common to all snails.

Any characteristic that can be used to identify or describe an organism is called a trait (trāt). Some traits shared by all the peppers in the basket are similar structure, texture, and odor. What do you think are some of the traits that snails have?

Sunflowers have edible seeds that are great for snacks.

Vegetable gardens grow best in bright, full sunlight.

All living things inherit, or receive, their traits from their parents. The passing of traits from parents to offspring is called heredity (hə red´i tē). The traits shown by the peppers were in the seeds produced by each of the parent plants.

Every person in your class has traits that he or she has inherited from his or her parents. Some of these traits are those that make us all human beings. But some of them are traits that make each person different from another and similar to his or her parents.

Look at the sunflowers. In your Science Journal, describe traits that the sunflowers have in common with many other kinds of plants. Also describe traits that make the sunflowers different from all other kinds of plants.

Pull weeds because they compete with garden plants for water, food, and light.

Explore Activity

What traits do you share with your classmates?

MINDS-ON ACTIVITY

Process Skills

Communicating, Collecting data, Making a graph

Observe and Collect Data

1. Having an attached or an unattached earlobe is an inherited trait. Look at the photographs on these pages to see the difference between these traits.

2. **Predict** how many of your classmates have either attached earlobes or unattached earlobes. Then do a survey of your classmates. Make a chart in your Activity Journal and record the number of people in your class with attached earlobes and the number with unattached earlobes.

3. **Predict** how many of your classmates can wiggle their ears. Do another survey and record how many of your classmates can wiggle their ears without touching them. Being able to do this also is an inherited trait.

4. **Predict** how many classmates can curl their tongues. Do a third survey of your classmates to determine how many have the trait which enables them to curl the tips of their tongues. Record the results in your Activity Journal.

Share Your Results

1. How many people in your class have each of the traits you examined? Share your results with your classmates.
2. Make a bar graph showing the number of people in your class who have each trait.

Draw Conclusions

1. What percentage of your class has each of these traits?
2. Find out the number of students in your school. **Predict** how many people in your school have these traits. Use what you know about the percentage of people in your classroom with these traits.

Apply What You Know

Make a list of other traits that you think are inherited. Do another survey examining who in your class has these traits. Could these traits be influenced by the environment or by the person's behavior? How?

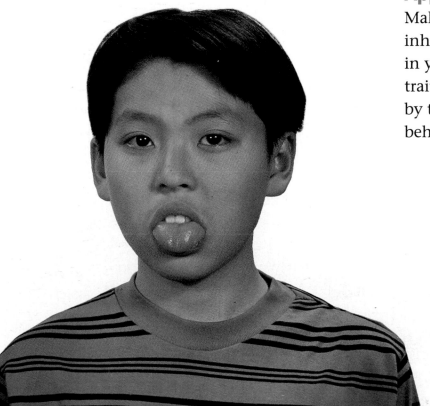

What are DNA and genes?

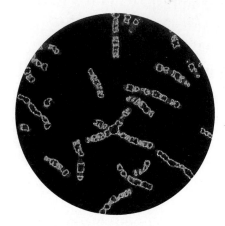

▲ These human chromosomes contain genes.

▲ A chromosome is made of a tightly wound DNA molecule. Imagine taking a rubber band and twisting it until it is a knotted jumble of rubber. This is what happens to the DNA molecule as it gets twisted into a chromosome.

How do living things pass on traits to their offspring? How is it possible that offspring of the same parents are different from one another and different from their parents? Many scientists all over the world are working to answer these and other questions related to heredity. The study of heredity is called genetics (jə net´iks).

These scientists focus much of their attention on chromosomes. Recall that chromosomes are structures found in the nuclei of most living cells. They control the activity of the cell. Before a cell divides by the process of mitosis, the number of chromosomes in its nucleus doubles so that both new cells formed by cell division receive the same number of chromosomes.

Scientists have learned that every chromosome contains proteins and deoxyribonucleic (dē äks´ə rī´bō-noo klē´ik) acid, or **DNA**. As the model shows, this spiral-shaped molcule is a long, twisted strand of material.

DNA carries information in a kind of code. To understand how a code works, think of the letters of the alphabet. If the letters are jumbled, they don't mean anything. But when arranged in a certain order, they can mean a great deal. Suppose you have a pile of alphabet blocks. By selecting and arranging the blocks, you can form words from the letters. Once the words are formed, they can be arranged to make sentences.

Just as words and sentences are made up of letters, DNA is made up of smaller units called bases. Linked together, these bases form the long, double-stranded chain that is the DNA molecule.

Be a Scientist

MINDS-ON ACTIVITY

Can you make your own code?

1. Try making a secret code to describe things in your classroom. Select any four letters from the alphabet to use in your code. Decide the rules for your code and write them in your Activity Journal.

2. For each particular trait you want to describe, choose a sequence of letters. For example, suppose you choose the letters *a, b, c,* and *d.* The sequence *abcd* might stand for flat, and *bcda* might stand for round. Other sequences can be used to stand for other traits, such as colors or sizes.

3. Select an item in the classroom that you want to describe. After you have written the code for that item, have your classmates try to guess what item you are describing. Then have them try to "solve" your code.

Every chromosome is made up of genes. A **gene** is a section of a chromosome. If you think of a chromosome as being like a chain, each link in the chain is a gene. The 46 chromosomes in a human cell contain about 100,000 genes.

Genes tell cells what functions they will perform. Every cell in your body has the exact same genes. However, bone cells make other bone cells because the genes that make other kinds of cells are turned off. Scientists are still only beginning to find out how living cells are able to turn genes off and on.

Carrots have 18 pairs of chromosomes.

How are genes and traits related?

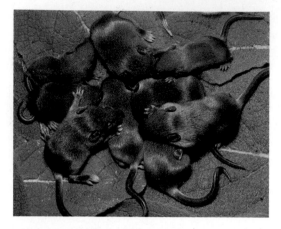

▲ What traits have these mice inherited from their parents?

Have you ever heard an adult refer to a young person as "a chip off the old block"? This means that the young person shows certain similarities to one or both parents. Such similarities are common. Children inherit their traits from their parents.

How are traits passed on from parents to children? Recall that every person starts out as a single cell—a zygote. Like all human cells, a zygote contains 23 pairs of chromosomes. Half of those chromosomes came from the father and half came from the mother. As an individual grows and develops, every single cell produced by cell division contains exact copies of those 46 chromosomes.

These lettuce leaves show a variety of inherited traits. Do you think they all came from the same plant? ▶

Laboratory Technician

Many laboratory technicians are curious about science. They are good observers, able to follow instructions, and can accurately measure and record their findings. They are like detectives looking for clues to find the causes of colds, allergies, blindness, cancer, or AIDS. After they help find the causes, they then can help find cures.

66 My name is Koreen Keith and I'm a laboratory technician. I research ways for people to maintain a good quality of life. Some of my responsibilities are weighing, measuring, and making calculations to determine how much of a chemical to use in an experiment. I'm able to perform experiments over and over, which requires patience.

"Not all lab technicians go to college. Some have laboratory experience and a high school diploma. Some learn their skills from on-the-job training.

"I studied biology and math. I was always interested in science, but was unsure how to apply my knowledge. Now I have a career in which I can use my skills in lab science. My responsiblities are critical for finding answers about new drugs that might save someone's life.**99**

The chromosomes carry the genes that instruct the cells that make up your body. Instructions from the genes determine traits. Genes determine physical traits such as hair color, eye color, and shape of the earlobe. Genes also determine general body structure and appearance. For example, if your parents are tall, you probably will be tall. The shape of your head and your facial features probably will be similar to those of your parents. What other traits do people have that are similar to those of their parents?

How are you doing?

1. How are chromosomes, genes, and DNA related?
2. What are inherited traits? Give some examples.
3. **Think** Suppose you were to create a code using only two letters. How many different traits could you code? Explain your answer.
4. **Think** What happens to genes when chromosomes are doubled before mitosis?

How are traits passed on?

Your garden has produced a fine crop of peas. Many people grow peas for food, but more than 100 years ago, one man grew peas for an experiment. Gregor Mendel was an Austrian monk who loved gardening, science, and mathematics. He combined these interests in a study of pea plants.

Mendel noticed variations in the pea plants. One of the variations was in the height of the plants. Some were tall; others were short. He suggested that such variations were due to traits passed on from generation to generation. To test his ideas, Mendel designed and tried some experiments.

Mendel bred some plants by hand pollinating. He transferred pollen from the male organ of a tall plant to the female organs of short plants. He collected the seeds produced by the short plants and planted them. All the plants produced from these seeds were tall!

Next Mendel bred these tall plants with one another. He then planted the seeds produced by this generation of plants. The new crop produced one short plant for every three tall plants produced. The question was, How could seeds from tall parent plants produce any short plants?

Today scientists know that traits are determined by genes on the chromosomes that are passed from parent to offspring. The offspring receive two complete sets of genes, one set from each parent. So offspring receive

Mendel's Experiment

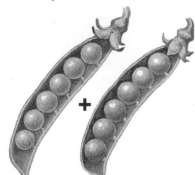

1 Mendel crossed green seed plants with yellow seed plants.

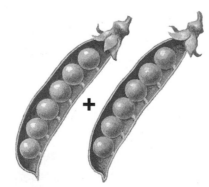

2 He planted seeds from hybrid plants and got only yellow seeds.

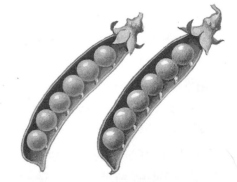

3 He crossed yellow second-generation seeds and got green and yellow seeds.

Development of a Hybrid Pea Parent

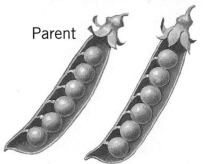 Parent

+

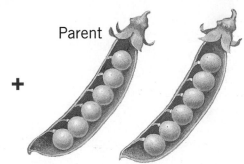 Parent

=

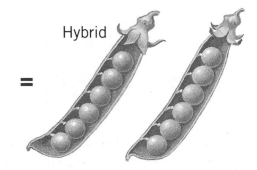 Hybrid

1 The first-generation plants all produced yellow peas. Were these purebred or hybrid peas?

2 Some second-generation plants produced green seeds and some produced yellow seeds.

3 The ratio was about three yellow-seed plants for every one green-seed plant. Were any of these plants purebred?

two genes that control each trait. For example, a pea plant receives a gene that controls height from its female parent and another gene for height from its male parent.

In pea plants, the gene for tallness is dominant over the gene for shortness. A **dominant gene** is one that blocks the effect of another gene for the same trait. A **recessive gene** is one whose effect is blocked, or hidden, by a dominant gene. In pea plants, the gene for shortness is recessive.

An organism that receives two dominant or two recessive genes for a trait is said to be purebred for that trait. An organism that receives one dominant and one recessive gene for a trait is hybrid for the trait. A hybrid pea plant always will be tall because it contains one dominant gene for tallness. However, a hybrid

plant does have a recessive gene for shortness. This gene can be passed on to the next generation of offspring. When two hybrid parents both pass on a recessive gene, the offspring will show the recessive trait. This explains how two tall pea plants, both hybrids, can produce a short pea plant.

The drawings above show an experiment in which Mendel explored another trait of peas—color.

 SCIENCE JOURNAL

Visit the produce section the next time you go to a supermarket or grocery store. You may find that a particular kind of fruit or vegetable, such as lettuce, comes in a variety of types. In your Science Journal, list the varieties you find of each different kind of fruit and vegetable.

BACK HOME

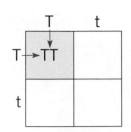

1 Combine the first gene of the Tt plant with the first gene of the Tt plant.

Mendel crossbred, or crossed, many different pea plants to learn about their traits. One way to follow what can happen during a cross is by making a Punnett square. A Punnett square is a diagram that shows all of the possible gene combinations for a trait that can be expected to show up in the offspring. A Punnett square has four boxes. Each box has a possible combination of genes for one inherited trait from each parent.

MINDS-ON ACTIVITY

Be a Scientist

What can you learn from a Punnett square?

1. Suppose you want to raise guinea pigs. You know that the trait for a rough coat of fur is dominant and the trait for a smooth coat is recessive. You decide to mate a rough-coated male with a smooth-coated female. All of the offspring have rough coats. Set up a Punnett square to find out what genes each parent probably carried.

2. Now suppose you mate a second rough-coated male with a second smooth-coated female. This time half the offspring have rough coats and half have smooth coats. What genes did the parents carry in this case?

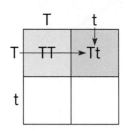

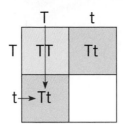

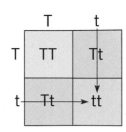

2 Combine the first gene of the Tt plant with the second gene of the Tt plant.

3 Repeat steps 1 and 2 using the second gene of the Tt plant.

4 The possible gene combinations resulting from a cross of two hybrids.

Shown on these pages are steps in completing a Punnett square for a cross between a hybrid tall pea plant and another hybrid tall pea plant. A letter is chosen for the trait being studied, in this case, plant height. The dominant trait for height is tallness, which is shown by T. The recessive trait, shortness, is shown by t. The tall plant's genes are Tt.

The two genes from one parent are placed along the top of the diagram. The two genes from the other parent are placed at the side. The possible gene combinations are written in the squares.

When this Punnett square is completed, you can see that the offspring from crossing a hybrid tall plant with another hybrid tall plant are tall and short plants. These plants are like second-generation plants in Mendel's experiment.

What happened when Mendel crossed these plants? Look at step 4 of the Punnett square, which shows the possible gene combinations from a cross between two hybrid pea plants. The possibilities are: purebred tall (TT), purebred short (tt), and hybrid tall (Tt).

From this square, you also can predict the expected number of each type of offspring. For example, if 100 offspring are produced from a hybrid cross, you could expect that 75 would be tall and 25 would be short. The short would all be purebred tt. Of the 75 tall plants, you could expect that 25 would be purebred TT and 50 would be hybrid Tt.

How are you doing?

1. How does a cross between two tall pea plants produce some short offspring?

2. If a black cat and a white cat have 10 black kittens, what can you say about genes for fur color?

3. **Think** If the gene for green peas is recessive and yellow is dominant, what might the color of a cross between two green pea plants be?

4. **Think** If a tall and short pea plant are crossed, half the offspring are short, and half are tall. Show how you can determine the parent's genes.

What causes variations in traits?

The world would be a duller place if all flowers were yellow, all birds were blue, and all vegetables looked and tasted the same. One of the greatest things about nature is the variety it offers.

For example, form an image of a butterfly in your mind. What do you see? All butterflies have certain traits in common. They have delicate, scaly wings, antennae, and sort of "fuzzy" bodies. And they all seem to fly about in a random, zigzag pattern. But think of the variety among butterflies. Some are large. Some are small. And they seem to come in an endless variety of colors and patterns.

All of the traits of butterflies are determined by genes. Different kinds of butterflies have different genes for such traits as color and size.

Yet, some variations come from combinations of genes. This can be best observed in some flowers. Red is determined by one gene and white by another gene. A plant that receives a gene for red from one parent and a gene for white from another parent will produce pink flowers. This is a blending of traits.

Many traits are determined by instructions from several pairs of genes. In such cases, the trait an organism shows depends on the combination of gene pairs that are inherited.

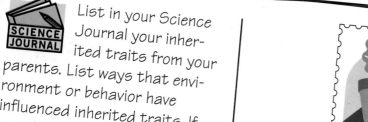

List in your Science Journal your inherited traits from your parents. List ways that environment or behavior have influenced inherited traits. If your hair color has been lightened by the sun, that trait has been influenced by environment. If you're a good swimmer, the trait of muscular coordination has been influenced by practice, which is a behavior.

BACK HOME

Selective Breeding

Modern genetics is one of the most exciting and fast moving fields of science. However, hundreds, perhaps thousands, of years before Mendel performed his experiments, people were applying many of the principles he used and identified.

The most widely used ideas related to genetics were those of selective breeding. That is the breeding of a male and female based on the most desirable traits of each parent.

The history of the dog is one example of the use of selective breeding. All dogs are probably descended from a wolflike animal that appeared on the earth about 15 million years ago. Fossil evidence indicates that people in what is now Europe tamed dogs some 10,000 to 20,000 years ago. The dogs were used to help people hunt.

Although there is no record of this, probably only the fastest and strongest dogs were used for breeding, so these traits became highly developed. Records do show that between 6000 to 7000 B.C., Egyptians developed Saluki dogs specifically for hunting. The Saluki is probably the oldest known purebred dog.

Since that time, dogs have been tamed and bred for a variety of purposes. American Indians tamed dogs as early as 4,000 years ago. In ancient Greece, large dogs were bred to hunt lions. The Romans kept dogs as pets and also used them to herd sheep and to hunt.

Today, many people have dogs as pets. However, there are still many working dogs that are bred for their speed, hunting, or herding abilities. So the next time you see someone's dog enjoying life, remember that it has a rich ancestry.

What is bioengineering?

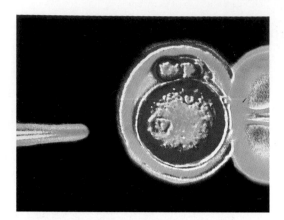

▲ Scientists can develop animals with specific traits. They do this by inserting genes with the desired traits into fertilized animal eggs. An animal will develop with the wanted traits.

▲ These Venus' flytraps were cloned from one parent.

Scientists have learned so much about genetics that they can now "redesign" some organisms. This is what genetic engineering, or bioengineering (bī´ō en´jə nir´ iŋ), is all about. Bioengineering is a treatment of genetic material that causes a change in the makeup of an organism. Using bioengineering, scientists can create superplants, oil-eating bacteria, and drugs similar to natural substances found in the human body. Such advances can help increase the world food supply, clean up pollution, and fight disease.

The following briefly describes some bioengineering breakthroughs.

Cloning is a technique by which a cell or organism is grown directly from one parent. A clone is genetically identical to its parent. Scientists use cloning to make medicines and new types of plants. You can make a clone by snipping some ivy and growing the cut piece in a glass of water.

Gene machines are computer-controlled machines that put together custom-made pieces of DNA. These DNA fragments then can be combined to create genes. Gene machines also can be used to change existing genes. The genes created with gene machines can be used in medical research and in the development of drugs.

In gene splicing, genes from two different species are joined. Gene splicing is used to make drugs and to develop plants that are resistant to disease or drought. In one type of gene splicing, scientists use bacteria for

▲ Biological fermenters create a controlled environment where genetically engineered organisms can flourish. For example, genetically engineered yeast cells can be used to produce a vaccine for a viral infection.

the production of many new drugs. A gene from a human is added to a DNA structure inside bacteria. Every time the bacteria reproduce, they make more copies of the human gene. The changed bacteria will make any substance that is coded by the human gene, such as insulin. Because bacteria reproduce so quickly, they can serve as insulin-making factories.

DILEMMA

Engineering Plants

Scientists are working on what may be your dinner in the future. Try to imagine a potato with a chicken gene. Experiments are being conducted to find ways to make potatoes resistant to rot. These experiments involve adding a chicken or an insect gene to the DNA of a potato. The added gene may help the plant grown from that potato to stay healthier longer and help increase the food supply.

However, some people think that it is dangerous to interfere with nature. Some new technologies are so different from anything that has been done before, it is feared that the foods produced may have unexpected harmful side effects.

Think About It Because of these concerns, some people refuse to buy or eat genetically engineered food. Discuss the issue with your family, friends, and neighbors. Ask them how they feel about genetically engineered foods. Find out if your local stores sell genetically engineered fruits or vegetables. Would you buy these foods?

How might bioengineering affect the future?

▲ Frostproof strawberries
Biotechnology combines engineering and technology to solve problems involving living things. For example, a strawberry plant has been developed that can survive freezing temperatures. Bacteria called "ice-minus" are inserted in the blossom, resulting in a frost-free plant.

Petroleum-eating bacteria
Scientists can splice the DNA of several types of bacteria to make a supergerm that is capable of consuming large quantities of petroleum. These bacteria can be used to clean up oil spills. ▶

The possibilities for bioengineering seem endless. Scientists may one day be able to locate, identify, and study all of the human genes. Genetic disorders may be corrected by changing or replacing faulty genes. Or they may be corrected by artificially producing the substance usually produced by a normal gene.

Twenty years ago, probably few people had imagined bacteria that could eat oil, break down chemical wastes, or protect plants from frost. But today, these super-germs are a reality. If advancements continue at the present rate, bioengineering will continue to change our lives in ways we might never have imagined. What are some of the ways that bioengineering might affect your future?

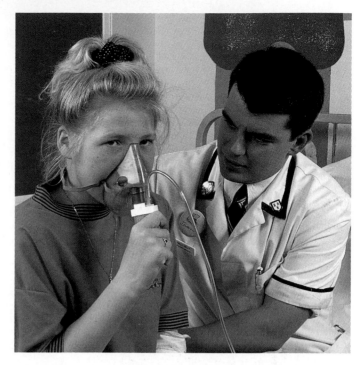

▲ **Cystic fibrosis**

Cystic fibrosis (sis´tik fī brō´sis) is a genetic disorder. The disorder causes the lungs to become clogged with mucus, making breathing difficult. In 1993, scientists discovered the gene that causes the disorder. Based on this knowledge, some day a cure may be found.

▲ Some tomatoes have received a spliced gene from a bacterium that is resistant to a disease-causing virus. The tomato plants produced are protected against the virus, which can destroy tomato crops.

How are you doing?

1. How can the blending of traits cause a variation?
2. Give an example of a trait being influenced by the environment.
3. **Think** Why are bacteria useful in making synthetic drugs?
4. **Think** How might bioengineering help the environment in the future?

Looking Back

Words and Concepts

Read each statement. If a statement is true, write *true* as your answer. If a statement is false, change the underlined word or phrase to a word or phrase that will make the statement true.

Potatoes are thickened underground stems called tubers.

1. Any characteristic, such as height or color, that describes an organism is called a <u>trait</u>.
2. A chromosome contains a molecule of <u>DNA</u>.
3. The passing of traits from parents to offspring is called <u>genetics</u>.
4. A trait that can block, or hide, another trait is caused by a <u>recessive gene</u>.
5. Growing a cell or an organism from one parent is called <u>cloning</u>.
6. Gene splicing is an example of <u>bioengineering</u>.

Applied Thinking Skills

Answer the following questions. You can use words, drawings, and diagrams in your answers.

7. Offspring receive genes from both parents. If each parent has one gene for a certain disease, how does this affect the chances that the offspring will get this disease? Does your conclusion depend on whether the traits are dominant or recessive? Use Punnet squares to find the answers.
8. Offspring that result from sexual reproduction are not identical to either parent. Explain why.
9. A treatment for the disorder known as sickle-cell anemia lies in the difference between fetal and adult hemoglobin, a substance in red blood cells. If a person were given a new drug that turns on the gene for making healthy fetal hemoglobin, would this treatment prevent the disease from being passed on from parent to child? Explain your answer.
10. **Your World** Suppose you wanted to find out how a particular human trait is inherited. Because you can't crossbreed people in an experiment, how might you study the trait?

Show What You Know

How do chromosomes determine sex?

Observe and Collect Data

1. Use a piece of tape and a marker to mark one side of a coin with an X and the other side of the same coin with a Y. Each male sex cell has either an X or a Y chromosome.
2. Now mark both sides of the other coin with an X. The female sex cell always has an X chromosome. Shake the two coins in your hands and drop them on your desk. Record which sides face up. Do this nine more times, recording your results each time.
3. Write the number of times you got an XX result as a fraction over ten. For instance, if you got XX three times, write 3/10. Write the number of times you got an XY result as a fraction over 10.
4. Add all of the XX results obtained by your class and divide this number by the total number of shakes. If your class has 20 students, you should have a total of 200 shakes.
5. Add all of the XY results obtained by your class and divide this number by the total number of shakes.

Draw Conclusions

Using your observations, what are the chances of producing a female offspring if you try ten times? Do the chances increase, decrease, or stay the same with more tosses?

Process Skills

Predicting, Communicating, Collecting data

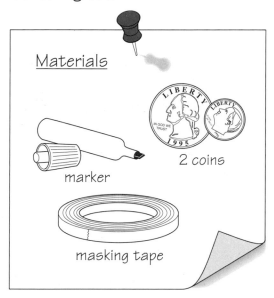

Materials

marker

2 coins

masking tape

One or two ears, on stalks that grow "as high as an elephant's eye"

Cells & Heredity

Show what you know about cells, heredity, traits, and reproduction. Work by yourself, with a partner, or in a group. Select one activity.

Model Maker Using common materials, build a model that shows the relationship among DNA, chromosomes, and genes.

Sculptor The city of Genes, USA, has asked you to make a head for a statue. You have decided to use the heads of two friends for models. Combine or blend their dominant traits. Use clay for the head.

Researcher Pretend you are a researcher who has just discovered the cause of a genetic disorder. You are about to go on television to announce your findings to the world. Hold a press conference. Ask your classmates to act like reporters and ask questions about your findings.

Science-Fiction Writer Write a short story about a clone that takes over someone's identity.

Choreographer Make up a dance showing cell division. Perform the dance for your class.

Playwright Make up a play in which the characters are different organelles of a cell. Perform the play for your class.

Glossary

asexual reproduction (ā sek´shoo əl rē´prə duk´shən)   Reproduction involving only one parent. (page B30)

cell membrane (sel mem´brān´)   A layer that surrounds the cell. (page B10)

cell wall (sel wôl)   A layer that surrounds the cell membrane in plant cells. (page B13)

cell (sel)   The basic unit of all living things. (page B6)

chloroplast (klôr´ə plast´)   An organelle that enables plant cells to make food. (page B13)

chromosome (krō´mə sōm´)   A structure in the nucleus of a cell. (page B26)

cilium (sil´ē əm)   A hairlike structure attached to the cell membrane of some types of cells. (page B11)

cytoplasm (sīt´ō plaz´əm)   The jellylike fluid that fills most of a cell. (page B10)

DNA   The material that makes up chromosomes. (page B44)

dominant gene (däm´ə nənt jēn)   A gene that blocks the effect of another gene for the same trait. (page B49)

gene (jēn)   A section of a chromosome. Each gene carries a piece of information for one trait. (page B45)

meiosis (mī ō´sis)   The process by which sex cells are formed. (page B29)

mitochondrion (mīt´ō kän´drē ən)   An organelle that releases energy to the cell. (page B10)

mitosis (mī tō´sis)   The process by which most types of cells divide. (page B26)

nuclear membrane (noo´klē ər mem´brān´)   A layer that separates the nucleus from the rest of the cell. (page B11)

nucleus (noo´klē əs)   The part of the cell that determines the cell's activity. (page B11)

organelle (ôr´gə nel´)   A tiny structure that makes up cells. (page B10)

recessive gene (ri ses´iv jēn)   A gene whose effect can be blocked by another gene. (page B49)

ribosome (rī´bə sōm´)   An organelle that makes proteins in the cell. (page B11)

sexual reproduction (sek´shoo əl rē´prə duk´shən)   Reproduction that involves two parents. (page B32)

vacuole (vak´yoo ōl´)   An organelle that performs the functions of storage and transport in the cell. (page B10)

zygote (zī´gōt´)   The new cell that results from the process of fertilization. The joining of an egg and a sperm produces a zygote. (page B32)

Unit B Index

Boldface numerals denote glossary terms. Italic numerals denote illustrations.

Credits

Photographs

1 Tom Bean/DRK Photo; 2–3 Renee Lynn*; 4 Renee Lynn*; 5 Ken Karp*; 6-7 Renee Lynn*; 6B Renee Lynn*; 6CL Roy Morsch/The Stock Market; 6T E. R. Degginger/Animals, Animals; 7 Renee Lynn*; 9B Ken Karp*; 9TL Bruce Iverson; 9TC Ed Reschke/Peter Arnold, Inc.; 9TR Breck P. Kent/Earth Scenes; 12 Eric Grave/Photo Researchers; 15BC Renee Lynn*; 15BL G. W. Willis, Ochsner Medical Institution/Biological Photo Service; 15BR G. W. Willis, Ochsner Medical Institution/Biological Photo Service; 15TC Cabisco/Visuals Unlimited; 15TL G. W. Willis, Ochsner Medical Institution/Biological Photo Service; 15TR Richard Green/Photo Researchers; 16 Jim Solliday/Biological Photo Service; 16–17 Renee Lynn*; 17B Charles Kingery/Phototake; 17TL Ken Karp*; 17TR John D. Cunningham/Visuals Unlimited; 18B Sapieha/Art Resource, New York; 18T Ken Karp*; 19 Elliott Smith*; 20 Bruce Iverson; 21 Ken Karp*; 23 Renee Lynn*; 24–25 Elliott Smith*; 25 J. Robert Waaland, U. of Washington/Biological Photo Service; 26–27 Michael Abbey/Science Source/Photo Researchers; 30BR Renee Lynn*; 30L Bruce Iverson; 30T Fred Bavendam/Peter Arnold, Inc.; 31BL

Renee Lynn*; 31R Wayland Lee*; 31T Biophoto Associates/Science Source/Photo Researchers; 33 Michael P. Gadomski/Bruce Coleman Inc.; 34 Lennart Nilsson, *A Child Is Born,* Dell Publishing Company; 35L Lennart Nilsson, *A Child Is Born,* Dell Publishing Company; 35T Jon Feingersh/Tom Stack & Associates; 38–39 Elliott Smith*; 40 Renee Lynn*; 41B Peter Beck/The Stock Market; 41TL Jim Foster/The Stock Market; 41TR Renee Lynn*; 42–43 Elliott Smith*; 44B Alfred Owczarzak/Biological Photo Service; 44T Custom Medical Stock; 45 Renee Lynn*; 46B Renee Lynn*; 46T Mary Clay/Tom Stack & Associates; 47T Anne Dowie*; 52 Renee Lynn*; 53 Tim Davis; 54–55 Alexander Tsiaras/Science Source/Photo Researchers; 54B Runk-Schoenberger/Grant Heilman Photography; 54T Jon Gordon/Phototake; 56BL Bob Daemmrich/Stock, Boston; 56BR J. B. Diederich/Contact Press Images/The Stock Market; 56T D. Cavagnaro/DRK Photo; 57B Renee Lynn*; 57T Simon Fraser/RVI, Newcastle-Upon-Tyne/SPL/Photo Researchers; 58 Steven King/Peter Arnold, Inc.; 59 Renee Lynn*

Special thanks to Malcolm X Elementary School, Berkeley, California; Franklin Year-Round School, Oakland,

California; Carl B. Munck Elementary School, Oakland, California; Hintil Ku Ka Child Care Center, Oakland, California.

*Photographed expressly for Addison-Wesley Publishing Company, Inc.

Illustrations

Nea Bisek 8T, 19, 21, 24T, 39, 59
Len Ebert 36–37
Jane McCreary 8B, 24B, 43, 57
Rebecca Merilees 22, 32, 48, 49, 50T
Rolin Graphics 50B
Patrice Rossi 10–11, 13, 26, 28, 34
Randy Vergoustraete 60–61

Text

36–37 From Laurence Yep, *Sea Glass* (New York: Harper & Row, 1979). Copyright ©1979 by Laurence Yep. Reprinted by permission of HarperCollins Publishers.

Yechhh!

GARBAGE

COMPOST

Landfill

Many of the things you throw away end up in landfills. A sanitary landfill is a huge pit lined with plastic. Garbage trucks dump loads of trash into the pit. Bulldozers spread the trash into layers. Huge tractors with wide, metal-spiked wheels pack down the trash. Also, bulldozers cover the trash with several centimeters of dirt to help keep away the flies and rats and to control the smell. The bulldozers will pile layer upon layer of garbage at this landfill.

Near this landfill is a compost pile, a recycling center, and an incinerator. Compost is food and yard waste that has rotted and changed into a natural fertilizer. A recycling center is a collection site for waste that will be made into useful products. An incinerator is a machine that burns trash. All of these places dispose of garbage in different ways. A landfill is also a good place to learn about heat and other forms of energy.

■ What is heat?

■ What happens when energy changes from one form to another?

■ How can energy resources be conserved?

ENERGY & RESOURCES

Where does all this garbage come from? Ugh!

Activities

Features

Chapter 1

Heat

What do a toaster, a hair dryer, a wool glove, and an outdoor thermometer have in common? The toaster heats food such as bread and frozen waffles. The hair dryer produces a stream of warm air. Gloves keep your hands warm. The thermometer can tell you how hot something is. All of these items have something to do with heat.

Heat is a form of energy. **Energy** is the ability to do work, or cause a change in matter. For example, the heat energy of a toaster changes bread from soft to crisp. The energy of a hair dryer changes your hair from wet to dry.

In your Science Journal, list ten things that you might find in a landfill. Write how we use these items. Think about how each item might be related to heat. Share your list with a classmate.

Metal trash

Household trash

Explore Activity

How does temperature affect dye in water?

HANDS-ON ACTIVITY

Process Skills

Controlling variables,
Interpreting data

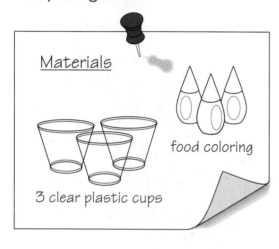

Materials

food coloring

3 clear plastic cups

Observe and Collect Data

1. ⚠️ Fill one cup with very cold water, one cup with water that is at room temperature, and one cup with hot tap water. Try to put the same amount of water into each cup.

2. Let the water stand for a few minutes until it is still.

3. Add two drops of food coloring to each cup, one right after the other.

4. 📓 Observe the coloring as it spreads through the water. Do not shake the cups or stir the water. In your Activity Journal, record your observations. You may describe what you see or make a series of drawings that show the changes taking place in each cup.

Share Your Results

1. In which cup did the food coloring spread fastest? What results did others in your class get?

2. In which cup did the food coloring spread slowest? What results did others in your class get?

Draw Conclusions

Describe how the temperature of water affects the spread of food coloring in water.

Apply What You Know

1. What do you think would happen if you heated the cold water shortly after adding the food coloring?
2. Why were you asked not to shake the cup or stir the water?

What is temperature?

Temperature is a measure of how hot or cold something is. Place your hand on your forehead. Does it feel warm? Now place your hand on your desk. Does it feel cooler or warmer than your forehead? Normal body temperature is 37°C. Your desk is probably close to the temperature of the room, which is probably about 20°C.

Whew! It's HOT!

Be a Scientist

Can you make an air thermometer?

Use a plastic soda bottle and a balloon to see if you can show air expanding. The object will act like a hot air thermometer. Test your design. How does your air thermometer respond when placed in a container of cold water? How does it respond when placed in a container of hot tap water? What is happening to the particles of air inside the air thermometer?

Record your observations in your Activity Journal. How is this similar to what happens to the liquid in an outdoor thermometer?

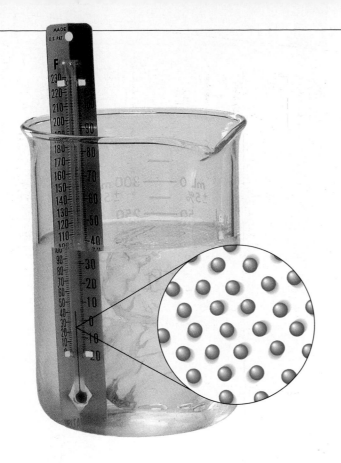

You can measure temperature by using an instrument called a thermometer. One type of thermometer is a narrow tube containing liquid. Outdoor thermometers contain colored alcohol. As the air and thermometer get warmer, the particles of alcohol vibrate faster. As the particles travel faster, they spread farther and farther apart.

The spread of the alcohol particles causes an increase in the volume of the alcohol. Because the particles can't go outward, they must go up. The heated particles of alcohol rise in the tube. The mark on the thermometer at the top of the alcohol tells you the temperature.

SCIENCE JOURNAL There are many different types of thermometers in the world. What kinds of thermometers can you find at your home or in your school? Where in your home or school are these thermometers located? In your Science Journal, draw a picture of the types of thermometers you found.

BACK HOME

What is heat?

At ten o'clock in the morning, two of the truck drivers got drinks for their morning break. One had a hot cup of tea, and the other had a cold glass of orange juice. Then something happened that needed their attention, and they had to leave their drinks. You can guess what happened next. The tea cooled to the temperature around it and the orange juice warmed to the temperature around it.

When something is warmer than its surroundings, it becomes cooler. When something is cooler than its surroundings, it becomes warmer. These changes take place because energy is being transferred from one substance to another.

Energy that moves from one substance to another because of a temperature difference is called **heat.** Heat can also move from one part of an object to another if the two parts are at different temperatures. When a pan is heated on a stove, heat will flow from the burner to the bottom of the pan. Then it will flow within the pan from the bottom to the sides and then to the handle.

There are two important points to remember about heat. First, the direction in which heat flows is always from a warmer substance to a cooler substance. Second, energy is called

YOU CAN HELP

Turn your heat down in the winter. If every household in the United States turned down the heat by about $3\frac{1}{2}$°C for just one day in the winter, the fuel saved would equal enough oil to fill 28 large swimming pools.

◀ Does a garbage truck use heat energy to do work? The truck's engine generates heat energy by burning fuel. This energy helps the truck to move.

▲ This special photograph shows heat escaping from a car. The yellow, orange, and red shading shows heat escaping. The blue and green shading shows the cooler parts of the car.

heat only when it is *moving* from one place to another. A substance can give off heat or take in heat, but it doesn't "have" heat. The energy that is inside a substance is called internal energy.

Heat, then, can increase the internal energy of something. In addition, like all forms of energy, heat can do work. Work is done when something is moved. The garbage truck in the photograph, for example, is able to move because of heat energy.

How are you doing?

1. What is temperature? How is it measured?
2. What is heat? In what direction does it flow?
3. **Think** Explain how a thermometer works. Why is alcohol used rather than water in outdoor thermometers?
4. **Think** Which has more internal energy— bath water with a temperature of 38°C or a person with a temperature of 37°C? Which one would increase in internal energy if the person got into the bath?

How are temperature and heat related?

As you learned in Lesson 1, when a substance gains heat energy, its temperature often increases. In general, how much its temperature changes depends on the mass of the substance. The greater mass a substance has, the less its temperature will change. Suppose you add a certain amount of heat to one liter of water and its temperature increases by 10°C. If you add the same amount of heat to two liters of water, its temperature will increase by only 5°C.

The relationship between heat and temperature is also affected by the kind of substance that is being heated. Different substances require different amounts of heat to cause the same change in temperature. For example, less heat is needed to increase the temperature of a metal than is needed to increase the temperature of water by the same number of degrees.

Sometimes heat energy can be added to a substance and its temperature will not increase. This happens when a substance changes state. Suppose, for example, that you add heat to some ice, which has a temperature of 0°C. The temperature will not increase, even though heat is continually being added. Instead, the ice will begin to melt. When all the ice has become liquid water, the temperature will start to increase.

Compost is a mixture of decaying food and yard waste that makes a good fertilizer. Many communities use compost piles to decrease the amount of waste that goes into landfills.

Inside a compost pile, the temperature can reach 66°C. Why is the temperature so high? As the material in the compost pile decays, energy stored in the molecules of the material is changed to heat. The process is similar to what happens when fuels are burned.

Be a Scientist

How do temperatures change?

1. **ACTIVITY JOURNAL** Place very cold water in a resealable plastic bag. Measure the temperature of the water and record this temperature in your Activity Journal. Close the bag securely.

2. Fill a container with hot water and measure the temperature of the hot water. Record the temperature. Place the plastic bag of very cold water into the container of hot water. Wait 15 minutes and then remove the bag from the container of hot water.

3. Measure and record the temperature of the water in the plastic bag. What happened to the temperature of the water in the plastic bag? Then measure and record the temperature of the hot water in the container. What happened to its temperature?

4. In your Activity Journal, explain why the temperatures changed.

How does heat travel?

Heat travels in three ways: by convection, by conduction, and by radiation.

▲ **Convection** (kən vek´shən) is the transfer of heat that happens when the particles of a gas or liquid flow within the material itself. For instance, when air is warmed, its particles move faster and begin to take up more space. Cooler, more dense air pushes the warm air upward. As the warm air rises, it loses heat, becomes cooler, and sinks. This is how wind currents are produced.

Radiation (rā´dē ā´shən) is the transfer of energy. One example of this **radiant energy** is the energy from the sun, which travels through empty space. Although radiation does not need matter to move it from one place to another, it can travel through some kinds of matter. The heat from a space heater, for example, radiates through air. ▶

▲ **Conduction**
(kən duk´shən) is the transfer of heat between objects that are touching, or from one part of an object to another part. Conduction happens best in solids. When a hot material and a cold material come together, the faster-moving particles of the warmer material collide with the slower-moving particles of the cooler material. Heat is passed from particle to particle.

Metals are good conductors of heat. Most cooking pans are made of metal. The handles of pans, however, are usually made of wood or plastic. These materials are poor conductors. Poor conductors are called insulators. An insulator slows down the transfer of heat.

Warm Houses

During the winter, most houses lose heat through their roofs, walls, and windows. To prevent heat loss, builders put insulation (in´sə lā´shən), such as fiberglass, inside the walls and in the roofs or ceilings of new houses. Insulation is a substance that slows heat transfer. Windows made of two layers of glass also help insulate homes. The double-paned windows trap a pocket of air between them. The air is a good insulator and helps keep heat inside your house.

Homes in Japan use the same idea. Traditional Japanese houses have partitions and sliding doors made of thin paper. Paper is a very good insulator. Some of the walls are made of layers of paper that trap air between them just as double-paned windows do.

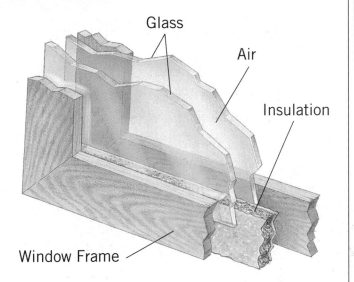

Glass

Air

Insulation

Window Frame

How are you doing?

1. What makes the temperature of an object increase?
2. How do the mass and substance of an article affect a change in its temperature?
3. **Think** What is the difference between a good conductor and a good insulator?
4. **Think** What are the differences among the three ways that heat travels?

Trash

Do you know what was in the trash your family threw out last week? Do you think anyone cares what was in your trash? You might be surprised to learn that many people think trash is interesting.

For recyclers, knowing what is in the trash is important. These people want to find out what materials can be taken out of the trash and recycled or reused.

For archaeologists, trash is a wonderful source of information. Archaeologists are scientists who search for clues about human cultures, especially those of the past. In their studies of ancient cultures, scientists have found that trash was sometimes used to fill foundations of buildings. By digging up these foundations and ancient dump sites, the archaeologists find tools and household items such as dishes. These items are clues about how people worked and lived.

Similar research is being done by garbologists, modern-day archaeologists who study garbage. They dig into landfills and find many surprises. In some areas, very little decay has taken place. There, hot dogs and other food scraps can be identified. Such scraps indicate the kinds of food that people have eaten. Dated materials, such as forty-year-old newspapers, tell the scientists when the trash was dumped.

Think again about what your family threw out last week. What would recyclers, archaeologists, or modern garbologists learn from your trash?

Archaeologists examine a find and discuss its purpose.

Garbologists try to discover what people dump and why.

Explore Activity

Does a rubber band have energy?

Process Skills
Inferring, Making models

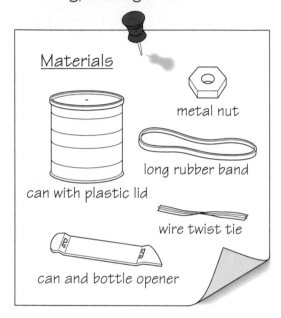

Materials

metal nut

long rubber band

can with plastic lid

wire twist tie

can and bottle opener

In this activity you will use a rubber band to make a can roll without any visible force—a "magic" can!

Observe and Collect Data

1. Work with a partner. As shown in the illustration, punch two holes in the bottom of the can and matching holes in the lid.
2. Cut the rubber band and put each end through the holes in the can.
3. Pull the rubber band taut. Tie the nut onto the rubber band with the twist tie, as shown. Make sure that the nut is close to the middle of the can.
4. Put the ends of the rubber band through the holes in the lid. Put the lid on and tie the ends of the rubber band together.
5. Roll the can away from you. As you might expect, it will slow down and stop. Then find out what will happen next.

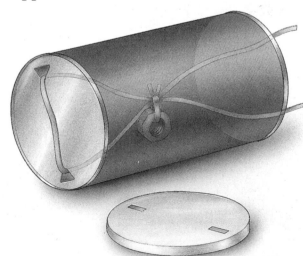

Share Your Results

1. Did your can roll back to you? How did your can compare to those of the others?

2. Does this activity work better if you roll the can gently or forcefully? Does it work better on a rough surface or a smooth surface? Share your ideas with your class.

Draw Conclusions

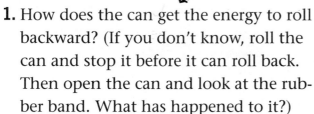

1. How does the can get the energy to roll backward? (If you don't know, roll the can and stop it before it can roll back. Then open the can and look at the rubber band. What has happened to it?)

2. This activity shows energy of motion changing to stored energy and then to energy of motion. In your Activity Journal, describe what happens.

Apply What You Know

How else could you use the stored energy of a rubber band to make something move? Write your ideas in your Activity Journal.

What are different forms of energy?

Energy is very important to scientists, and it is equally important in our daily lives. Nonetheless, it is a difficult idea to understand. One reason for this difficulty is that energy has a number of forms that are very different from one another. As you read these two pages, you will learn about or review various forms of energy such as light, sound, and electrical energy. You may wonder why they are all called energy. There are two reasons: They can all change from one form to another, and they can all do work, or cause change in matter.

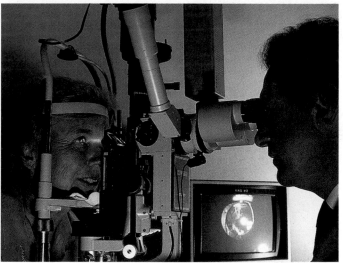

▲ **Light energy**
Lasers make a concentrated beam of light that can be used during surgery. Surgeons use lasers to treat conditions that can cause blindness.

Be a Scientist

HANDS-ON ACTIVITY

Can heat be made from mechanical energy?

Take two wooden blocks and briskly rub them together. Touch the blocks. How do they feel? In your Activity Journal, describe the energy changes that happen in this demonstration.

◀ Sound energy

When you play a drum, the skin over the cylinder vibrates. These vibrations move through the air as waves, setting molecules in the air in motion. When vibrating molecules reach your ears, your eardrums vibrate, too. A message is sent to your brain, and you hear the sound of the drum.

▲ Mechanical energy

Mechanical energy is the energy an object has due to its motion, position, or condition. The speedboat has energy of motion. This is also called **kinetic energy**. If an object is raised above the position it was in—perhaps a ball thrown into the air—it has stored energy because of its position. If an object is compressed, or squeezed together—a spring, for example—it has stored energy because of its condition. Stored energy is also called **potential energy**.

Heat energy

Heat from this campfire keeps the campers warm. It also provides a way for them to cook their dinner. ▼

▲ Electrical energy

Lightning is an example of electrical energy. An electric charge builds up in the clouds, causing a spark to move through the air. The spark can move from one cloud to another or it can strike the ground. Sometimes fires start when a lightning bolt hits a tall tree. Many homes are protected from lightning by rods that direct the spark into the ground.

What are some ways that energy changes form?

Energy changes form in many ways. Your body turns chemical energy from food into energy that helps you to move. When you clap your hands, you change the mechanical energy of the movement of your arms into sound energy. If you rub your hands together very fast, you change mechanical energy into heat energy. Here are some other examples of energy changing form.

▲ Gulls search the landfill for food. Sometimes they drop objects to break them apart. When the gull flies upward, it gives the object potential energy. When the gull drops the object and the object falls, its energy is changed to kinetic energy.

TEXAS INSTRUMENTS **TI-108**

▲ As electricity flows through the wire inside the light bulb, electrical energy changes into both heat energy and light energy.

▲ Energy stored in the bonds that hold atoms together is called **chemical energy**. This comb jellyfish has stored chemical energy that can be changed to light.

◀ A solar cell changes light energy into electricity. Only a few solar cells are needed to run this pocket calculator, while large groups of solar cells can provide energy to a satellite.

Be a Scientist

Can you make candy spark?

Some hard candies give off light when they are crushed. Find out which candies spark by trying this experiment.

1. ⚠ Select a variety of wintergreen candies. One person in the group will be the candy crusher. Other students will be observers. The candy crusher will use a pair of pliers to crush the candy. Everyone should wear safety goggles to make sure that flying bits of candy don't get in their eyes. Turn out the lights and crush the candy.

2. 📝 **ACTIVITY JOURNAL** After you have crushed the candy, turn on the lights and record the results in your Activity Journal.

3. Did the candy give off light? What was the color of the light? How bright was the light?

4. Repeat the experiment using different flavors of hard candy, including wintergreen, root beer, pineapple, cherry, butterscotch, lemon, grape, or spearmint. Which candies give off more light? What causes candy to give off light?

What is a common result of energy changes?

▲ Your TV set changes electrical energy into light, sound, and heat.

When an energy change occurs, one form of energy often changes to several different forms of energy. Some of these new forms of energy are useful, but others are not. When you turn on your television set, electrical energy changes to light and sound. In this case, both light and sound are useful to you. But have you noticed that your TV also gets warmer while it is on? This heat energy is not of any use. In fact, the heat shows that some of the electrical energy put into your TV is wasted.

Look at the energy changes on these two pages and on the two previous pages to find out what forms of energy are not needed in each example. Sometimes light isn't needed. Sometimes sound isn't needed. And almost always there is unwanted heat.

What does it matter if heat results when energy changes form? Sometimes heat makes people uncomfortable. For example, you probably don't want to be near warm machinery on a hot summer's day. More importantly, however, excess heat represents energy that is not available for us to

SCIENCE JOURNAL Look for energy changes in your home or neighborhood. Make a list of five of these changes in your Science Journal. Try to include all of the energy forms that result from the change.

BACK HOME

use. It cannot run a TV, for example, or light a lamp.

You could compare excess heat to the discarded objects in a landfill. Those worn out or broken objects cannot be used again. Instead of being useful, they cause problems by taking up space in the landfill. Excess heat is equally useless, and too much of it can cause problems as well. Too much unwanted heat is called thermal pollution.

▲ The mixer changes electrical energy to mechanical energy, but it also produces some unneeded sound and heat.

Four kinds of energy!

▲ Chemical energy changes into heat energy and light energy when the fuel of the blow torch is lit. The heat energy cuts the metal. Sparks flying from the metal show extra wasted heat energy and light energy. The chemical energy of the fuel also changes into sound energy as the fuel burns.

How are you doing?

1. Name three different forms of energy and give examples of each.
2. If there were an "energy landfill," which forms of energy might you find in it?
3. **Think** Both a candle and a lamp give off light. Compare the ways these objects produce light.
4. **Think** Suppose you stretched a rubber band until it broke. What energy changes take place when a rubber band breaks?

How does the sun release energy?

Energy produced by the sun in the form of heat and light is called **solar energy**. It is created by a process inside the sun that releases energy from matter. Very high temperatures separate electrons from the nuclei of their atoms. The nuclei of some forms of hydrogen atoms can join together to produce helium nuclei. The matter that isn't contained in the helium and the released neutron is changed to large amounts of energy. This process, called nuclear fusion, leaves less matter at the end than there was to begin with.

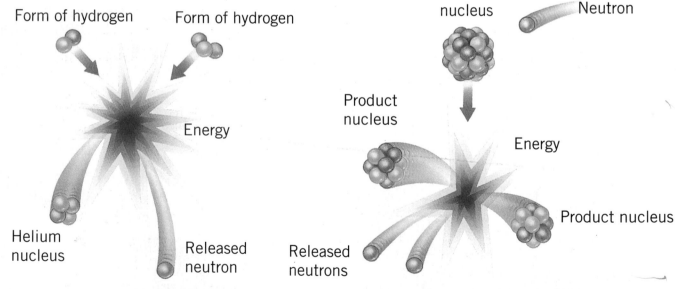

Form of hydrogen   Form of hydrogen

Energy

Helium nucleus

Released neutron

Uranium nucleus   Neutron

Product nucleus

Energy

Product nucleus

Released neutrons

▲ **Nuclear fusion** (fyoo´zhən) is a process that releases energy by joining the centers, or nuclei, of atoms. When the nuclei of some forms of hydrogen atoms fuse together, they form helium. This reaction produces huge amounts of energy.

▲ Unlike the sun, people produce energy from matter through **nuclear fission** (fish´ən), a process that splits atoms by bombarding their nuclei with smaller particles. As an atom splits, it gives off more particles, which collide with other atoms. This starts a chain reaction that creates a great amount of energy.

◄ The sun provides the energy that helps maintain livable temperatures on the earth and creates convection currents that circulate the earth's air. The sun's energy also powers the earth's water cycle by evaporating water from rivers and oceans.

Energy from Nuclear Fusion

Scientists have helped us better understand how the sun releases energy by nuclear fusion. By understanding it more, we may someday harness this kind of energy.

Nuclear fusion can release great amounts of energy. But there is a problem. It's hard to push atoms close to one another. To get hydrogen atoms to come together takes very high temperatures. High temperatures cause atoms to lose their electrons. This makes it much easier for the atoms to smash into each other and join together.

How hot does it have to get before atoms join forces? In one fusion reactor, hydrogen gas is heated to nearly 40 million degrees Celsius. Creating such high temperatures uses great amounts of energy. Often this is more energy than the reactor can produce, so it is not economical. Scientists around the world are studying fusion to try to overcome this problem.

How is the sun's energy used?

Although the sun is 150 million kilometers away from the earth, we receive enough light energy to help us to see and to help plants grow. Heat energy from the sun also warms the earth. Almost all of the energy we use comes from the sun. Look at the pictures below to see how the sun supplies energy for living things.

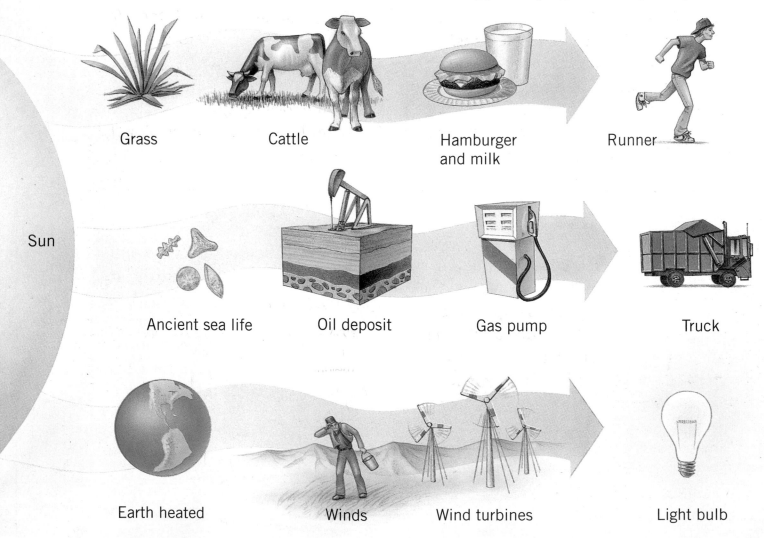

Sun

Grass   Cattle   Hamburger and milk   Runner

Ancient sea life   Oil deposit   Gas pump   Truck

Earth heated   Winds   Wind turbines   Light bulb

Solar Service Technician

Solar energy is one of our renewable resources. We cannot use it, however, without the necessary equipment. Mike Anchondo installs, services, and repairs solar equipment that heats the water for homes. He did not have to go to college to learn his trade. He learned mostly by hands-on experience as an apprentice.

66 To do my job, it is important to know how to get the greatest amount of heat from solar panels. I need to know about solar energy, electricity, and the transfer of energy. It is also important to my work that I can explain to customers how their system works, how it saves them money, and how solar energy use is better for the environment and for the community.

"We need to look for alternative energies for the future. The sun is there for us right now. There is a cost to the equipment, but the energy is free! I look forward to the day when the majority of houses use solar equipment. I take pride in my work, knowing I am helping the environment.**99**

The sun's energy helps grass grow. Dairy cows eat the grass and produce the milk that you drink. Milk and other foods give you the energy to run and jump. The sun provides energy for tiny sea creatures such as diatoms. The diatoms die and eventually turn into oil deposits. The oil goes to a refinery, where it is made into the gasoline that powers vehicles such as garbage trucks.

The sun also supplies heat energy that warms the air. This creates wind currents that can turn wind turbines that produce electricity for our lights.

How are you doing?

1. How does the sun affect some of your daily activities?
2. What is the difference between nuclear fusion and nuclear fission?
3. **Think** How does the amount of matter change during a nuclear reaction?
4. **Think** Starting with the sun's energy, trace the energy transformations that allow a kangaroo to hop.

How do plants and animals store energy?

Plants use energy from the sun to make food. This happens through a process called photosynthesis, which changes light energy into chemical energy. Food contains stored chemical energy.

Plants make food to meet their own energy needs. They use some of the food right away, but some is stored for future use in their roots, stems, or other parts. In many cases, the food that plants store for themselves can also be used as food by people and animals.

When you eat plants, you take in stored energy. Then chemicals in your body break down the food and release the energy. Your body uses that energy for various activities, including movement and growth. Often energy that is not used is stored as fat.

Some animals, as you know, do not eat plants. Instead, they get the energy they need by eating other animals. Energy is passed along on a food chain from plants to plant-eaters to animal-eaters. This flow of energy can be thought of as an energy pyramid. At the bottom of the pyramid are plants. This level has the greatest amount of stored energy. As the pyramid narrows, less and less food energy is available. The living things at each level have used some of that energy for their life activities.

▲ This is the energy pyramid for a food chain in a field that borders a landfill. Study the plants and animals in an area near you. Draw an energy pyramid for that area in your Science Journal.

◀ You can't go on putting trash into a landfill forever. Once a landfill is full, workers cap it with a layer of clay and several meters of soil. Often, workers plant trees and plants in landfills and turn the landfills into parks, golf courses, or sites for businesses or warehouses. Why must the landfill be capped with clay before it can be used for other purposes?

How is energy stored in fuels?

▲ Scientists are not completely sure how oil was formed. The most accepted theory is that oil formed from the remains of ancient sea life that may have looked like these one-celled diatoms.

A **fossil fuel** is an energy resource, such as coal, oil, or natural gas, that was formed from organisms that died long ago. The remains were buried under layer after layer of sediment. After a long time, the remains were so deep inside the earth's crust that very high temperatures and great pressure changed them into coal and other fossil fuels.

Where did the energy in fossil fuels come from? Plants and many microscopic living things get their energy from the sun. The energy that comes from fossil fuels is really stored energy from the sun.

SIDE TRIP

Uses of Methane

If you look closely at a landfill, you might see tall pipes coming out of the ground. As garbage decays, it gives off a gas called methane. As the methane accumulates in the landfill, it is vented into the air through pipes.

Some landfills collect the gas and sell it as fuel. Companies that buy the methane often use it to produce electricity.

Power companies also buy methane and mix it with other natural gas. You might use this mixture in your home for cooking and heating.

Some vehicles have engines that run on methane. Methane works well as a fuel for vehicles. Why do you think most vehicles do not use methane? Do you think that someday they will?

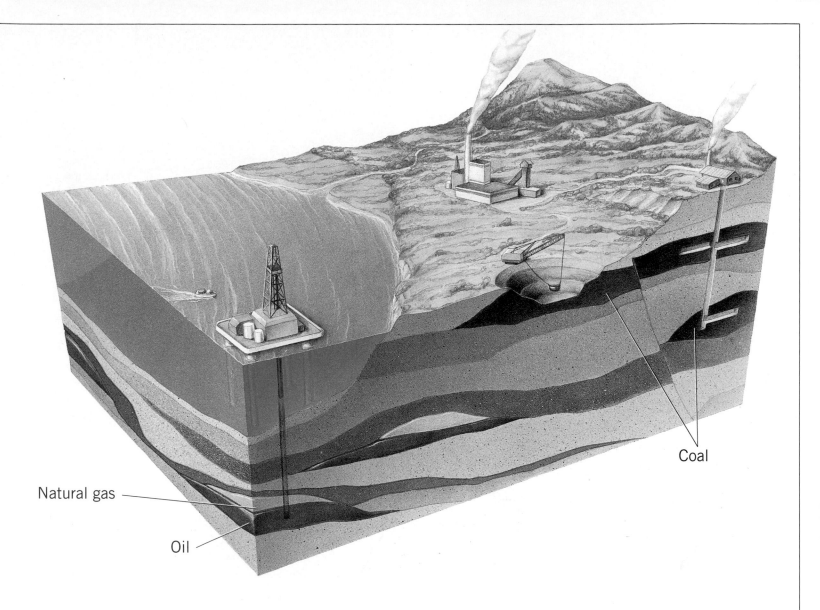

Natural gas

Oil

Coal

For many centuries, layers of sediment covered the remains of ancient sea life. Sediment is dirt, silt, and other matter that is deposited by water or wind. High pressure and temperature changed the remains of living things into pockets of gas and oil, which were trapped in the sediment. Eventually, the sediment turned into rock. Workers must drill through many layers of sedimentary rock to get to the pockets of oil and natural gas.

To find coal, miners often must dig many meters beneath the earth's surface. Layers of coal deposits are called coal beds. Some coal beds are only a meter thick, while others can be 100 meters thick. Coal is found in layers because the remains of ancient land plants from which coal formed were covered with dirt and mud that turned into rock. Coal beds are sandwiched between these layers of rock. There are two kinds of coal mines—a surface mine and an underground shaft mine.

How else is energy stored?

The world is a storehouse of energy. Nuclear fuels such as uranium and plutonium store great amounts of energy. Mechanical potential energy and chemical energy are other examples of stored energy. Your body stores energy, too.

▲ When released, the elastic potential energy of compressed springs decreases and their kinetic energy increases. Furniture that contains springs feels bouncy because the elastic potential energy is changed into kinetic energy that pushes you up after you sit down.

▲ Candles store chemical energy. When they burn, their chemical energy changes to heat and light.

◀ Nuclear fuels are powerful energy sources. Many small pellets of uranium, each about 2.5 cm long, will go into fuel rods for use in a nuclear reactor, such as the one shown here. In the reactor, the nuclei of atoms are split apart. This process, called nuclear fission, creates a huge amount of energy.

Some of the chemicals in dry-cell batteries are poisons that can harm the environment. Find out if there is a way to recycle dry cells in your community.

Chemical paste

Negative terminal

Positive terminal

Zinc jacket

Carbon rod

▲ Dry cells, commonly called batteries, store energy in chemicals. When you use the batteries in a flashlight, calculator, or radio, you use the cells' stored energy.

How are you doing?

1. Where do fossil fuels get their energy?
2. Describe different ways that energy can be stored.
3. **Think** Compare and contrast elastic potential energy and chemical energy. Give examples.
4. **Think** How does the human body store the chemical energy from food?

Science & Literature Connection

Where it comes from Garbage Where it goes

by Evan and Janet Hadingham

In this excerpt, the authors quote a magazine article from 100 years ago.

A century ago, Americans were already throwing out more garbage than the people of many other nations. The writer of this passage from an old issue of *Scientific American* noted that the citizens of Paris, France carefully saved and reused items that Americans generally thought of as trash:

"Even the smallest scrap of paper, that which every one throws away, here becomes a source of profit. Old provision tins, for instance, are full of money; the lead soldering is removed and melted down into cakes, while the tin goes to make children's toys. Old boots, however bad, always contain in the arch of the foot at least one sound piece that will serve again, and generally there are two or three others in the sole, the heel, and at the back. Scraps of paper go to the cardboard factory, orange peel to the marmalade maker, and so on. . . . The most valuable refuse—that which fetches two francs the kilo—is hair; the long goes to the hair dresser [for wigs], while the short is used, among other things, for clarifying oils."

Scientific American, September 1, 1894

Think About Your Reading

1. If you could generalize from this passage, how would you say the citizens of Paris viewed garbage in 1894?
2. What is your prediction? Will Americans ever be as careful about recycling as the Parisians of 1894? Why or why not?

Collecting data Keep track of everything your household throws away for one week. Measure how much space it takes up. Estimate how much space you could save in a landfill per week and per year by recycling or reusing some items.

Where to Read More

Brenda Guiberson, *The Turtle People*, (Atheneum, 1990)
Richie finds an ancient bowl along a river and imagines the American Indian people who crafted it.

Looking Back

Words and Concepts

Complete the following statements.

1. A(n) _____ is an energy resource that was formed from living things that died long ago.
2. Stored energy is called _____ energy.
3. Lightning is an example of _____ energy.
4. Energy stored by living things is in the form of _____ energy.
5. The energy given off by the sun is called _____ energy.
6. Energy released from matter is called _____ energy.

Yechhh!

Applied Thinking Skills

Answer the following questions. You can use words, drawings, and diagrams in your answers.

7. Look at the photograph of the exhaust from the bulldozer. What form of energy would you find here? Describe all the energy changes that led to the energy in its current form.
8. What forms of energy are found in each of the following: gasoline in a car, uranium atoms, a worker's jackhammer, crackers, light bulb, gas stove, and electric blanket?

9. Predict several things that would happen to the earth if the radiant energy that comes from the sun were drastically reduced.
10. **Your World** Describe the energy changes that allow you to write answers to these questions. Include chemical, electrical, mechanical, heat, and light energy in your description.

Show What You Know

Can you make dominoes climb?

Observe and Collect Data

1. To understand how transformations of energy can start a chain reaction, try constructing a domino path that will make the dominoes climb uphill.
2. Construct a dominoes path that includes an inclined plane made by raising one end of a piece of cardboard. Stand the dominoes close to one another over the course of the path.
3. When you push the first domino, you will start a chain reaction. Experiment with different paths that will make your dominoes climb over other objects.

Process Skills

Making models, Inferring, Controlling variables

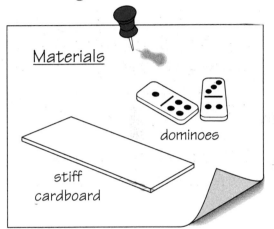

Materials

dominoes

stiff cardboard

Draw Conclusions

1. What energy transformations are happening in this experiment? Write your observations in your Activity Journal.

2. What form of energy are you providing to start the chain reaction?

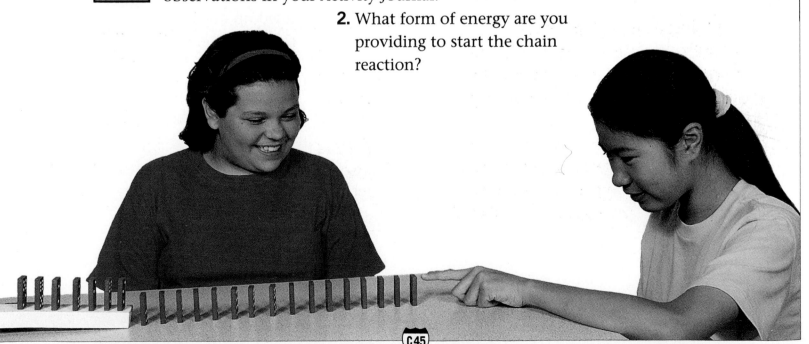

Chapter 3

Energy Resources

Future greeting cards

Ready for cleaning

It is Saturday morning, time to recycle. **Recycling** is the collection and treatment of discarded materials to make them into useful products. You reach into the trunk of the car and grab a box of plastic bottles. You walk to the recycling bins, where you dump out the boxes. Each bin has a label. One is for glass, one for aluminum, and another for different kinds of plastic.

This place is busy and many of your friends are helping with recycling, too. It is great to see your friends and neighbors at the recycling center. It may have been easier to throw all of these things out in the trash. What would have happened to all of these bottles and cans if you and your neighbors had not brought them to the recycling center? You are right if you guessed that they may have ended up in a landfill. Aluminum, glass, and plastic do not break down in landfills. Now, instead of taking up landfill space, these items can be made into useful products.

I didn't know all these plastics could be recycled.

We recycle every Saturday.

Explore Activity

How can you build a solar house?

Process Skills

Making models, Measuring, Predicting

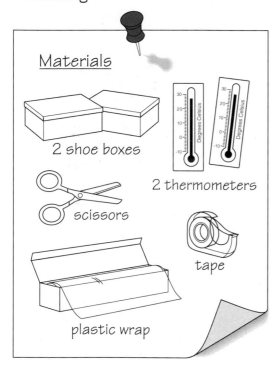

Materials

2 shoe boxes

2 thermometers

scissors

tape

plastic wrap

Only a small amount of the sun's energy reaches the earth. If we could harness all of that energy, however, it would be enough to provide for all of our energy needs. Building energy efficient solar homes is one way to work toward this goal. Find out how you can build a model solar house by trying this experiment.

Observe and Collect Data

1. First make a nonsolar house. Make a small hole in the lid of a shoe box. Put the lid on the box and insert a thermometer (bulb down) into the box.
2. Now make a model of a solar house. A solar house often has structures that absorb energy from sunlight. Plan your design. Think about the materials you will use to build your model.
3. Insert a thermometer into the solar house.
4. Measure the temperature in both houses. Record each temperature in your Activity Journal.
5. **Predict** what will happen to these temperatures when you place the houses in a sunny spot for an hour.
6. Place both boxes near a sunny window in your classroom. Measure and record the temperatures after one hour in the sun.

Share Your Results

Compare your results with those of other groups. Which houses have higher temperatures?

Draw Conclusions

Radiant energy from the sun travels through space in waves. What happened to these waves of energy when they reached the solar house? What happened when the waves of energy reached the nonsolar house?

Apply What You Know

1. Using what you have learned about insulation, what are some ways to keep heat in your solar house longer?
2. What does this experiment tell you about ways to keep your family's home warmer in the winter?

What are nonrenewable energy resources?

When you go somewhere by automobile, you use energy from petroleum. When you turn on a light, you may use energy made from nuclear fuels or from burning coal or oil at a power plant. If you have a gas stove, you use natural gas to cook your food.

Nuclear fuels, coal, oil, and natural gas are natural resources. A **natural resource** is something that comes from the earth that we use to sustain our lives.

▲ Nuclear power stations can produce large amounts of energy. But many people oppose them because of the possibility of accidents and the difficulty of disposing of nuclear waste safely. Still, the United States gets 22 percent of its electricity from nuclear power.

▲ Workers drill wells to find oil deposits. Crude oil, or petroleum, is a brown or black liquid or a sticky tar. We use petroleum to make fuels such as gasoline and kerosene. We also use petroleum to make electricity and to make products such as pesticides, fertilizers, and plastics.

Trees, air, water, minerals, plants, and animals are all natural resources. Some resources replace themselves in just a few years. A natural resource that is *not* replaced after it is used is called a **nonrenewable resource**. It took millions of years for nuclear fuels, coal, oil, and natural gas to form. Once we use them up, we cannot make more.

YOU CAN HELP

Walk, ride a bike, or ride the bus. By driving less, people can decrease the use of fossil fuels, which take millions of years to create.

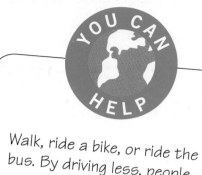

▲ Natural gas is mostly methane, but it can also include other gases. Workers drill into the earth to find natural gas. Companies sell the natural gas to power plants that make electricity.

▲ The United States is one of the biggest users of coal. In fact, 56 percent of the energy used to make electricity in the United States comes from coal. Coal is also used to make heat to process metals such as iron and steel.

What are renewable energy sources?

The world is running out of fossil fuels. Where will we get our energy once we use up all of our coal, oil, and natural gas? Scientists and conservationists have been looking for alternative energy resources for many years. Many of our energy alternatives are renewable energy resources. **Renewable resources** are resources that the environment is more easily able to replace or recycle. Water power, wind power, solar energy, and geothermal energy are renewable resources.

▲ Wind provides another energy source for the production of electricity. Most of the world's wind turbines are located in California. In one year, California wind farms provided energy equal to the output of one nuclear plant.

Hydroelectric (hī´drō ē lek´trik) **energy** is the use of the energy of moving water to make electricity. Workers build a dam across a river to create a waterfall. The potential energy of the water is turned into mechanical energy as it turns the turbines. ▶

Solar energy is energy harnessed from the sun. One solar farm covers 988 hectares of land and uses more than a million mirrors to focus the sun's energy. Computers help the mirrors move and follow the sun during the day. The mirrors have tubes on top. These tubes are filled with oil, which absorbs the sun's energy. The oil heats water to make steam and electricity. ▶

Burning Trash

We throw away millions of tons of garbage every year, and landfills in the United States are quickly filling up. Few people want new landfills in their communities. What are we to do with all our trash?

Large machines called incinerators can make electricity by burning trash. Burning 1 ton of garbage releases as much energy as 160 liters of petroleum. Burning trash also can reduce the volume of waste that goes into landfills by about 80 percent.

However, there are some problems with incinerators. Poisonous ashes are produced, which are then buried in landfills. In landfills that are not properly lined, rainwater may wash poisons from the ash into the ground water.

Burning trash also creates air pollution. Incinerators are equipped with filters and air scrubbers that clean the gases in the smokestack. Unfortunately, some pollutants still escape into the air.

Think About It There are good and bad sides to burning trash. What do you think? Find out if your community uses incineration to get rid of trash. Describe how other ways of handling trash could be used.

◀ We can use the earth's heat as an energy source. Energy from heat trapped inside the earth is called **geothermal energy**. *Geo-* means "earth," and *thermal* means "heat." There are many places where steam and hot water are trapped underground. We can dig wells into these underground energy stores and use the hot water and steam to make electricity.

How are you doing?

1. How do we use water to make electricity?
2. Describe several alternative energy sources.
3. **Think** In what types of climates is it most practical to use solar energy?
4. **Think** Which renewable energy resource is most available where you live?

How are materials recycled?

While scientists and conservationists are busy working on renewable energy sources, we must find ways to conserve the nonrenewable energy supply we already have. One way to conserve energy resources is by recycling. It often takes less energy to make products from recycled materials than to make them from raw materials.

Aluminum is made from a mineral called *baux-ite*. To get aluminum from bauxite takes a lot of electricity. Making aluminum products from recycled aluminum takes only about 10 percent of the energy required to make aluminum from bauxite ore. Recycling aluminum uses fewer natural resources and saves minerals. ▼

▲ When plastic jugs, bottles, and containers are recycled, they are first shredded and washed. Next, the tiny bits of plastic are melted and pressed through a machine that makes the plastic look like long strings of spaghetti. These strings are cut into tiny pellets. New plastic products can be made from these pellets. It takes up to 90 percent less energy to make a plastic product from recycled plastic than it does to make it originally.

▲ Glass is another material that can be recycled. Used glass is crushed, melted, and formed into new glass products. Crushed glass is sometimes used in paving roads.

▲ Much of the trash that ends up in landfills is paper, which could have been recycled. At a paper-recycling plant, used paper goes into a machine that washes out the ink and turns the paper into a milky substance called pulp. The pulp gets pressed into thin layers, rolled out in sheets, and dried. Products such as cardboard boxes, toilet paper, paper towels, newsprint, and stationery come from recycled paper. To make these paper products without recycling, you would have to cut down trees.

MINDS-ON ACTIVITY

Be a Scientist

Can you discover wasteful packages?

Classify packaging that you and your family throw away into the following categories: glass, aluminum, paper, plastic, and other. What raw materials do you think went into making these packaging items? Which of these items can you recycle?

Some packaging prevents damage to the product. Some keeps the product fresh. Other packaging encourages people to buy the product. Identify the purpose of each packaging item you found. How can you cut down on the amount of packaging you buy? How would you design a useful package?

Amazing!

You could heat five million homes for 200 years with the amount of paper and wood Americans throw away in one year.

What can you do?

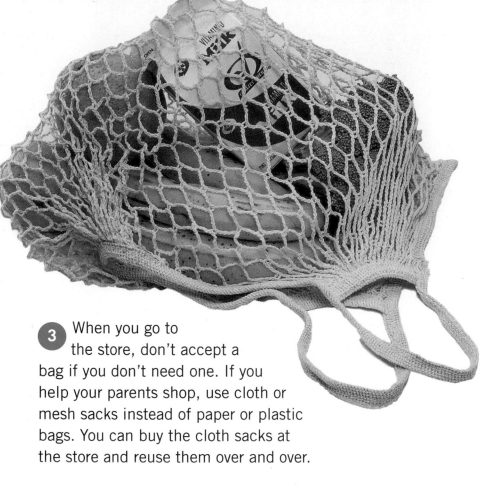

 Less than 5 percent of the world's population lives in the United States. Yet we use more than 23 percent of the world's energy resources. Many of our energy resources are limited. But by doing little things, you can make a big difference. Here are some ways to save energy resources.

1 Flip a switch. Turn off the lights and household appliances when you are not using them. Let your hair air dry naturally instead of using a hair dryer. If you must use a dryer, use it on the low setting. This saves electricity and prevents split ends.

2 Keep the refrigerator closed. Think about what you want before you open the refrigerator door.

3 When you go to the store, don't accept a bag if you don't need one. If you help your parents shop, use cloth or mesh sacks instead of paper or plastic bags. You can buy the cloth sacks at the store and reuse them over and over.

4 Don't pay for the package. Much of the paper and plastic that ends up in landfills is from packaging. Don't buy overpackaged products.

 SCIENCE JOURNAL Look around you. How many of the things you use at home and at school are made from recycled materials? Make a list in your Science Journal.

BACK HOME

Be a Scientist

How can you do an energy audit?

1. You can find out if your home is using energy efficiently by doing an energy audit. Check the doors and windows for drafts. Do this on a cold or windy day so that you can easily tell where heat may be escaping. Record your results in your Activity Journal.

2. With the help of an adult, see if the water heater in your home is insulated. Check the hot-water temperature setting by holding a thermometer under the hot water faucet in the kitchen, letting the water run until it's hot. Record the temperature and compare it to the temperatures recorded by your classmates.

3. Check to make sure that your refrigerator is not letting warm air in. Check the seal around the refrigerator door by closing a piece of paper in the door. Try pulling the paper out. If it slides out easily, the seal around the door needs to be replaced. What other ways can you think of to make your home more energy efficient?

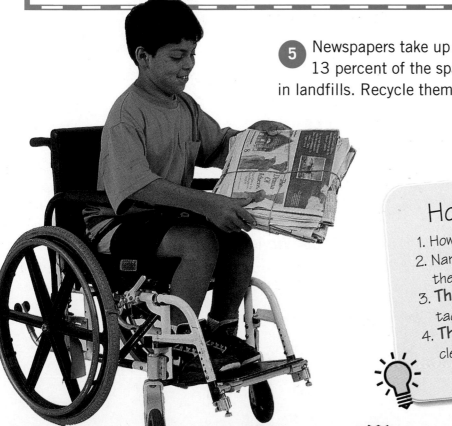

5 Newspapers take up 13 percent of the space in landfills. Recycle them!

How are you doing?

1. How does recycling save energy resources?
2. Name five things that you can do to help the environment.
3. **Think** What are some of the disadvantages of disposable products?
4. **Think** Name five products made of recycled products. How many do you use?

Looking Back

Words and Concepts

Read each statement. If a statement is true, write *true* as your answer. If a statement is false, change the underlined words to make the statement true.

1. Minerals, air, and soil are <u>fossil fuels</u>.
2. Batteries in your camera get energy from <u>film</u>.
3. You can save energy by <u>crushing</u> plastic, aluminum, and glass.
4. Coal, oil, and natural gas are made from <u>living</u> things.
5. Hydroelectric power is a <u>nonrenewable</u> energy resource.
6. <u>Conduction</u> is an energy resource that comes from heat from the earth.

Applied Thinking Skills

Answer the following questions. You can use words, drawings, and diagrams in your answers.

7. Compare the stored energy in fossil fuels to the stored energy in food. How are these energy sources similar and different?
8. The United States gets most of its energy from the burning of fossil fuels and from nuclear power. What factors might cause an energy shortage? What measures would you propose to prevent future shortages?
9. If a natural resource is renewable, can we use it in any way we want? Why or why not?
10. **Your World** Make a log of your daily activities. Next to each activity, list a way that you can change your activity to save energy resources.

Show What You Know

What's in the trash?

Observe and Collect Data

1. To understand how decisions about trash disposal affect the environment, try this game. Work in a group to think of all the things you might find in the trash. Make a paper label for each of about fifty common trash items. Put them all into a container. Pretend this container is your trash can.
2. Make another set of labels that say *recycle, reuse, compost,* and *landfill*. Attach each label to a separate container.
3. Select an item from your trash can and decide how to dispose of it. If you can recycle it, put it into the recycle container. If you can reuse it, put it into the reuse container. If you can compost it, put it into the compost container. If you can't recycle, reuse, or compost the item, put it in the landfill container. Try to keep as much trash as possible out of the landfill. Record in your Activity Journal the number of trash items in each container.

Draw Conclusions

1. What fraction of your trash were you able to keep out of the landfill?
2. What can you and others do to reduce the amount of trash that goes to landfills? Why is this important?

Process Skills
Classifying, Communicating

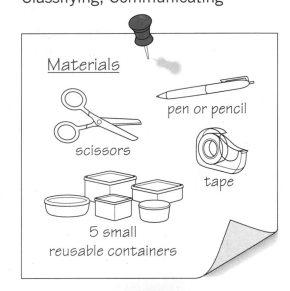

Materials

scissors

pen or pencil

tape

5 small reusable containers

Energy & Resources

Show what you have learned about landfills, energy resources, and recycling. Work with a partner, in a group, or by yourself. Select one activity.

Landfill Ambassador Pretend you are going to another state to share information about how to design and manage a landfill. Make a presentation or video on the subject.

Jingle Writer TV and radio programs use catchy jingles or songs to sell products. Come up with your own jingle or rap song to encourage people to recycle.

Trash Artist Make a sculpture, a musical instrument, or a toy out of trash.

City Planner Many people don't want to live near a landfill. Design a city with all the necessary structures: schools, houses, a water treatment plant, roads, landfill, and anything else you think is necessary. Will your city need an incinerator?

Archaeologist Make a list of all of the things thrown away at school. Of the things tossed out, what was probably not around when your parents were your age?

Poster Artist Design a poster that makes people realize that they can save energy resources by recycling.

Glossary

chemical energy (kem´i kəl en´ər jē) The stored energy that is released during a chemical change. (page C29)

conduction (kən duk´shən) The transfer of heat between objects that are touching or from one part of an object to another. (page C16)

convection (kən vek´shən) The transfer of heat from one part of a gas or liquid to another part by the movement of the material itself. (page C16)

energy (en´ər jē) The ability to cause change in matter. (page C6)

fossil fuel (fäs´əl fyoo´əl) An energy resource formed from organisms that died long ago. (page C38)

geothermal energy (jē´ō thər´məl en´ər jē) Heat from the earth. (page C53)

heat (hēt) Energy that moves from one place to another because of a temperature difference. (page C12)

hydroelectric energy (hī´drō´ ē lek´trik en´ər jē) The use of water to make electricity. (page C52)

kinetic energy (ki net´ik en´ər jē) The energy of motion. (page C27)

natural resource (nach´ər əl rē´sôrs´) Something that comes from the earth and is used by people. (page C50)

nonrenewable resource (nän ri noo´ə bəl rē´sôrs´) A natural resource that is not replaced after it is used. (page C50)

nuclear fission (noo´klē ər fish´ən) A process that releases energy by splitting atoms. (page C32)

nuclear fusion (noo´klē ər fyoo´zhən) A process that releases energy by joining the nuclei of atoms. (paage C32)

potential energy (pō ten´shəl en´ər jē) Stored energy. (page C27)

radiant energy (rā´dē ənt en´ər jē) Energy from the sun. (page C16)

radiation (rā´dē ā´shən) The transfer of heat and other forms of energy. (page C16)

recycling (rē sī´kliŋ) The collection and treatment of discarded materials to make them into useful products. (page C46)

renewable resource (ri noo´ ə bəl rē´sôrs´) A natural resource that the environment replaces or recycles. (page C52)

solar energy (sō´lər en´ər jē) Energy from the sun. (page C32)

temperature (tem´pər ə chər) A measure of how hot or cold something is. (page C10)

Unit C Index

Boldface numerals denote glossary terms. Italic numerals denote illustrations.

Credits

Photographs

1–3 Tim Davis*; 4L David Weintraub/Photo Researchers;
4R Tim Davis*; 5 Tim Davis*; 6BL Tim Davis*; 6BR David
Weintraub/Photo Researchers; 6T Tim Davis*; 7B Tim
Davis*; 7T Thomas Kitchin/Tom Stack & Associates; 9
Elliott Smith*; 10T Ken Karp*; 10B Ken Karp*; 11 GHP
Studio*; 12–13 Larry Lefever/Grant Heilman Photography;
12B Ken Karp*; 13B Geoff Williams/SPL/Photo
Researchers; 16L Tim Davis*; 16TR Rafael Macia/Photo
Researchers; 16–17 Dan McCoy/Rainbow; 18B Bob
Daemmrich/Stock, Boston; 18T Ken Karp*; 18C Tom
Bean/DRK Photo; 20 Ken Karp*; 22BL Tim Davis*; 22BR
Breck P. Kent/Animals, Animals; 22T Kevin Schafer/Peter
Arnold, Inc.; 23 Thomas Kitchin/Tom Stack & Associates;
25 Elliott Smith*; 26B Hank Morgan/Rainbow; 26T Jim
Cummins/AllStock; 27BR Robert Daemmrich/Tony Stone
Images; 27L Keith Kent/Peter Arnold, Inc.; 27TR Vince
Streano/The Stock Market; 28BR GHP Studio*; 28L GHP
Studio*; 28T Thomas Kitchin/Tom Stack & Associates; 29
Runk-Schoenberger/Grant Heilman Photography; 30 Mike
Price/Bruce Coleman Inc.; 30(TV) GHP Studio*; 31B Tim
Davis*; 31T M. Dwyer/Stock, Boston; 33 NASA; 35 Anne
Dowie*; 37 Tim Davis*; 38 Jim Zuckerman/Westlight;
40TR Karen Kasmauski/Woodfin Camp & Associates; 40L

Tim Davis*; 41BR GHP Studio*; 41 Ken Karp*; 43 The
Bettmann Archive; 44 Andrew Rakoczy/Bruce Coleman
Inc.; 45 Elliott Smith*; 46B Mike Massaschi/Stock, Boston;
46T Gordon R. Gainer/The Stock Market; 47B Peter
Beck/The Stock Market; 47TR Tim Davis*; 47TL
Mugshots/The Stock Market; 49 Ken Karp*; 50L David M.
Doody/Tom Stack & Associates; 50R Ken Graham/AllStock;
51L Kristin Finnegan/AllStock; 51R Fred
McConnaughey/Photo Researchers; 51T Ken Karp*; 52–53
Don & Pat Valenti/DRK Photo; 52B Peter Menzel/Stock,
Boston; 52C John S. Flannery/Bruce Coleman Inc.; 52T
Grant Heilman/Grant Heilman Photography; 54L Roberto
Soncin Gerometta/Photo 20–20; 54R Phil Degginger/Bruce
Coleman Inc.; 55B R. Ian Lloyd/The Stock Market; 55T
Hank Morgan/Rainbow; 56 GHP Studio*; 57B Tim Davis*;
58 Larry Lefever/Grant Heilman Photography; 59B Elliott
Smith*

Special thanks to Malcolm X Elementary School, Berkeley,
California; Franklin Year-Round School, Oakland,
California; Carl B. Munck Elementary School, Oakland,
California; Hintil Ku Ka Child Care Center, Oakland,
California.

*Photographed expressly for Addison-Wesley Publishing
Company, Inc.

Illustrations

Nea Bisek 8T, 19T, 21, 24T, 45, 48T, 59
Brian Evans 39
Different Strokes 11
Marilyn Keiger 16, 16–17B
Michael Maydak 32T–33T, 36, 37
Jane McCreary 8B, 24BL, 48B, 55B
Rolin Graphics 17T, 19B, 32B, 34, 41
Randy Vergoustraete 60–61
Sarah Woodward 14–15

Text

42–43 Evan and Janet Hadingham, *Garbage! Where It Comes
From, Where It Goes* (New York: Simon & Schuster Books for
Young Readers, 1990). Copyright ©1990 by Evan and Janet
Hadingham and WGBH Educational Foundation; Scientific
American, September 1, 1894.

Amusement Park

Here at the amusement park, many objects and people are in motion. Roller-coaster riders are pressed back into their seats as the ride moves uphill, and they lean sideways into each other as it tilts and turns. People on some rides are flattened against a spinning cylinder as the floor moves away. Riders on the carousel move up and down as well as in a circle.

Many types of forces are acting on objects and people at the amusement park. The force of gravity pulls roller-coaster riders toward the center of the earth. The force of friction acts to slow and stop the roller-coaster cars. What other forces can you identify?

The amusement park is a great place to have fun while studying the energy of motion. And even though people are relaxed, work is being done with almost every move. Get ready to ride!

■ How can you describe motion?

■ What laws describe the motion of people and objects?

■ How are work and motion related?

MOTION & ENERGY

AMUSEMENT PARK

Activities

Features

Chapter 1

Motion

Have you ever been on a loop roller-coaster ride? If you like to move up and down and upside down, this might be the ride for you.

What sensations do you think riders feel as they move up the loop and are turned upside down? How do their feelings change as their cars slow to a halt at the end of the ride? What do the riders see at different points along the ride? Compare the view at different points on the ride with the view of people watching from the ground.

Think about the loop roller-coaster ride. What forces are involved as the cars move along the track? In your Science Journal, describe the points along the ride where you think the cars speed up. Where do you think they slow down? Why?

Wind in our faces and stomachs left behind

It doesn't get better than this!

Cooool! Is this how astronauts feel?

Look, Ma! No hands! (Good thing we've got seat belts.)

Explore Activity

What can a race teach you about speed?

HANDS-ON ACTIVITY

Process Skills
Predicting, Measuring, Collecting data

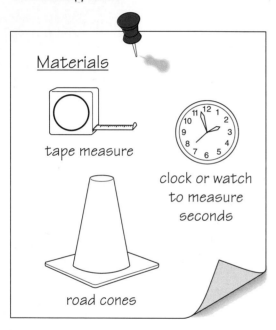

Materials

tape measure

clock or watch to measure seconds

road cones

Observe and Collect Data

1. Design three races, each one with the same total distance. At least one race may be an obstacle course. Make a drawing of the course for each race that you design. Briefly describe each race in your Activity Journal.
2. **Predict** in which races you will run fastest and slowest. Write your predictions in your Activity Journal.
3. Have a friend measure the seconds it takes you to run the first race. Record this time next to the description of the race in your Activity Journal.
4. Repeat step 3 for the other two races you designed.

Share Your Results

1. Describe the races that students ran in less time.
2. Describe the races that took the most time.

Draw Conclusions

1. How did running on a straighter course affect the time it took to go the distance?
2. How did changing direction affect the time needed?
3. What other factors affected the time it took to run different races?

Apply What You Know

1. Which courses were similar to amusement park rides? Which rides were they similar to?
2. Which courses might be good ideas for amusement park rides?

What is motion?

When you take part in a race, you start at one place and move to the finish line. Like all moving things, you change position. **Motion** is a continuous change of position. Moving objects can travel in a straight line or on a path that changes direction. Sometimes moving objects speed up. Sometimes they slow down. But all moving things are alike in that they are changing position.

Clues to motion are found by looking at other objects. When you ride the carousel, the people standing in line might seem to move past you. But you know that it is the carousel that is moving because you know that the people in line are staying in one place. You have used the line of people as a reference object. A **reference object** is something to which you compare the positions of a moving object. By using reference objects, you can follow changes in the motion of things.

How you describe an object's motion depends on the reference object you choose. It also depends on your own motion. Suppose you and a friend ride on a carousel car that does not move up and down. If you consider your friend as a reference object you are not moving. You do not change position relative to your friend, but stay seated next to him or her during the entire ride.

Be a Scientist

How can you tell what has moved?

HANDS-ON ACTIVITY

1. **ACTIVITY JOURNAL** Place five objects on your desk. Ask your partner to close his or her eyes. Move one object. Ask your partner to look and tell which object you moved. In your Activity Journal, explain how your partner could tell what had been moved.
2. Repeat this exercise. This time, mark the starting position of the object you move with a piece of transparent tape.
3. After your partner identifies the object that moved, find out how it moved in relation to the reference objects. How far and in what direction did it move?

▲ What do these riders see from the carousel? The world seems to move past them. But the child and her mother remain the same distance apart. Using each other as reference points, they aren't moving.

▲ Compared to a reference point off the carousel, the carousel riders are moving side to side, as well as first away and then back.

On the other hand, if you choose the people standing in line as a reference object, you are moving because you are changing position relative to them. They stay in one place, and you move first away from them and then back toward them again as you ride in a circular path on the carousel.

Think again about your friend sitting next to you. Suppose you are sitting on a carousel horse that moves up and down during the ride, while your friend is on one that is broken. If you use your friend as a reference object now, you will see that you have another kind of motion too. You are moving up and down in relation to your friend.

The kind of motion you describe can differ depending on the reference object you use. As you have learned, the earth is constantly in motion. The earth orbits the sun. It also rotates. If you consider the sun as your reference object, you are always in motion, even when, relative to the earth, you are standing still!

Motion is always relative. When scientists say the earth is moving in orbit, they mean that it is moving relative to the sun. When roller-coaster riders move up and down a hill, they move relative to the earth.

 Imagine you are riding on a bus past your school. In your Science Journal, describe your motion using the school as your reference object, using the bus driver as your reference object, and then using the sun as your reference object.

How does friction affect motion?

As you look around the amusement park, you see objects moving. One ride is just starting, while another is slowing to a stop. In a game booth, a plastic ring is moving toward the neck of a bottle. All of these changes in the speed or direction of objects are caused by forces.

A force is a push or a pull. When you pick up a book, pull open a door, or throw a ring toward a bottle, you are using forces. Almost everything you do involves forces. What causes the ring to drop after you throw it toward the bottle? One force causes this change in motion—gravity.

Friction (frik´shən) is a force that resists motion between objects that are touching. Friction keeps

▲ Hockey players are glad that there is not much friction between the puck and the ice. People who have to walk on icy sidewalks, however, wish there were more friction.

PEOPLE

SCIENCE TECHNOLOGY & SOCIETY

Galileo

Galileo Galilei (1564–1642) is famous for his experiments concerning motion. He showed that moving objects slow down and stop because of friction. Without friction, he said, objects in motion on a horizontal surface would continue in motion forever.

Actually, Galileo was not the first scientist to express this idea. Thousands of years earlier philosophers in China wrote, "Motion stops due to an opposing force. If there is no opposing force, the motion will never stop."

things from moving or slows moving objects until they eventually stop. The force of friction exists between all objects that are touching one another and that are either moving or trying to move relative to each other. For example, your chair stays in place because of friction between the chair legs and the floor. The ball you roll across the floor will slow down and eventually stop. The amount of friction depends on how rough the surfaces of touching objects are. There is more friction when the surfaces are rough. If you roll a ball across a carpet, it will stop sooner than a ball rolled across a wood floor.

Although friction resists motion, it helps you control motion. If you are running on a slippery gym floor, the treads of the sneakers keep you from slipping. Imagine trying to run on the same floor while wearing smooth, leather-soled shoes! The treads of tires keep cars from slipping too. Look at an old tire or the soles of old sneakers. Why have these things worn down?

Grease and oil reduce friction in machines. Grease makes the parts of a machine slide over each other smoothly. When friction is reduced, the machine lasts longer. ▶

Can you reduce friction?

Friction can cause things to heat up and wear out. Think of something you could do to your hands to reduce the friction when you rub them together. Test your idea. In your Activity Journal, describe your results. Tell how a similar idea could be used to reduce friction in machines.

How does gravity affect motion?

▲ Riders are pulled to the top of the vertical-drop ride and then plunge downward because of gravity. What forces keep the riders from dropping too fast?

When you zoom to the top of a hill on a roller-coaster track, you sometimes feel as if you might fly into space. But this is only a brief feeling, because you are pulled to the earth by a force called gravity. **Gravity** (grav´i tē) is a force of attraction between objects. The earth's gravity pulls all objects toward its center. Things on the earth stay on the ground because of gravity.

But the earth is not the only thing with gravitational pull. All objects exert this force. For example, the pull of gravity exists between you and a friend. Why, then, don't you and your friend slide into each other?

Two factors affect the pull of gravity between two objects: their masses and the distance between them. The greater the masses of the objects, the greater the pull of gravity between them. The pull is very small unless the mass of at least one object is large. In addition, the pull becomes greater if objects are closer to each other.

The reason you and your friend don't slide into each other, even if you are close together, is that your masses are too small. The earth has a great mass, so that is why on the roller coaster you always come back toward the earth after feeling as if you will fly off into space.

The force of gravity between you and the earth is so strong that it can be measured. You can easily measure the amount of this force by standing on a bathroom scale—your weight is a measure of the gravitational pull between you and the earth.

The Moon

What happens if you jump up high? The pull of gravity brings you back to the surface of the earth. If you were to jump on the moon, you would jump higher than you would on the earth. You wouldn't go soaring into space, however. Even for moon walkers, gravity is still in effect.

The moon's gravitational pull on you is weaker than the earth's. Can you explain why? That also means that you would weigh less on the moon.

What would it be like to drink a glass of water on the moon? What would it be like to throw a ball? In your Science Journal, describe how these or two other daily activities

would be different on the moon, where the force of gravity is less than it is on the earth.

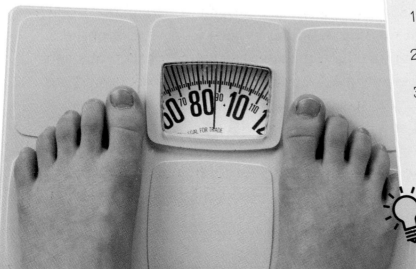

You pull on the earth and the earth pulls on you with equal force. ▼

How are you doing?

1. How do you know you're moving when you climb a flight of stairs?
2. What factors affect the force of friction? What factors affect the force of gravity?
3. **Think** Is it easier to push a box of books across a floor if the floor is made of wood, covered with tile, or carpeted? Why?
4. **Think** Where would the earth's gravity pull more strongly on you, at sea level or on top of a mountain? Why?

What is speed?

Headgear on … Moving on out!

YOU CAN HELP

Traveling at about 88 km/hr saves fuel. Encourage adults who drive on the highway to maintain a constant speed of 88 km/hr.

You and your friend ride your bikes to the amusement park. You start earlier than your friend, but your friend passes you and gets there before you do. You both traveled the same distance, but your friend did it in less time. Your friend had the faster speed.

When figuring speed, you need to know two things. First, you need to know the distance traveled. Also, you need to know the time it took to move that distance. **Speed** is the distance an object moves in a certain amount of time. You can figure out an object's speed by dividing the distance traveled by the time it took to go that distance. Speed = Distance ÷ Time.

Suppose you rode your bike 18 kilometers to the amusement park in two hours. To find your speed, divide the distance by the time. Eighteen divided by 2 is 9. Your speed was 9 kilometers per hour, which is abbreviated 9 km/hr. Your friend, who passed you, rode the 18 kilometers to the amusement park in one hour. What was your friend's speed?

During your ride to the amusement park, you did not actually always travel at the same speed. Going up hills, your speed was slower. When you went down hills, it was faster.

Your speed at any given moment is called instantaneous speed. If you had a speedometer on your bicycle, it would have shown your instantaneous speed for every moment of your ride.

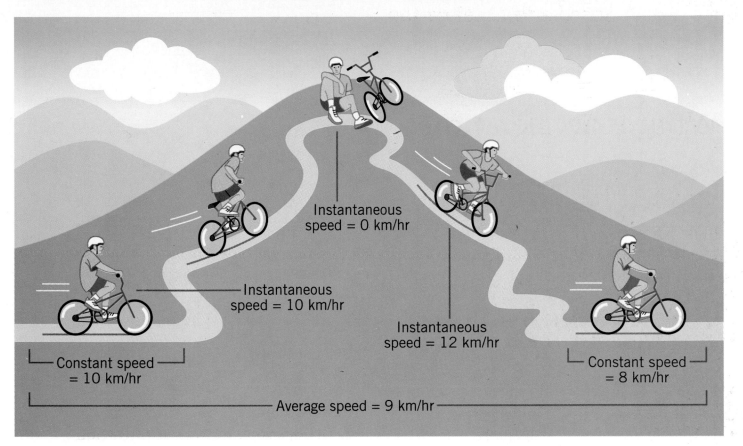

Instantaneous speed = 0 km/hr

Instantaneous speed = 10 km/hr

Instantaneous speed = 12 km/hr

Constant speed = 10 km/hr

Constant speed = 8 km/hr

Average speed = 9 km/hr

▲ For the first part of your ride, you rode at a constant speed of 10 km/hr. Your instantaneous speed for each moment of that part of the ride was also 10 km/hr. Then your speed slowed as you rode up a large hill. While you stopped for a rest, your instantaneous speed was 0 km/hr. Going down the hill, you picked up speed rapidly until you were going 12 km/hr. From there on, you kept a new constant speed of 8 km/hr.

If your speed remained the same (maybe 8 km/hr) for a period of time, you were moving at a constant speed for that part of your trip. You might have traveled at a different constant speed (maybe 10 km/hr) for another part of the trip.

Nine km/hr was your average speed. Average speed is the average pace of the whole trip.

A speedometer is a device that shows a vehicle's instantaneous speed. The next time you ride in a car or on a bus, watch the speedometer. Does the car travel at a constant speed for any part of the trip? When is the instantaneous speed greatest? When is it the least?

BACK HOME

What is acceleration?

Objects in motion may change speed and direction many times. When you ride on a roller coaster, a log ride, or the bumper cars, you are constantly changing direction and speed. Any change in an object's speed or direction is called **acceleration**.

The change in speed during acceleration can be a speeding up or a slowing down. Scientists use the term *acceleration* for both increases and decreases in speed. Speeding up is called *positive acceleration*. Slowing

Ready. Set. Go!

down is called *negative acceleration*. In everyday language, however, we often call decreases in speed *deceleration*.

You can experience acceleration on the bumper cars. When you first sit down and press the pedal, the car's speed increases. This is acceleration. When you turn the wheel to head toward another car, you are changing the direction of movement. This is also considered acceleration. Acceleration occurs again when you bump into another car and your car suddenly stops. This kind of acceleration is a decrease in speed.

Acceleration can affect the way your body feels. When you go up the ramp of a roller coaster, gravity pulls on the cars and your speed decreases. When you reach the top of the ramp, you experience a feeling of weightlessness. Gravity seems to have gone away.

Amazing!

Some roller coasters can accelerate from 0 to 97 km/hr in fewer than 4 seconds! Riders may experience a force of 4 G's on these rides. During a rocket launch at the Kennedy Space Center, astronauts are subjected to a force of 5 G's.

▲ What kinds of acceleration have these riders just experienced? What kind are they about to experience?

Then you accelerate downward as gravity pulls on you.

Forces that make you feel as if gravity has changed are called G-forces. The force of 1 G is equal to the earth's gravity. The G-forces increase when speed is increased or direction is changed. Astronauts experience increased G-forces as their space vehicle is launched. Roller-coaster riders experience changing G-forces as their cars go up and down and make sharp turns along the track.

How are you doing?

1. Give examples of instantaneous, constant, and average speed in a race.
2. What is acceleration? How does it differ from speed?
3. **Think** If a sprinter can run 100 meters in 10 seconds, what is his or her speed?
4. **Think** When you dive off a high diving board, when is your speed the greatest?

Art in Motion

How do you think an artist might view motion? The sculptor Alexander Calder made motion sculptures called mobiles. These abstract works of art are made of wire and sheet metal and they move! They hang in many places around the world, including Paris and New York.

Think of other types of artists and how they might view and represent motion. What might a musician do? What role does motion play in dance? How might an architect design a building to incorporate a sense of movement?

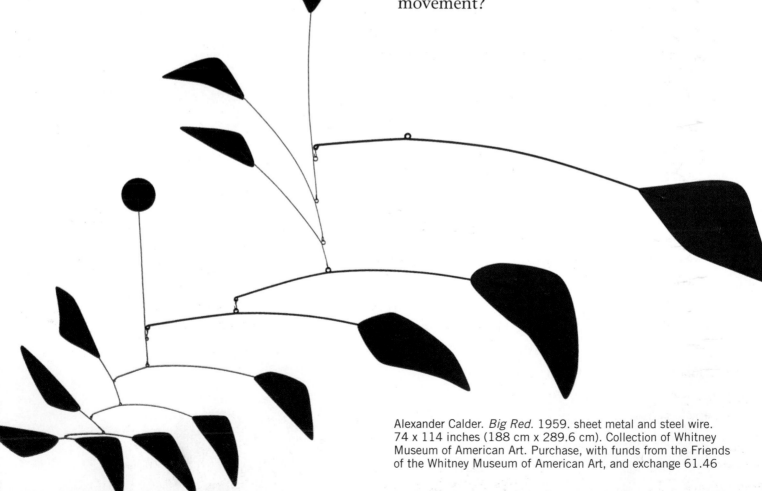

Alexander Calder. *Big Red*. 1959. sheet metal and steel wire. 74 x 114 inches (188 cm x 289.6 cm). Collection of Whitney Museum of American Art. Purchase, with funds from the Friends of the Whitney Museum of American Art, and exchange 61.46

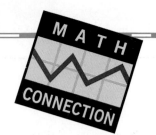

How can you slow a marble?

Observe and Collect Data

1. Stack the books. Make a ramp by placing one end of the board on top of the stack and the other end on the floor. Place the cup at the bottom of the ramp to catch the marble.

2. Release a marble at the top of the ramp. Time the number of seconds it takes for the marble to reach the bottom. Record the time in your Activity Journal. Repeat this step two times. Calculate and record the average time it takes for the marble to reach the bottom of the ramp.

3. Design a maze to make the marble move down the ramp more slowly. Release a marble at the top of the maze and time its descent. Repeat this step twice. Calculate and record the average time it takes for the marble to travel down the maze.

Draw Conclusions

1. What part of the maze slowed the marble the most?

2. How did gravity and friction act on the marble?

Process Skills

Making models, Measuring, Controlling variables

Materials

board   marble   glue

masking tape

2-3 books

scrap materials

plastic cup

clock or watch
to measure seconds

Looking Back

Words and Concepts

Complete the following statements.

1. _____ is a change of position.
2. _____ is a change of speed or direction.
3. If you threw a piece of popcorn into the air, the force of _____ would make it fall back toward the earth.
4. Skiers wax the bottom of their skis to reduce the force of _____ , a force that opposes motion.
5. If a roller coaster travels 1,000 meters in 40 seconds, the average speed of the roller coaster is _____ .

Applied Thinking Skills

Answer the following questions. You can use words, drawings, and diagrams in your answers.

6. At the amusement park you ride on a Ferris wheel. Describe your motion relative to the seat. Describe your motion relative to the people waiting in line for the Ferris wheel.
7. Describe a bus ride, telling the average speed, as well as examples of instantaneous speed and constant speed during the trip.
8. Tell how to change the drawing on this page in a way that reduces friction between the girl's feet and the ground.
9. If the moon had twice as much mass, how would the force of gravity between the earth and moon be affected? Explain your answer.
10. **Your World** Give an example of how friction helps you. How does friction create problems?

Show What You Know

How can you show acceleration?

Observe and Collect Data

1. Tape one end of the string to the inside of the lid. Using the T-pin, attach the other end of the string to the cork.
2. Fill the jar with water. Screw on the lid with the cork inside.
3. Turn the jar upside down and then on its side. Roll it across the floor. Change the motion of the jar as it rolls. Write your observations in your Activity Journal.
4. Take the jar with you on a bus, car, or other ride. Observe the cork while the jar is in motion. In your Activity Journal, record your observations.

Draw Conclusions

1. How does a change in direction affect the cork?
2. Compare the motion of the cork during an increase in speed with its motion during a decrease in speed.

Process Skills

Making models, Observing, Controlling variables

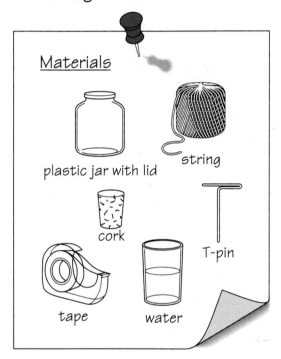

Materials

plastic jar with lid

string

cork

T-pin

tape

water

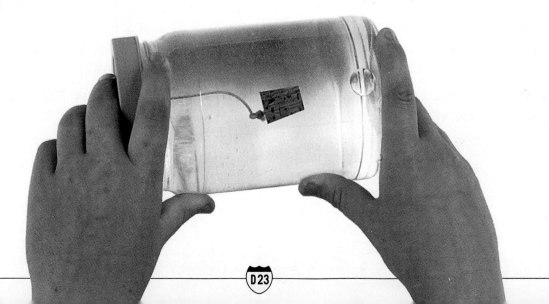

Chapter 2

Laws of Motion

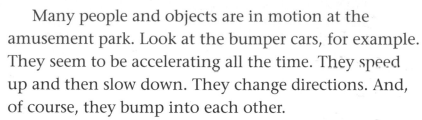

Many people and objects are in motion at the amusement park. Look at the bumper cars, for example. They seem to be accelerating all the time. They speed up and then slow down. They change directions. And, of course, they bump into each other.

When someone bumps into the side of your car, you can feel your car being pushed sideways. If someone bumps into your car from behind, you can feel your car being pushed forward.

When you bump into someone else's car, your car stops moving right away. But you don't. Your body keeps moving forward. It's good that you're wearing your seat belt!

SCIENCE JOURNAL In your Science Journal, explain why wearing seat belts is important.

Watch out for reckless drivers!

So this is what topsy-turvy means.

Explore Activity

How do changes affect motion?

Process Skills

Observing, Measuring, Communicating

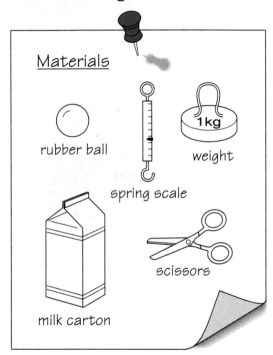

Materials

rubber ball

spring scale

1kg
weight

scissors

milk carton

Observe and Collect Data

1. Cut off the top and one side of a quart-size milk carton. You should now have a three-sided box. Put it on its side and poke a hole in the bottom of the box with your pencil.

2. Put the rubber ball in the box. Make the open end of the box face forward. Push the box quickly over the top of your desk with your hand. When the box gets to the edge of the desk, stop it suddenly. Record your results in your Activity Journal.

3. Attach the spring scale to the box by putting its hook through the hole. In your Activity Journal, record the force needed to pull the box.

4. Add the weight to the box. Pull the box using the spring scale. In your Activity Journal, record the amount of force needed.

Share Your Results

1. What did you and the other groups observe when you stopped the milk carton suddenly?

2. Compare the amount of force it took you to move the box in step 3 and in step 4 with your classmates' results.

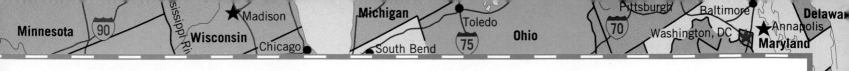

Draw Conclusions

1. How did the motion of the box and the motion of the ball differ? What conclusion can you draw from this difference?
2. Compare the amounts of force needed to pull the box in steps 3 and 4. Explain.

Apply What You Know

1. Describe the sensation you feel when a car, bus, or bike that you are riding in or on stops suddenly.
2. Do you think it takes more force to start a freight train or a bicycle? Explain your answer.

What is the first law of motion?

In science, a law is a statement that describes events or relationships that exist in nature. During the 1660s, the English scientist Isaac Newton studied what happens when objects move. He developed three laws of motion that describe how things move. Stated simply, Newton's first law says that an object continues to do whatever it has been doing unless a force causes it to change. If an object is in motion, it tends to stay in motion. If it is at rest, it tends to stay at rest. If it is moving in a certain direction, it tends

to continue in that direction. This tendency of an object to resist any change in its state of motion is called **inertia** (in ər´shə).

When you first press the pedal of a bumper car, it feels as if you jerk backward as the car moves forward. According to the first law of motion, your body is at rest and it tends to stay at rest as the bumper car surges forward. You haven't really jerked back. You sat still when the car moved.

You also feel the effects of inertia when your bumper car turns. When you swerve to the left toward another car, it feels as if your body leans toward the right of the car. This is because your body was traveling in a straight line before you turned. When you change the car's direction, your body resists this change and tends to continue in a straight line.

If your car bumps another car, you also feel the effects of inertia. When the car suddenly stops, you feel as if you surge forward in your seat. This is because your body, or any object, tends to stay in motion once it is in motion.

How does the first law of motion affect you when you are riding on your bicycle?

The first law of motion
Unless a force acts on an object to move it or to change its motion, an object at rest stays at rest, and an object in motion stays in motion in a straight line at a constant speed.

WOOSH

▲ When the miniature train begins to move, you feel as if a force has pushed you backward. Actually, the train starts moving, and you stay put. The inertia of your body resists moving forward with the train. If something is at rest, it stays at rest unless a force acts on it to move it.

Sharp curve ahead. Hang on!

Be a Scientist

Can you show inertia?

ACTIVITY JOURNAL

Set a glass on a flat surface and put a card on top of the glass. Then put a nickel or a quarter in the center of the card. Flick the card off of the glass with your fingers. In your Activity Journal, describe what happens to the coin. Why does it happen?

◄ On this ride, you have been traveling in a straight line. Suddenly, the car makes a sharp right turn. You feel your body pressed against the left side of the car. What happened? The car changed its direction, but you continued moving in a straight line. You didn't move to the left—the car moved to the right. An object in motion stays in motion in a straight line at a constant speed unless a force changes that motion.

What is net force?

We almost always find that more than one force is acting on an object at the same time. Sometimes these forces work together and sometimes they work against each other. Either way, the combination of all the forces working on an object is called the **net force**.

When two forces work in the same direction, the net force is equal to the sum of the two forces. For instance, if a hot dog vendor pushes her cart with the help of her assistant, then the net force is the same as if one person pushed as hard as the vendor and her assistant combined. When two forces work against each other, then the net force is equal to the difference between them. Gravity pulls down on a roller-coaster car, but friction opposes that force and keeps the car from falling too rapidly. Finally, suppose two children both want a toy and pull it in opposite directions with equal force. If the forces are balanced, the toy won't move. The net force might be said to be zero.

Often the different forces acting on an object are balanced. They cancel each other out. When forces are balanced, the object stays at rest or stays in motion at a constant

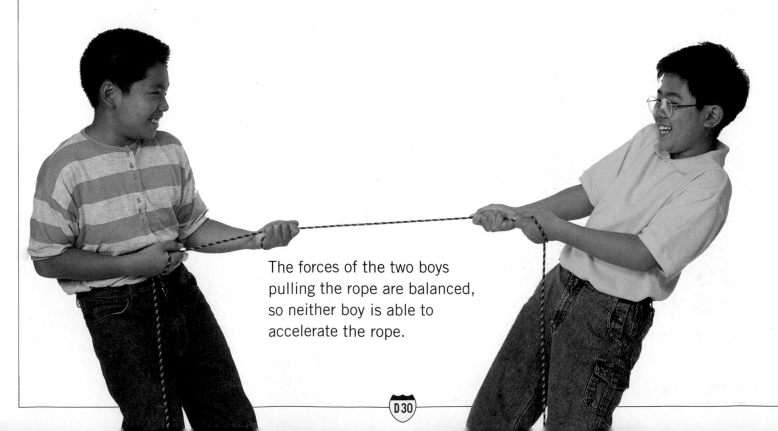

The forces of the two boys pulling the rope are balanced, so neither boy is able to accelerate the rope.

Isaac Newton

One of the greatest scientists in history, Sir Isaac Newton, not only formulated the laws of motion, but also discovered the law of gravity, invented a new form of math, and discovered some properties of light and color. He lived from 1642 to 1727, a period rich in scientific discovery and invention. Newton wrote, "If I have seen further . . . it is by standing upon the shoulders of Giants." Newton knew that scientific discoveries in any period depend on the work of earlier scientists. One "giant" who preceded Newton was the Italian scientist Galileo, who died the year Newton was born. In his experiments concerning friction, Galileo established the foundation for Newton's first law of motion.

speed. No acceleration occurs. If something happens to unbalance the forces, then direction or speed will change. In the picture below, **centripetal force** keeps the riders moving in a circular path. If a rider accidentally dropped a shoe, the net force on the shoe would change. In which direction would the shoe travel? How does your knowledge about inertia and gravity help you answer this question?

Centripetal (center-seeking) force

How are you doing?

1. What was Isaac Newton's contribution to the study of motion?
2. What is net force?
3. **Think** You are playing miniature golf. Use Newton's first law of motion to explain what happens to the ball after you hit it.
4. **Think** Which objects are constantly changing direction, the cars on a train or the horses on a carousel? Explain your answer.

What is the second law of motion?

Isaac Newton observed situations in which acceleration was affected by the mass of the object or by the force acting on it. He put his observations together into the second law of motion. The law says that an object will begin to move (or change its motion) in the direction that a net force is acting. It also says that to accelerate a large mass at the same rate as a smaller mass, you have to add more force. The photos on these pages show how acceleration is related to the mass of an object and the force applied to it.

The second law of motion
An object's acceleration depends on the mass of the object and the magnitude and direction of the force acting on it.

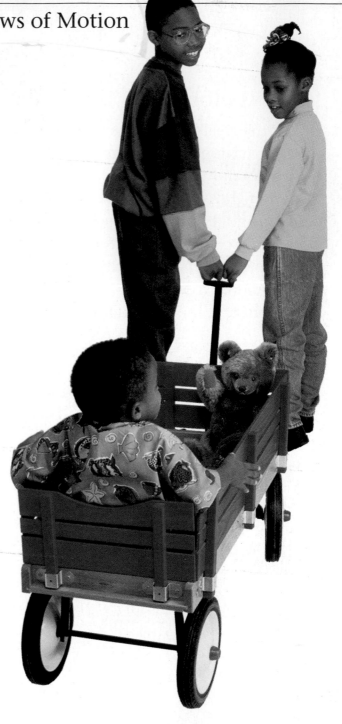

▲ When the boy pulls with enough force, the wagon accelerates. If he pulls harder, it accelerates more. With the girl's help, it accelerates even faster. Added net force causes acceleration. As net force increases, acceleration increases.

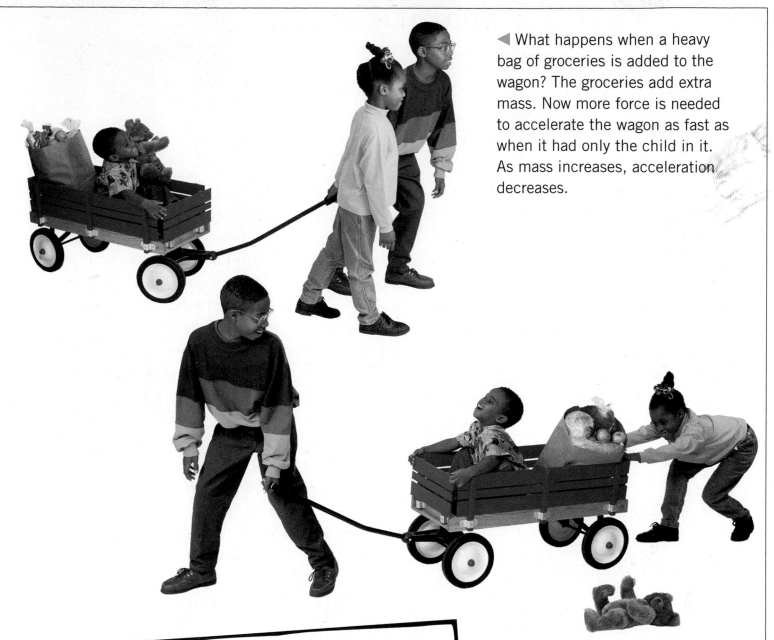

◄ What happens when a heavy bag of groceries is added to the wagon? The groceries add extra mass. Now more force is needed to accelerate the wagon as fast as when it had only the child in it. As mass increases, acceleration decreases.

▲ What happens if the girl pulls the wagon in the opposite direction from the boy? If the two forces are equal, the wagon stands still. But if the forces are not equal, the wagon accelerates toward the person pulling with the most force.

Next time you go to the grocery store, use your grocery cart to experiment with Newton's second law. In your Science Journal, record how the mass in your grocery cart affected acceleration.

BACK HOME

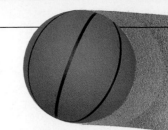

What is the third law of motion?

Imagine you are trying to lift a heavy box by its handles. You can feel the box pulling down on your hands. At the same time, your hands are pulling on the box.

Newton's third law of motion explains how forces work in pairs. Newton showed that if you press on a stone with your finger, the stone presses back on your finger. That is like saying that whatever you touch touches you back. You could also say that whatever you pull pulls you back, or whatever you push pushes you back. Newton described this in his third law of motion.

Did you ever blow up a balloon and then let it go? The motion of the balloon is an example of the third law of motion. Before you released the balloon, air pushed inside the balloon in all directions. When you released the balloon, you allowed air to escape through the open end of the balloon. The balloon pushed the air out while the escaping air pushed on the balloon. This force pushed the balloon forward.

WHAP!

The third law of motion
When one object exerts a force upon a second object, the second object exerts an equal and opposite force upon the first object.

To throw a basketball, you push on it. The basketball pushes on you, and if there isn't much friction to hold you in place, you move backward.

Be a Scientist

How can you show the third law of motion?

1. Connect two spring scales. Hold one scale steady while your partner pulls on the other. Observe the needles on the spring scales. In your Activity Journal, record how hard your partner is pulling on you. Record how hard you are pulling on your partner.

   ACTIVITY JOURNAL

2. Keep the spring scales connected. Attach one spring scale to a fence, stop sign, or other large object fixed to the earth. Pull on the other scale. Observe the needles on the scales. Record how hard you are pulling on the object. Record how hard the object is pulling on you.

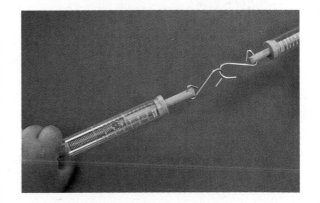

What are some examples of the laws of motion?

Think about experiences that illustrate the laws of motion. You kick a door with your foot. You ride a bicycle into a trash can. You bounce a ball against a wall. Try to tell how the pictures on this page provide examples of Newton's laws.

Newton's second law of motion

Newton's first law of motion

▲ The bumper boats tend to stay in motion unless a force acts to change that motion. What happens when one boat bumps another boat?

▲ The acceleration of the child onto the carousel horse depends on the mass of the child and the magnitude and direction of the force. In other words, how quickly the child gets lifted depends on how much mass she has and how forcefully her mother lifts her. How would the amount of force needed change if the child had twice as much mass?

Travel light! It takes more energy, and therefore more gas, to carry more mass in a car or bus.

▲ You push on the ground. The ground pushes on you with equal force.

Newton's third law of motion

▲ The girl pushes on the boat. The boat pushes on the girl. What happens if she pushes too hard?

How are you doing?

1. What is the second law of motion?
2. What is the third law of motion?
3. **Think** How does throwing a ball illustrate Newton's second law of motion?
4. **Think** How do you think jet engines illustrate Newton's third law of motion?

Burton's
Zoom Zoom Va-Rooom Machine

Dorothy Haas

This is an excerpt from a book about Burton Bell Whitney Knockhurst,
a born inventor. This time, he is working on a very special skateboard.
His little brother is helping with research.

"Rockets," recited Little Brother, checking out the information he had on hand. "Mmm-mmm . . . discharge a thrust of air, thus producing forward movement." He looked bewildered. "What have you got in mind?"

"What I'm thinking," said Burton, keeping his excitement under control with great difficulty, "is, the board is pretty good right now as it is—"

"But you haven't road tested it yet," said Little Brother in his practical way. "So you don't know that for sure."

"I'll get to it. I'll get to it," murmured Burton. "I'm thinking beyond that. Like . . . the thing that could make the big difference between this board and the regular kind, the thing that could make it take off, would be a little extra power."

"You mean *really* take off?" asked Little Brother, interest lighting his face. "You mean like into the *air?*"

Think About Your Reading

1. Why do you think it might help a scientist to have a helper with a practical mind? Give an example from the excerpt.
2. How does a rocket work? Use what you know about motion, as well as Little Brother's information.

"You've got it!" Burton nodded solemnly. "Not a whole lot, you understand. Just enough to get up high enough to . . . to . . . well, do some really interesting stuff on it."

Little Brother's eyes were round with wonder as he thought about the great "stuff" a rocket-powered skateboard could do. Then the practical side of his nature surfaced once more. "Wouldn't the rockets have to be really small?"

"Uh-huh." Burton welcomed Little Brother's input. Whatever he had to say always made sense. "See if you can find anything on midget rockets."

"How would you stay on the thing?" asked Little Brother. "I mean, what if it zips right out from under you?"

Burton thought about that, biting his lip. "Now that you mention it . . . The rider could fall back into the exhaust and . . . and . . . "

"Get barbecued?" asked Little Brother.

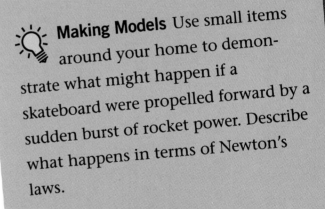

Making Models Use small items around your home to demonstrate what might happen if a skateboard were propelled forward by a sudden burst of rocket power. Describe what happens in terms of Newton's laws.

Where to Read More

Peter Lafferty, *Force and Motion* (Dorling Kindersley, 1992)
The whole world is in motion, and this book tells you all about it, from Newton's laws to spinning tops to the science of a cannonball.

Looking Back

Words and Concepts

Match the terms in Column A with the sentence completions in Column B.

Column A

1. Newton's first law of motion
2. Newton's second law of motion
3. Newton's third law of motion
4. Inertia
5. Net force
6. Centripetal force

Column B

a. is the tendency of moving objects to stay in motion or of nonmoving objects to stay at rest.

b. describes what happens when one object exerts a force on another object.

c. keeps an object moving in a circular path.

d. describes how an object behaves if no force acts upon it.

e. is the combination of forces that act on an object.

f. explains that mass and force affect an object's acceleration.

Applied Thinking Skills

Answer the following questions. You can use words, drawings, and diagrams in your answers.

7. Think about rolling a ball across a carpet. What would happen if there were no friction?

8. Are the forces acting on a skateboard that is turning balanced or unbalanced? Why?

9. How does a canoer make use of Newton's third law?

10. **Your World** If you were a bicycle racer, would you want a lightweight bicycle or a heavy bicycle? Explain.

Show What You Know

Can a structure exert an upward force?

Observe and Collect Data

1. Design a structure or group of structures to support a book so that it is 5 to 10 centimeters above your desk. You may use only masking tape, glue, and uncooked fettuccine to build your structure. Draw your design in your Activity Journal.

2. Assemble your structure. Gently place the book on your structure.

3. If the structure breaks, look for ways to make your design stronger, and try again. Record your results.

Draw Conclusions

1. What exerted the downward force?

2. What exerted the upward force?

3. Were the forces balanced? How could you tell?

Process Skills

Making models, Inferring, Controlling variables

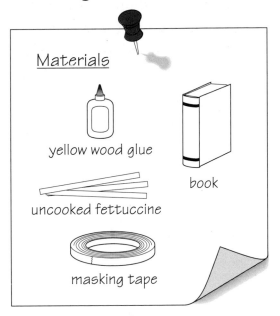

Materials

yellow wood glue

uncooked fettuccine

book

masking tape

Chapter 3

Work and Energy

You can see and experience all sorts of energy changes at the amusement park. Energy is the ability to cause a change in matter. Energy has several different forms, such as heat, light, and sound. You can see examples of many different kinds of energy in an amusement park, but on this trip, we will focus on one form of energy—mechanical energy. **Mechanical energy** is the energy an object has due to its motion or position.

Energy enables a person or object to do work. There are many different people who work at the amusement park. Employees sell and collect tickets, operate rides and games, cook food, plant flowers, and clean the grounds. Some people at the park use machines to make their work easier.

 Suppose you did all the activities pictured on these pages in one morning. Would you be having fun, doing work, or both? Perhaps you would be tired or hungry afterward. How could you replenish your energy? Write what you think in your Science Journal.

Watch your step on the swinging bridge. Crocodiles below!

Up + down + all around = DIZZY!

Speeding down the track!

What a view from up here!

Alright! Eats!

Explore Activity

How does an object's mass affect its ability to do work?

Process Skills

Measuring, Predicting, Interpreting data

Materials

masking tape

4-5 books

board

marker

tennis ball

can

string

toy truck, car, or skate

meter stick

brick

Observe and Collect Data

1. Make a ramp on the floor with the board and books. The ramp should be about 15 centimeters high. Use the tape to make a starting line 45 centimeters from the bottom of the ramp.

2. Place the can against the bottom of the ramp. Have two team members hold the meter stick against the can as shown. Place the tennis ball on the other side of the meter stick. Center the ball against the can.

3. Place the truck or car at the starting line. Release it.

4. Measure the distance the tennis ball moves. Record this distance in your Activity Journal. Repeat steps 2 to 4 twice more and record these measurements also.

5. Use string to hold a brick on the car.

6. **Predict** whether the ball will roll farther than it did before. Repeat steps 2 to 4 using the weighted car.

Share Your Results

Compare your data with those of two other teams. Which team's tennis ball rolled the farthest?

Draw Conclusions

1. How much farther did the weighted car push the tennis ball than did the unweighted car? How did these results compare to your prediction?
2. How does an object's mass affect its ability to make something move?

Apply What You Know

Suppose you repeat the activity. Before releasing the car, you move the can forward so that it is 45 centimeters in front of the ramp. **Predict** how that change would affect the distance the tennis ball moves. Explain your prediction.

What is work?

Work is being done. The stroller is moving in the direction of the force that is applied. ▶

Make a mental list of the kinds of work you do every day. Your list could include making your bed, brushing your teeth, and reading a book. In everyday life, we regard all these things as work. In science, the term *work* means something very specific. Scientifically speaking, **work** is done when an object moves in the direction of a force that something or someone applies to it. Often work is done to change the speed of an object. In other cases, work is done to overcome the forces of friction or gravity.

If you apply the scientific definition of work to the tasks mentioned above, not all of them are work. Making your bed is work because a force was applied to pull your sheets in the direction of the headboard. Brushing your teeth is work because a force is applied to move your toothbrush. Reading a book, according to the scientific definition, is not considered work. No force was applied and nothing moved. In scientific terms, the only work done in reading is turning the pages.

A force does not always do work. If you hold a child in your arms, the force you use against gravity may tire you, but you are not doing any work on the child. In order for work to be done, a force must move something through a distance. If you lift a child off the ground, you are doing work. The child moves through a distance in the same direction as you lift.

Up we go!

▲ Work is being done. As the mother lifts her child, she is applying a force opposite to the force of gravity.

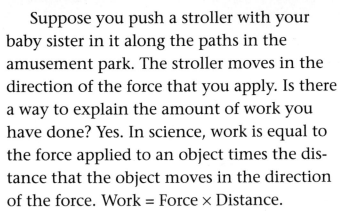

Suppose you push a stroller with your baby sister in it along the paths in the amusement park. The stroller moves in the direction of the force that you apply. Is there a way to explain the amount of work you have done? Yes. In science, work is equal to the force applied to an object times the distance that the object moves in the direction of the force. Work = Force × Distance.

What is power?

The power needed to carry riders around on the auto-whirl is greater than the power needed to carry riders the same distance on the Ferris wheel. Why? ▼

Energy can be used to do work quickly or over a long period of time. Take riding your bike to the amusement park, for example. If you take a long period of time to ride your bike to the park, your power output is small. If you ride as fast as you can, you produce more power. You need more energy to do work faster.

The rate at which work is done is called **power**. Some of the machines that run rides at the amusement park are more powerful than others. If you take your little brother on the Ferris wheel, you slowly travel 10 meters vertically. Then, when you and your friends go on the auto-whirl ride, you go toward the sky the same

distance, but in just a few seconds. Work was done on both rides. Both rides used a certain amount of force to carry you 10 meters. The ride you and your friends took requires more power because the time it took to do the work was less.

How can you explain the amount of power used to do work? It's simple. Power is equal to the amount of work done divided by the time required to do the work. Power = Work ÷ Time.

The slide down is worth the climb up!

▲ Compare walking up a flight of stairs with running up the stairs. Which takes more time? Which takes more power?

How are you doing?

1. What must happen for work to be done?
2. What is power?
3. **Think** Two girls of the same weight ran up a flight of stairs. One girl got to the top before the other. Which girl used more power? Explain your answer.
4. **Think** In the example in question 3, did the girl who used more power also do more work? Explain your answer.

What are potential energy and kinetic energy?

The objects at the amusement park do not have to be moving to have energy. Energy, remember, is the *ability* to do work. A compressed spring has energy. A person sitting at the top of a slide has energy. They have what is called **potential energy,** energy that is stored and ready to use. Some potential energy represents work that has already been done. Work was done to compress the spring, and work was done to take the person to the top of the slide.

When you stretch or compress a spring, you give it the ability to do work. The spring has potential energy. ▶

▲ When the spring is released, it can move an object.

◀ The position of an object gives it potential energy. A boy at the top of the slide has more potential energy than the boy who is just reaching the bottom of the slide. But the boy nearing the bottom has more kinetic energy than the boy who is waiting at the top. What about the women and children sliding together? Do they probably have more or less kinetic energy than the boy who is ahead of them? Why?

The amount of potential energy an object has depends on the position of the object and its mass. If people were at the top of a taller slide, they would have more potential energy because of their higher position. If several people who weighed more got on the slide together, they would have more potential energy because of their greater mass.

Once an object is in motion, it also has a different kind of energy. **Kinetic energy** is energy of motion—it is energy that is being used. The boy on the spring shoes has kinetic energy when he is bouncing up and down. Once the people start down the steep slide, they have kinetic energy.

The amount of kinetic energy a moving object has depends on two things. First, it depends on the object's speed. The faster the object goes, the more kinetic energy it has. For example, if one go-cart speeds around the track and another drives at a leisurely pace, then the fast car has more kinetic energy than the slow car. As a moving object slows down, it loses kinetic energy. When it stops, it has zero kinetic energy.

The amount of kinetic energy also depends on the mass of the moving object. The larger the mass, the greater its kinetic energy. If the amusement park train and the go-cart travel at the same speed, the train has more kinetic energy because it has greater mass. How might the amount of kinetic energy change if a large adult went down the slide instead of a sixth grader? How would it change if two adults slid down on one mat?

How is energy conserved?

When you ride the roller coaster, you are experiencing changes in energy. When energy changes from one form to another, the total amount of energy neither increases nor decreases. It stays the same. A scientific law called the Law of Conservation of Energy states that energy can neither be created nor destroyed.

When the roller coaster moves uphill, for example, it gains potential energy. At its highest point, the car has its greatest potential energy. But it has almost no kinetic energy as it moves slowly over the top of the hill. When the roller coaster reaches top speed at the bottom of the hill, it has the greatest kinetic energy.

1 At the top of the hill, the car has a lot of potential energy. Gravity pulls the car downhill. The car accelerates as it falls. Potential energy changes into kinetic energy.

2 Kinetic energy increases as the car moves downhill.

3 Between its highest and lowest points, the car has some potential energy and some kinetic energy.

4 When it is at its lowest point, the car has its greatest kinetic energy and least potential energy.

5 At the end of the ride when the car stops at the bottom of the hill, it has neither potential nor kinetic energy.

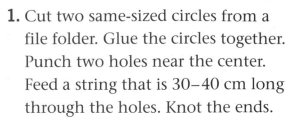

Be a Scientist

How can you show changes in energy?

1. Cut two same-sized circles from a file folder. Glue the circles together. Punch two holes near the center. Feed a string that is 30–40 cm long through the holes. Knot the ends.

2. Hold one end of the string in each hand. Loop each end of the string around one finger. Twirl the string to wind it up. Then, move your hands repeatedly in and out.

3. In your Activity Journal, describe what happens. Where was the energy stored that made the circle spin?

How are you doing?

1. What is potential energy?
2. What is kinetic energy?
3. **Think** Describe the changes from potential to kinetic energy when you bounce a rubber ball. Does the total amount of energy that the ball has change? Explain.
4. **Think** What changes between potential energy and kinetic energy occur as you swing back and forth on a swing?

How do machines change forces?

Large machines, like those in the amusement park, are made up of combinations of simpler machines. You already learned that Work = Force × Distance. Even simple machines help us to do work more easily by changing forces. Some machines change the direction of a force. Some machines increase the strength, or magnitude, of a force. Some can do both. The amount by which any machine increases the magnitude of a force is called the **mechanical advantage** of the machine.

▲ Scissors are made of two levers.

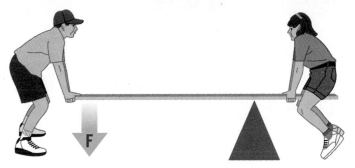

▲ A **lever** is made up of a bar that pivots on a fixed point called a fulcrum. A seesaw is an example of a lever. If you push down on one end of a seesaw, your friend on the other end goes up into the air easily. Two things happen. First, the seesaw changes the direction of the force from down to up. Second, the seesaw increases the force you apply, allowing you to lift your friend easily.

▲ An **inclined plane** is a machine that helps people raise heavy objects without lifting them straight up. Increasing the distance over which the force is applied means that the task becomes easier. The wheelchair goes up a long, gently sloped ramp more easily than on a short, steep ramp.

DILEMMA

How to Protect People's Jobs as Machines Do More

Because machines usually work faster, factories are using machines more and more to do work that people once did. What happens when a factory starts using machines to do jobs that used to be done by people? Workers can lose their jobs.

Machines will continue to change how people run factories, businesses, hospitals, and schools. How government and business should respond to these changes is a dilemma. Should companies retrain workers whose jobs are made obsolete by new machines? Should the government provide funds for retraining or special protection for older workers?

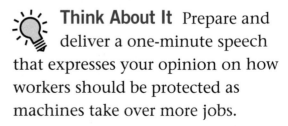 **Think About It** Prepare and deliver a one-minute speech that expresses your opinion on how workers should be protected as machines take over more jobs.

What other machines change forces?

Two other machines that change forces are based on the wheel. One is the pulley and one is the combination of wheel and axle. Both machines make work easier by changing forces.

Mechanical Engineer

Bill Kelley climbs aboard the newest roller coaster, fastens the safety restraint, and prepares for an exciting ride. Lots of people do this for fun, but for Kelley it's all part of his job. Kelley designs roller coasters and other amusement park rides, and he tests the rides he creates.

66 When the actual roller coaster is built, it is tested in a variety of ways. We run the ride with sandbag 'passengers' that have twice the weight of the human passengers to come. We measure stress on various parts of the roller coaster. And we use an accelerometer to make sure the accelerations aren't so extreme that they could cause injury. Then I ride the roller coaster myself to make sure there aren't any rough spots.

"To be a designer of amusement park rides, you should be interested in physical science, mathematics, and mechanical things—but you must also *love* the rides!**99**

▲ A **wheel and axle** is two attached wheels of different sizes rotating together. The smaller one is called the axle and is often shaped like a rod. When the larger wheel is turned, it moves over a longer

distance than the smaller axle does. This increases the force and makes the axle easier to turn. When you turn a steering wheel, your force turns the axle to which it is attached, and the axle turns the mechanisms that turn the car.

▲ A **pulley** is a wheel with a rope around it. A single pulley will change the direction in which a force acts, but will not change the magnitude of the force. In a sailboat, when you pull backward on the rope, the sail is pulled sideways, closer to you. If two or more pulleys are combined, they can change both the direction and the magnitude of the force. Larger sailboats sometimes have such pulley combinations.

F

10kg

How are you doing?

1. What are two ways that machines change forces?
2. In what way does a pulley change the force applied to it?
3. **Think** What kind of machine is a doorknob? How does it make work easier?
4. **Think** What kinds of simple machines do movers use when they load and unload furniture from their trucks? How are forces changed by using these machines?

Looking Back

Words and Concepts

Complete the following statements.

1. Force × Distance = _____
2. Work ÷ Time = _____
3. The stored energy in a rock on the top of a hill is _____ energy.
4. When you ride your bike down a hill, potential energy is converted to _____ energy.
5. _____ is the law that energy can be neither created nor destroyed.

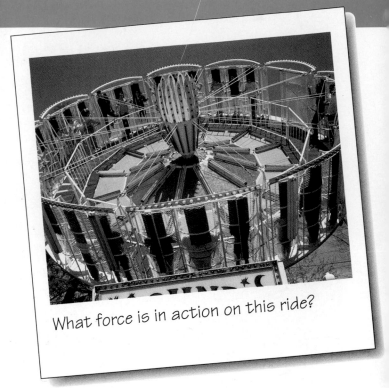

What force is in action on this ride?

Applied Thinking Skills

Answer the following questions. You can use words, drawings, and diagrams in your answers.

6. Give an example of how you could get tired without doing any work.
7. Look at the picture to the left. What happens to a car's energy at each of the points marked?
8. Could you bowl as well with a basketball as with a bowling ball? What characteristics of these objects would make the difference?
9. Give an example of a simple machine and explain how it helps you do work.
10. **Your World** You want to pass over a wall that is higher than you are. Describe a simple machine that could help you get over the wall.

Show What You Know

Can you construct a roller coaster?

Observe and Collect Data

1. Use the tubing to construct a roller coaster. Hold it against the cardboard backing. Select the marble that will travel fastest through the tubing.

2. Design the roller coaster to maximize the distance that the marble moves through the tubing. Experiment by holding the tubing in different positions against the cardboard and sending the marble through.

3. When you have found the best design for your roller coaster, tape the tubing into position on the cardboard. Draw your design in your Activity Journal.

4. Send the marble through the roller coaster. Measure the distance that it travels through the tubing. Also measure the time it takes to travel through the tubing. Do three trials. Calculate and record the average speed.

Draw Conclusions

1. Compare your roller coaster and data recorded in step 4 with those of other groups. Which roller coaster works best? Why?

2. On your drawing of your model, indicate the kinds of energy changes that took place as the marble passed through the tubing. Explain your answers.

Process Skills

Making models, Observing, Measuring

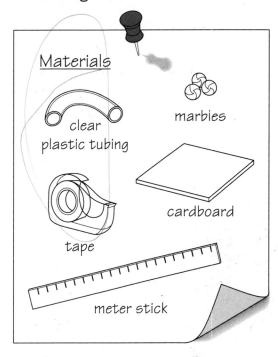

Materials

clear plastic tubing

marbies

cardboard

tape

meter stick

Motion & Energy

Show what you know about the way things move. Work by yourself, with a partner, or in a group. Select one activity.

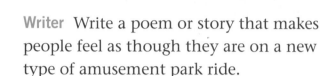

Writer Write a poem or story that makes people feel as though they are on a new type of amusement park ride.

Inventor Combine two or more simple machines, such as a pulley and a lever, to create a new machine. Draw a picture of your machine, give it a name, and explain what it can do. Add labels that point out the simple machines.

Mechanical Engineer Make a model of an amusement park ride. Ask your classmates whether they would like to try this ride. Have them give reasons.

Songwriter Compose a song that makes people feel as though they are on an amusement park ride. Listeners should experience the forces, speed, and acceleration of the ride.

Science Historian Choose either Galileo or Newton. Do research to find out more about the scientist you chose. Prepare a brief report about some interesting part of his life or work.

Dancer Create a dance that includes the following characters: potential energy, kinetic energy, and amusement park visitor. Perform your dance for the class.

Glossary

acceleration (ak sel´ər ā´shən) Any change in an object's speed or direction of motion. (page D18)

centripetal force (sen trip´ət'l fôrs´) A force that keeps objects moving in a circular path. (page D31)

friction (frik´shən) A force that resists motion between objects that are touching. (page D12)

gravity (grav´i tē) A force of attraction between objects. (page D14)

inclined plane (in klīnd´ plān´) A simple machine that helps people raise objects without lifting them straight up. (page D55)

inertia (in ər´shə) The tendency of an object to resist any change in its state of motion. (page D28)

kinetic energy (ki net´ik en´ər jē) The energy of an object due to its motion. (page D51)

lever (lev´ər) A machine made up of a bar that pivots on a fulcrum. (page D54)

mechanical advantage (mə kan´i kəl ad vant´ij) A measure of how much a machine reduces the force needed to do work. (page D54)

mechanical energy (mə kan´i kəl en´ər jē) The energy an object has due to its motion or position. (page D42)

motion (mō´shən) A continuous change of position. (page D10)

net force (net fôrs) The combination of all the forces acting on an object. (page D30)

potential energy (pō ten´shəl en´ər jē) Stored energy that an object has due to its condition or its position. (page D50)

power (pou´ər) The rate at which work is done. Power = Work ÷ Time. (page D48)

pulley (poo´lē) A wheel with a rope around it that changes the direction of a pull. (page D57)

reference object (ref´ər əns äb´jikt) Something to which the positions of a moving object are compared. (page D10)

speed (spēd) The distance an object moves divided by the amount of time to move that distance, such as 75 km/h. Speed = Distance ÷ Time. (page D16)

wheel and axle (hwēl and ak´səl) A simple machine made of two wheels of different sizes rotating together. (page D57)

work (wərk) The force applied to an object times the distance that the object moves in the direction of the force. Work = Force × Distance. (page D46)

Unit D Index

Boldface numerals denote glossary terms. Italic numerals denote illustrations.

Credits

Photographs

1 Hank Morgan/Rainbow; 2–3 Bob Daemmrich/Stock, Boston; 3 Roy King; 4BR Charles Krebs/The Stock Market; 4L Dan McCoy/Rainbow; 4T GHP Studio*; 5 Ken Karp*; 6BL Brian Stablyk/AllStock; 6BR Michael Grecco/Stock, Boston; 6TR Charles Krebs/AllStock; 7(inset) Stephen Frisch*; 7 Christian Grzimek/OKAPIA/Photo Researchers; 9 Ken Karp*; 10T GHP Studio*; 11L F.S. Maroon/Photo Researchers; 11R Michael P. Gadomski/Bruce Coleman Inc.; 12 GHP Studio*; 13 Bob Daemmrich; 14 Roy Bishop/Stock, Boston; 15B Ken Karp*; 15T NASA; 16B Ken Karp*; 16T Tim Davis/Photo Researchers; 18 Steve Solum/Bruce Coleman Inc.; 19 Tom Bean/AllStock; 20B Alexander Calder. *Big Red.* 1959. Sheet metal and steel wire. 74 × 114 inches (188cm × 289.6cm). Collection of Whitney Museum of American Art. Purchase, with funds from the Friends of the Whitney Museum of American Art, and exchange 61.46; 20T Ken Karp*; 21 Elliott Smith*; 23 Tim Davis*; 24BL Ann Purcell/Photo Researchers; 24BR Hank Morgan/Rainbow; 24T GHP Studio*; 25 C. Bruce Forster/AllStock; 27 Elliott Smith*; 29B Roberto Soncin Gerometta/Photo 20-20; 29R Tim Davis*; 29C Elliott Smith*; 30 Ken Karp*; 31 Ken Straiton/The Stock Market;

32 Ken Karp*; 33 Ken Karp*; 34 GHP Studio*; 35L Ken Karp*; 35R Elliott Smith*; 36L Bob Daemmrich; 36R Elliott Smith*; 37B Bob Daemmrich; 37TL Ken Karp*; 37TR Ken Karp*; 40 Benn Mitchell/The Image Bank; 41 Tim Davis*; 42B Bob Daemmrich/Stock, Boston; 42T Dan McCoy/Rainbow; 43(background) Philip Bailey/The Stock Market; 43B Peter Menzel/Stock, Boston; 43C Coco McCoy/Rainbow; 43T Mike Mazzaschi/Stock, Boston; 45 Elliott Smith*; 46 Elliott Smith*; 46–47 Nita Winter*; 47 Ken Karp*; 48 W. Eastep/The Stock Market; 49B Lawrence Migdale/Stock, Boston; 49T Thierry Cariou/The Stock Market; 50 Ken Karp*; 51 Dan McCoy/Rainbow; 52–53 Karl Weatherly/AllStock; 54B Tim Davis*; 54T Elliott Smith*; 55 Stephen Frisch*; 56–57 Annie Griffiths Belt/Westlight; 56 Anne Dowie*; 57 Bob Firth/International Stock Photo; 58B David Travers/The Stock Market; 58T Jeff Persons/Stock, Boston

Special thanks to Malcolm X Elementary School, Berkeley, California; Franklin Year-Round School, Oakland, California; Carl B. Munck Elementary School, Oakland, California; Hintil Ku Ka Child Care Center, Oakland, California; Kelley Park, San Jose, California.

*Photographed expressly for Addison-Wesley Publishing Company, Inc.

Illustrations

Nea Bisek 8T, 21, 23, 26T, 41, 44T, 59
Marilyn Kreiger 1
Michael Maydak 34, 35
Jane McCreary 8B, 18, 26B, 38–39, 44B
Randy Vergoustraete 60–61
Nina Wallace 9, 17, 54, 55, 57

Text

38-39 Dorothy Haas, *Burton's Zoom Zoom Va-Rooom Machine* (New York: Macmillan Publishing Co., 1990). Text copyright ©1990 by Dorothy F. Haas. Reprinted with the permission of Bradbury Press, an affiliate of Macmillan, Inc.

A dream had come true! Your friend had managed to get seats near the dugout for the third game of the 1989 World Series in San Francisco, California. You were excited as you settled into your seat. You had never been this close to the action before. The umpire was sweeping off home plate. The game was about to begin and suddenly you felt your seat wiggle and shake. In fact, everything began to shake! What was happening?

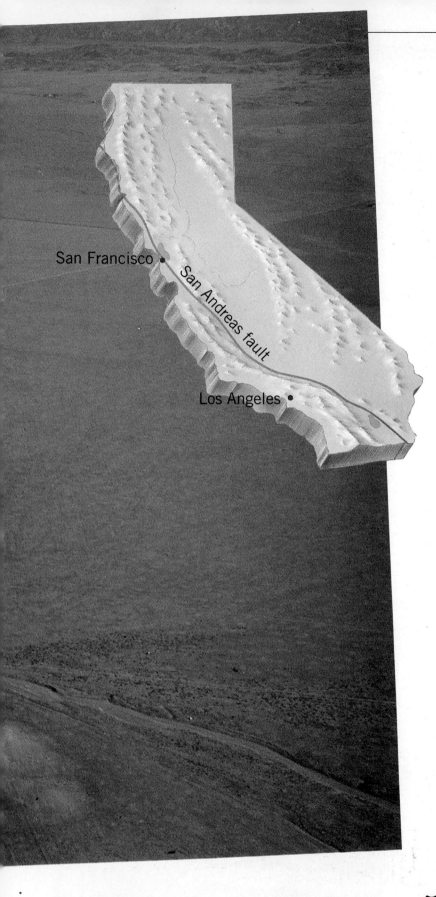

San Francisco •

San Andreas fault

Los Angeles •

San Andreas Fault

The aerial photograph on this page is of the Carrizo Plain. It shows a part of the San Andreas fault. The fault is a group of fractures, or cracks, in the earth's rocky surface where earthquake movements have taken place. It runs roughly parallel to the coastline of California. In some places, the fault can be seen at the earth's surface. In other places, it lies beneath the surface or is under water.

A fault is also a line where rock on one side of the fault might move up, down, or sideways in relation to rock on the other side. An earthquake is a sudden, rapid shaking of a part of the earth's crust caused by the release of energy stored underground in rocks. On October 17, 1989, movement along the San Andreas fault caused one of the strongest earthquakes along the fault in recent history. The earthquake began in the Santa Cruz Mountains near Loma Prieta Peak. Yet, people as far away as the states of Oregon and Nevada felt the shaking.

■ What does the inside of the earth look like?

■ How old is the earth?

■ What causes earthquakes?

EARTH MOVEMENTS

Using a map to help locate the fault

Activities

Features

Chapter 1

The Earth's Layers

A broken fence showing displacement along the San Andreas fault.

▲ Damage caused by the 1906 San Francisco earthquake. Note the twisted tram tracks, cracks in the street, and buckled sidewalks.

Much of the movement along the San Andreas fault is horizontal. This horizontal movement occurs when great blocks of rock move sideways slowly past each other. Land on the western side of the fault moves toward the northwest. Land on the eastern side of the fault moves toward the southeast.

Railroad tracks, roads, fences, or anything that crosses the fault can be broken or offset when movement occurs. Even stream beds may turn sharply where they cross the fault. In fact, movement along the fault in 1857 offset some stream channels by almost 10 meters.

The students in the photograph are standing along the San Andreas fault. Imagine that you are with them. What might you see if you looked down at the fault? You might expect to see a single fracture or crack in the ground. However, the San Andreas fault is a system of many fractures about 1,200 kilometers long and as much as 16 kilometers deep.

Now imagine that you could go down into the earth to investigate the San Andreas fault. What kinds of rocks do you think you would see? What would you see if you could continue your journey toward the center of the earth? What do you think the earth's interior would look like? How would the temperature change as you plunged toward the center of our planet?

SCIENCE JOURNAL

The earth has three layers. Rocks and soils make up most of the crust, or outer layer. Look around your home and neighborhood. In your Science Journal, list ways that people use rocks and soils.

Explore Activity

How are the earth's layers studied?

Process Skills

Making models, Inferring, Communicating

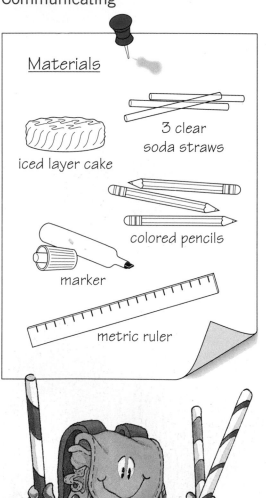

Materials

3 clear soda straws

iced layer cake

colored pencils

marker

metric ruler

Observe and Collect Data

1. Observe the cake. In your Activity Journal, write down as many properties about the cake as you can. Some properties you will be able to see, such as the color of the icing. Other properties, such as the flavor of the cake or the number of layers, you will have to infer, or guess, based on your observations.

2. Now, gently push one straw straight into the top of the cake. Do not tilt the straw. Push the straw until it reaches the bottom of the cake.

3. Carefully remove the straw from the cake. Label the straw "A" with the marker.

4. Repeat steps 2 and 3 with the two remaining straws in different parts of the cake. Make certain that the samples are taken along a straight line. Label the straws "B" and "C."

5. Place the three straws in order in front of you. Use the ruler and colored pencils to draw a cross section of the cake from what you see in the straws. A cross section is a cutaway, or side, view of an area. In this case, it is a sketch of what the cake would look like if you cut it in half and viewed it along the cut.

Share Your Results

How is your cross section like other students' cross sections? How is it different?

Draw Conclusions

1. Which of your inferences about the cake were like your observations?
2. Which inferences were different from your observations?
3. How did the straws allow you to "see" inside the cake?

Apply What you Know

1. Scientists who study the earth's soil use a similar method to take soil samples. Their instruments are much like your straws, but the instruments are made of a different material. What do you think this material is? Explain your answer.
2. Would it be possible to use this method to sample rocks deep within the earth? Explain your answer.

How did the earth's layers form and what are they like?

Our planet might have formed in stages.

▲ Early in its formation, the earth was a vast collection of unsorted particles.

▲ As it heated and cooled, denser elements moved toward the earth's center.

▲ Lighter elements moved toward the earth's surface to form its crust.

If you could cut the earth in half, you would see that it is made of layers. The outermost layer is the **crust.** The innermost layer is the **core**. The **mantle** (man´təl) lies between the crust and the core. How do you think these layers might have formed?

Most scientists think that the earth, and the other planets, formed from a huge, hot ball of gases, dust, and other elements. As the ball heated and cooled over millions and millions of years, the densest elements sank to the earth's center. Other elements accumulated to form the middle layer. The lightest elements rose and became the earth's outermost layer. Many of the gases combined to form the oceans and atmosphere.

The earth's rocky crust is its thinnest layer. There are two types of crust: continental crust and oceanic crust. Continental crust forms the earth's landmasses. Mountains and valleys are made of continental crust. The highest point on the earth's crust is Mount Everest in Asia. It is nearly 9 kilometers high.

Oceanic crust is found below the earth's oceans. The deepest point on the earth is found in the Pacific Ocean. It is the Mariana Trench, and it reaches to a depth of more than 11 kilometers below sea level.

Below the crust is the mantle, the thickest layer of the earth. The mantle has two parts. The upper 100 kilometers of this middle layer are rigid, or stiff. Below this rigid part, the mantle is partly melted. Sometimes this partly melted material behaves like a brittle solid. Sometimes it behaves like soft putty.

Crust

The crust is the thinnest layer of the earth. Continental crust is about 35 kilometers thick. Oceanic crust is about 8 kilometers thick.

Outer Core

The earth's core has two parts. The hot, liquid, outer core is about 2,270 kilometers thick.

Inner Core

The earth's solid inner core is about 1,210 kilometers in radius.

Mantle

The earth's mantle is about 2,900 kilometers thick. The mantle is a hot layer of rocks. Temperatures in this layer might be as high as 4,000°C and the rocks can bend like red-hot metal.

The core is the innermost layer of the earth. This hot, dense sphere has two parts. The outer core is liquid. A recent hypothesis suggests that the outer core has ridges, peaks, and valleys several kilometers deep and high over its surface. This liquid outer core surrounds a solid inner core.

Be a Scientist

How is an egg like the earth?

1. ⚠️ Carefully cut a hard-boiled egg in half with its shell on. On one half, put a small dot in the center of the yolk with a permanent marker.

2. **ACTIVITY JOURNAL** Study the flat side of the egg. Make a sketch of it in your Activity Journal. To one side of the sketch, label the shell, egg white, yolk, and dot.

3. On the other side of the drawing, label the parts of the egg that could represent different layers of the earth. How accurate do you think your model is? What could you do to make it more accurate?

How do scientists know about the earth's interior?

Scientists have drilled nearly 12 kilometers into the earth's crust. In the drawing of the earth shown on page E11, you can see that the earth's diameter is almost 12,800 kilometers. How do you think scientists find out about the rest of the earth?

Much of what we now know about the earth's interior comes from studying meteorites. A meteorite is a chunk of rock that traveled through our solar system and fell to the earth's surface. Some meteorites are made mostly of iron. Which layer of the earth is mostly iron? Some meteorites are made of materials much like peridotite. Which layer of the earth is mostly peridotite?

Scientists believe that meteorites formed at the same time as our planet. They also think that the planets and meteorites formed from the same cloud of dust and gases. Thus, by studying meteorites, scientists can hypothesize about the composition of the earth's interior.

What evidence do scientists have that the earth is divided into three layers? The division of the earth into the crust, the mantle, and the core is based on studies of earthquake waves.

Most earthquakes occur along faults, such as the San Andreas fault. Waves of energy are caused by a sudden movement along a fault. These earthquake waves move through the earth in all directions. The waves behave differently when they travel through different materials. By studying the ways these waves travel through the earth, scientists are able to identify three major boundaries in the earth's interior.

▲ The earth's middle layer, the mantle, is possibly made of a rock called peridotite. Peridotite contains minerals rich in iron and magnesium. Earthquake waves travel faster through the mantle than they do through the earth's crust.

▲ The earth's core is a very hot, dense sphere probably made of iron and nickel. Iron and nickel are very heavy elements. Some earthquake waves travel only through solids. How do you think scientists found out that the outer core is liquid?

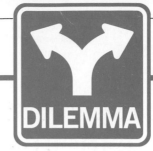

DILEMMA

Deep Drilling

Scientists are planning to drill deep into the earth along the San Andreas fault. The information they find may help us to better understand our planet. Perhaps the data will provide clues to some of the other planets in our solar system. Drilling these holes, however, could create huge amounts of waste rock materials.

SCIENCE JOURNAL **Think About It** Should the holes be drilled? Why or why not? What should be done with the waste? Write your opinion in your Science Journal and explain your reasons.

▲ There are two kinds of crust. Continental crust, which makes up the earth's landmasses, is made mostly of granite. Granite is a rock rich in elements such as silicon, potassium, aluminum, and magnesium. Oceanic crust makes up the ocean floors. Oceanic crust is mostly basalt. Basalt is rich in silicon, calcium, aluminum, iron, and magnesium.

How are you doing?

1. From the center of the earth outward, what are the layers of the earth? Which is the thinnest? The thickest?
2. Describe the earth's mantle.
3. **Think** Which fruit, an apple or a peach, is a better model of the earth? Explain why.
4. **Think** Which kind of crust—continental or oceanic—is more dense? Explain.

What are mountains?

Have you ever been mountain climbing? A mountain can be any feature that is higher than the surrounding land. It can be a very high hill. So if you've climbed a hill, you've been mountain climbing!

Whether you've climbed a hill or the peaks of the Rockies, the part of the mountain you saw above the earth's surface is only a small part of that mountain. Sometimes mountains are compared to icebergs. Have you ever heard the expression, "It's just the tip of the iceberg"?

An iceberg is a huge chunk of ice that has broken off a glacier. Nearly 90 percent of an iceberg is below water.

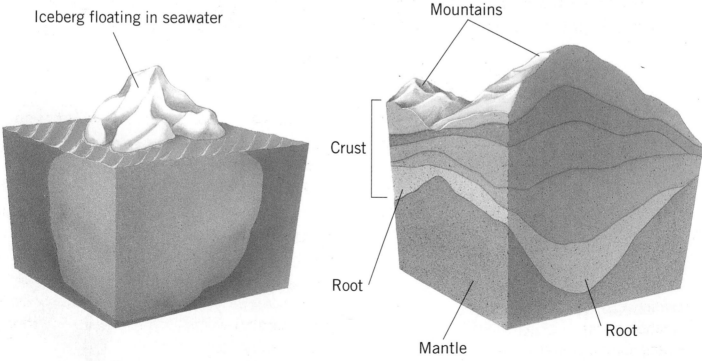

Iceberg floating in seawater

Mountains

Crust

Root

Mantle

Root

Be a Scientist

How can a mountain sink?

1. ⚠ Carefully cut off the top 8 centimeters of a 2-liter plastic bottle. Then fill the bottle with water to about 2–3 centimeters from the top.

2. Fill a baby-food jar half-full with water. Put the lid on the jar. **Predict** how much of the jar will be above the water level when you place it into the bottle. Use masking tape to mark the predicted level "A."

3. ACTIVITY JOURNAL Place the baby-food jar into the water. Note the water level on the outside of the jar. Use labels to mark this water level "B." How did your prediction, "A," match your observation, "B"? In your Activity Journal, use your results to estimate how much of your "mountain"—the baby-food jar—was below the earth's surface.

If these pieces of ice are so big, why do they float? Icebergs float because they displace, or push away, a certain volume of the sea water in which they are floating.

Recall that the earth's continental crust is made mostly of granite. The mantle is made of peridotite, a much denser rock. Just as an iceberg floats in water, the lighter crust "floats" on the denser mantle. The same volume of the earth's crust weighs less than the same volume of mantle. In fact, mountains are said to have vast "roots" that support them. The roots of a mountain are the thickest part of the mountain that sinks into the mantle. If a mountain's surface erodes away, the mountain weighs less and rises. The root also rises.

◀ Just as icebergs float in water, mountains on the earth "float" on the mantle below. The higher the mountain is, the deeper the root.

How do mountains form?

There are three major mountain systems in the world. One system is along the west coast of North and South America. Another system crosses Europe and Asia. The third system is the peaks of land in the Pacific Ocean, in east Asia, and Australia.

Mountains form as the result of many processes within the earth's crust and upper mantle. Geologists have identified several major processes of mountain building. These include folding, faulting, uplift, and volcanism. Folding produces mountains marked by

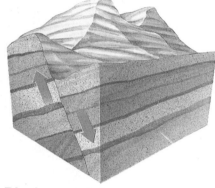

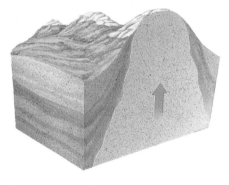

Fold mountains

When sections of the crust and upper mantle are squeezed from opposite sides, the crust wrinkles and fold mountains are formed. The Appalachians are fold mountains.

Block mountains

Block mountains have a fault along at least one side. These kinds of mountains have a steep side and a sloping side. The Teton Range in Wyoming are block mountains.

Dome mountains

Dome mountains form when large portions of the earth's crust are pushed upward by magma. The Black Hills in South Dakota are dome mountains, which are igneous rock.

valleys and parallel ridges. Faulting of large blocks of rock results in sharply rising block mountains. Uplifting results in dome mountains. What kind of mountains do you think are the result of volcanic activity?

Volcanoes

Volcanoes are cone-shaped mountains that form when melted rock material piles up and hardens. Note how Mount Hood, a volcano in Oregon, is cone-shaped.

Be a Scientist

HANDS-ON ACTIVITY

Can you model mountain building?

1. Use a plastic knife and three balls of clay. Flatten each ball into a slab about 1 centimeter thick.
2. Stack the clay slabs, separating the layers with plastic wrap. Use the clay to form fold mountains, then dome mountains, and, finally, block mountains.
3. **ACTIVITY JOURNAL** In your Activity Journal, record the way you formed each mountain type. Also include a sketch of each model and label it.

How are you doing?

1. How are mountains like icebergs?
2. How do fold mountains form?
3. **Think** Compare and contrast block, dome, and volcanic mountains.
4. **Think** The San Andreas is a fault, but along most parts of the fault, it does not form block mountains. Explain why.

by Diane Siebert

Sierra

*This is an excerpt from an illustrated story-in-rhyme about a
Sierra Nevada mountain speaking about herself and her
sister peaks.*

I am the mountain.
Tall and grand.
And like a sentinel I stand.

Surrounding me, my sisters rise
With watchful peaks that pierce the skies;
From north to south we form a chain
Dividing desert, field, and plain.

I am the mountain.
Come and know
Of how, ten million years ago,
Great forces, moving plates of earth,
Brought, to an ancient land, rebirth;
Of how this planet's faulted crust
Was shifted, lifted, tilted, thrust
Toward the sky in waves of change
To form a newborn mountain range.

. . .

I am the mountain.
From the sea
Come constant winds to conquer me—
Pacific winds that touch my face
And bring the storms whose clouds embrace
My rugged shoulders, strong and wide;
And in their path, I cannot hide.

And though I have the strength of youth,
I sense each change and know the truth:
By wind and weather, day by day,
I will, in time, be worn away;
For mountains live, and mountains die.
As ages pass, so, too, will I.

Think About Your Reading

1. What are the two causes and two effects of this poem?
2. Write a short paraphrase to explain the point you think this poem makes.

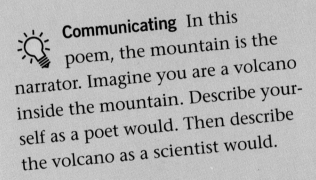

Communicating In this poem, the mountain is the narrator. Imagine you are a volcano inside the mountain. Describe yourself as a poet would. Then describe the volcano as a scientist would.

Where to Read More

Sara C. Bisel, *The Secrets of Vesuvius* (Scholastic, 1992)
Come along with an archeologist to the village of Herculaneum which was buried by one of the biggest volcanic disasters in history.

Looking Back

Words and Concepts

Use the correct word or phrase to complete the statement.

1. The _____ is the thinnest layer of the earth.
   - a. inner core
   - b. outer core
   - c. mantle
   - d. crust

2. Temperatures in the earth's _____ may be as high as 4,000°C.
   - a. inner core
   - b. outer core
   - c. mantle
   - d. crust

3. The earth's inner core is made mostly of _____.
   - a. granite
   - b. iron
   - c. meteorites
   - d. peridotite

4. The San Andreas fault is a feature of the earth's _____.
   - a. crust
   - b. mantle
   - c. inner core
   - d. outer core

5. _____ form when melted rock builds up and hardens to form mountains.
   - a. Block mountains
   - b. Volcanoes
   - c. Fold mountains
   - d. Dome mountains

6. When sections of the earth's crust and upper mantle are squeezed from opposite sides, _____ mountains are formed.
   - a. block
   - b. fold
   - c. volcanic
   - d. dome

Applied Thinking Skills

Answer the following questions. You can use words, drawings, and diagrams in your answers.

7. Which do you think is denser—the earth's inner core or the outer core? Explain.

8. Draw a model of Mount McKinley, an Alaskan mountain that towers about 6,200 meters above the earth's surface. Be sure to show the percentage of rock above and below the earth's surface.

9. What do volcanoes tell us about the earth's interior?

10. **Your World** Are there any faults in your state? Find out. Then explain why earthquakes could occur along any fault.

Show What You Know

Can you model the earth?

Observe and Collect Data

1. In this chapter, find the thickness of each layer of the earth. Record these values in a data table in your Activity Journal.
2. Decide on a scale to use for your model of the earth. For example, the diameter of the earth is about 12,800 kilometers. You might choose a scale of 3 centimeters = 1,000 kilometers. At this scale, the diameter of your model would be 38.4 centimeters.
3. Now, draw a cross section of the earth on the sheet of butcher paper. Draw the layers so they are the proper thickness for a model this size. Use different colors for different layers.
4. Label your model with the layer's name, thickness, and scale used. In your Activity Journal, write a brief description of each layer of the earth.

Draw Conclusions

1. Compare your model with other students' models. How are they the same?
2. How does your model differ from other students' models?
3. How accurate is your model?

Process Skills
Measuring, Communicating, Making models

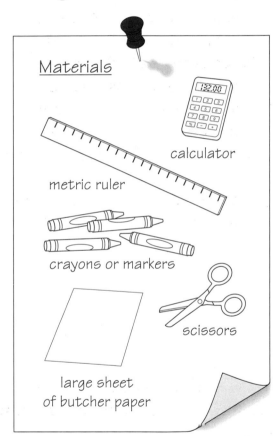

Materials

calculator

metric ruler

crayons or markers

scissors

large sheet
of butcher paper

Chapter 2

The Earth's History

What kind of creature do you think the students are observing? Does the animal remind you of any other kind of animal?

Some lizards look somewhat like animals that once roamed the earth. Can you guess which ones? If you said dinosaurs, you're right! Dinosaurs lived on our planet millions of years ago. Some were huge and might have been more than 40 meters long. Others were quite small—much like the lizard shown in the photograph. Some dinosaurs were meat eaters and some ate plants. Most lived on land while others spent some of their time in water.

Dinosaurs disappeared from our planet about 65 million years ago along with some marine creatures. What may have caused these creatures to become **extinct** (ek stiŋkt´)? Might the earth's climate have changed too quickly for them to adapt? Might erupting volcanoes or earthquakes have caused their extinction? Could a meteorite have collided with the earth and caused these creatures to die?

SCIENCE JOURNAL Imagine that you were a dinosaur that roamed the earth millions of years ago. Where did you live? How did you move from place to place? What did you eat? What did your neighbors look like? Remember, they were probably other dinosaurs—people didn't exist yet. Write your ideas in your Science Journal. Include a self-portrait.

Sometimes Western fence lizards are called blue-belly lizards.

This whale vertebra fossil was found in a sandstone layer of an ancient seabed.

Explore Activity

How do scientists find out about ancient animals?

MINDS-ON ACTIVITY

Process Skills

Inferring, Communicating, Hypothesizing

Observe and Collect Data

1. Study the fossil shown in the photograph.
2. [ACTIVITY JOURNAL] In your Activity Journal, draw a possible shape and possible body covering of the animal. Include as many features as you can infer from the fossil.
3. Describe the animal. **Predict** how you think it moved, what it ate, where it lived, and so on.

Share Your Results

Compare your drawing with those of several other students. How are the drawings the same? What reasoning did all of you use to draw similar conclusions about the animal?

Draw Conclusions

1. Now your teacher will show you how scientists think the animal looked. How is your drawing similar or different?
2. What can you tell from an animal's skeleton?

Apply What You Know

Imagine that scientists found some ancient animal's bones and teeth. From this evidence, do you think that the scientist might be able to tell what kinds of plants and animals once lived on the earth? Or what the earth's climate was like? What might they do or what information might they use to help them put the bones and teeth together? What was the earth like in the past?

What are fossils?

What was the earth like in the past? Some clues to the earth's past can be found in rocks. Certain rocks contain fossils. **Fossils** are preserved evidence of ancient living things. They usually form when organisms die and are covered by sediments. Fossils tell us about plants and animals that once lived on the earth. Scientists who study the prehistoric life of plants and animals are paleontologists (pā´lē ən täl´ə jists).

The soft parts of living things, such as leaves, skin, and muscles, decay quickly. Fossils usually are the remains of the hard parts of an organism, such as wood, shells, bones, and teeth.

Because not all parts of animals and plants become preserved as fossils, paleontologists often must piece together a few parts of an organism. In order to rebuild an ancient plant or animal, they use what they know about similar organisms from the past. They also use their knowledge of plants and animals that live on the earth today.

▲ Some fossils are the actual remains of a plant or animal. Animals like this fragile insect have been found preserved in hardened tree sap, called amber. Woolly mammoths, which were as large as modern adult elephants, have been discovered frozen in ice.

Sometimes after an organism is buried, water rich in minerals dissolves the original organic matter. When this original material is preserved, the plant or animal is petrified (pe´tri fīd´), or turned to stone. This fossil is petrified wood. ▶

▲ When an organism is buried and squeezed between layers of sediments, the fluids are removed from the organism. A thin film of carbon remains and an imprint is left.

Can you make a fossil?

1. **ACTIVITY JOURNAL** Choose an object to make your own mold and cast fossils. Coat your object with a thin film of petroleum jelly. Gently push the object into some modeling clay. Carefully remove the object. What kind of fossil did you make?

2. Now coat the impression you made with petroleum jelly. Fill the impression with plaster of Paris.

3. When the plaster is dry, remove it from the impression. What kind of fossil did you make? Exchange fossils with a classmate and try to write descriptions of the original objects. What information could you infer from this fossil? What information could you not infer?

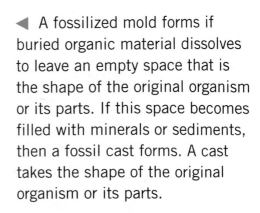

◄ A fossilized mold forms if buried organic material dissolves to leave an empty space that is the shape of the original organism or its parts. If this space becomes filled with minerals or sediments, then a fossil cast forms. A cast takes the shape of the original organism or its parts.

How do scientists determine the age of rocks?

▲ Trilobites are good index fossils because they were numerous and widely distributed over the earth for a short period of time.

Suppose you get a newspaper delivered to your home each day. After the newspaper is read, you put it into a box. If you do this after you read each paper every day, the oldest newspaper will be on the bottom of the box and the most recent paper will be on the top. If the pile is not disturbed, the newspapers will remain in this order, or sequence.

Much like your stack of newspapers, scientists have found that in areas where rocks are undisturbed, the oldest rocks are on the bottom. The youngest rocks are near the top. This kind of sequencing is called relative dating. Using this method, scientists are able to determine that one rock layer is older or younger than another. Often, relative dating is used to date sedimentary rock layers.

Then, too, scientists use fossils to determine the age of rocks. Different-aged rocks contain different fossil groupings. Fossilized organisms occur in a definite order within rocks. Thus, a time period in the earth's past can be recognized by the fossils contained in its rocks.

Some fossils clearly indicate the age of a rock. These are called **index fossils.** In order to be an index fossil, three conditions must be met. First, an

SCIENCE JOURNAL

Look at some old family photos. How have you and your family changed? How are you the same? Take several photos, each taken in a different year, and mix them up. Would you be able to sort the pictures from the oldest to the most recent? What clues would you use? Write your ideas in your Science Journal. Then have a family member try to put the pictures in order.

BACK HOME

Cenozoic

Mesozoic

Paleozoic

Precambrian

▲ Paleontologists use index fossils to date rocks. An index fossil can indicate a rock's age fairly accurately.

organism must have been abundant. Next, the organism must have existed for only a short period. Finally, the organism must have changed, or evolved, rapidly.

Trilobites (trī´lō bīts´) are animals that lived hundreds of millions of years ago. They are index fossils that have been found in a rock layer at the bottom of the Grand Canyon and in a rock layer in Wales. From this, scientists infer that both rock layers are about the same age.

What is another way that scientists determine the ages of rocks?

Think about the Back Home activity on page E28. Unless you knew when each photograph was taken, you could probably say only that one was newer or older than another. In the same way, when scientists use relative dating methods, they can say only that one rock layer is younger or older than another.

Imagine that your camera could record the date and time of day that a photo was taken. You could use this information to put the pictures in order according to the exact time each was taken. In a similar way, the actual ages of some rocks can be determined by a method called radiometric dating.

Scientists use a form of radiometric dating called carbon-14 dating to determine the age of once-living organisms. Also, scientists are able to date rocks that have fossils in them because fossils were once living. In this process, the amounts of two elements are measured. One of these elements is a radioactive element that changes at a constant rate into another element. The other element that is measured is the one that the radioac-

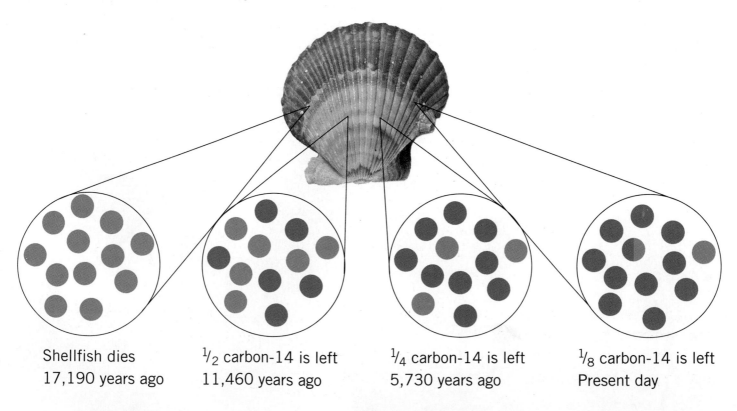

Shellfish dies
17,190 years ago

$\frac{1}{2}$ carbon-14 is left
11,460 years ago

$\frac{1}{4}$ carbon-14 is left
5,730 years ago

$\frac{1}{8}$ carbon-14 is left
Present day

The Age of the Earth

The San Andreas fault system is between 15 and 20 million years old. This is considered a very young feature on our planet! Most scientists agree that our planet is about 4.6 billion years old. What was the earth like 4.6 billion years ago? What is your theory on how it formed?

Most scientists believe that the universe formed about 15 billion years ago. The big-bang theory is about an explosion that caused matter to fly outward from a central point. A swirling cloud of hot gases and dust slowly cooled over billions of years to form our solar system. Gravity caused much of the matter to be pulled toward the center of the cloud. This matter eventually became our sun. Other particles collected to form the planets. Radiometric dating of meteorites, materials from the moon, and certain earth rocks suggests that the earth is about 4.6 billion years old.

tive element changes into. By comparing the amounts of each element, a fossil's age can be determined.

Organisms collect carbon-14 during their lives. When a plant or animal dies, no more carbon-14 enters the organism and the remaining carbon-14 in the organism continues to decay. If the amount of carbon-14 is compared to the amount of decay product, scientists can determine when the organism died.

The decay rate of radioactive elements, like carbon, never changes. Carbon-14 decays at a predictable rate. Thus, scientists can

◀ Radioactive elements decay, or change into new elements, at a constant rate. These elements can be used to determine the approximate ages of certain fossils.

measure the amount of carbon-14 in a once-living organism and use that measurement to calculate its age.

In the oldest rocks that have fossil remains, most of the radioactive elements have changed to other elements.

How are you doing?

1. What are some ways organisms can be preserved as fossils?
2. Name three ways the earth's rocks can be dated.
3. **Think** How is the radioactive element carbon-14 used to determine the age of fossils? Explain.
4. **Think** Worms have no hard parts. Yet, scientists know that they've been on the earth for millions of years. How might a scientist find out about ancient worms?

What is geologic time?

Cenozoic Era
Present

Mesozoic Era
65 million years ago

Paleozoic Era
225 million years ago

Precambrian Era
4.6 billion years ago

The earth's history is very long. Scientists have determined that the earth is about 4.6 billion years old. This is a great amount of time that is hard to imagine. If this time could be squeezed into one year, humans would be on the earth for less than a blink of your eye.

Scientists use a **geologic time scale** to show the earth's history and its life. The earth's history can be divided into four major segments that are called eras. Eras are defined by the different plants and animals that lived during that time. The close of each era is marked by many extinctions of plants and animals. Eras are not of equal lengths of time.

Precambrian Era
4.6 billion years before present

Earth's beginning, first crust   Oldest rock   Oldest fossil   Ancient continents and oceans formed   First cells

Precambrian Era

The Precambrian (prē kam´brē ən) Era is the longest unit of geologic time. It lasted for almost 4 billion years. Mountains formed and eroded away. Glaciers covered much of the land at times. Little is known about this era because few fossils have been found. After the earth began to take form, it was hundreds of millions of years before the first life evolved. About 3,500 million years ago the first cells appeared. Millions of years later fungi and algae evolved. Then organisms such as jellyfish and sponges appeared.

Paleozoic Era

During the Paleozoic (pā´lē̄o zō´ik) Era, the earth's land formed a supercontinent called Pangaea. Toward the end of the era, the Appalachian Mountains began to form. The climate was warm and the landscape barren. Many organisms lived in the warm, shallow seas that covered much of the planet. Sea animals with shells and external skeletons thrived. Many invertebrates, such as trilobites, became extinct. Plants and animals developed adaptations that allowed them to live on land.

Paleozoic Era
600 to 225 million years before present

First simple organisms

Appalachian Mountains began to form

First fish, reptiles, amphibians, and shellfish

Mass extinctions

Atlantic Ocean began to form

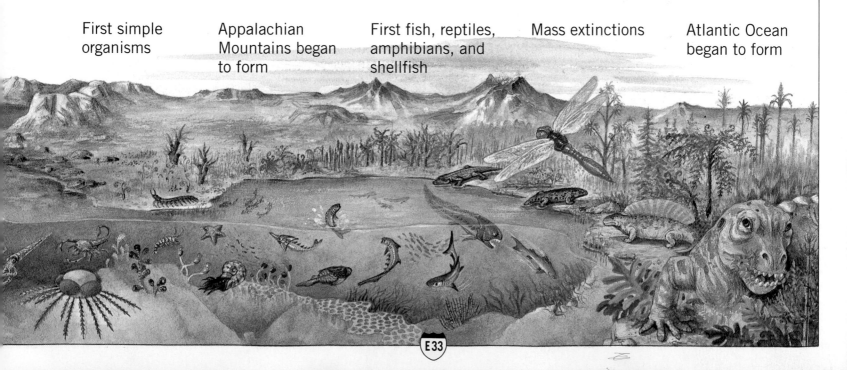

Burning fossil fuels pollutes the air you and other animals breathe. Plants, too, are harmed by pollution from fossil fuels. You and your family can help cut down on air pollution by reducing activities that involve burning fossil fuels, such as driving a car.

Mesozoic Era

The Mesozoic (mes´ō zō´ik) Era is marked by Pangaea breaking into separate continents and the Rocky Mountains forming. The climate was generally warm and sea levels rose. Dinosaurs roamed the earth for much of the era. For reasons still not known, they became extinct, along with other animals and plants. During this era fish, reptiles, and large mollusks lived in the seas. One mollusk, the ammonite, resembled some of today's snails. Small mammals, birds, snakes, and flowering plants appeared on land.

Mesozoic Era
225 to 65 million years before present

Pangaea began to break apart

First dinosaurs and mammals

First snakes, birds, and marsupials

Mass extinctions

Cenozoic Era

During the Cenozoic (sē´nə zō´ik) Era the landmasses continued to separate and moved to present-day positions. The Himalayas rose and ice built up on Antarctica. Mountain building took place over the world as slabs of the earth's crust collided. Movement along the San Andreas fault began. Some animals, such as the woolly mammoth, became extinct. Insects and flowering plants continued to be abundant. During this era, the first humans appeared.

Cenozoic Era
65 million years ago to present

First primates   Ice Age glaciers melted   Landmasses reach present position   First humans

Coal—One Source of Energy

Coal is the remains of plants that lived long ago. When plants died, they were attacked by bacteria that caused the plants to decay. This decayed matter was covered with sediments. Heat and pressure caused certain elements to escape, leaving behind carbon. Over millions of years, the carbon accumulated to form coal.

The living plants gathered and stored energy from the sun. When coal is burned, this stored energy is released. Explain why coal is a fossil fuel.

How are you doing?

1. On what are the divisions of the geologic time scale based?
2. Briefly describe some of the events that happened during the Paleozoic and Mesozoic eras.
3. **Think** Compare and contrast the dominant life forms in each era.
4. **Think** Describe a general pattern, or trend, in the kinds of life that lived on the earth over geologic time.

Earth Legends

Earthquakes and other natural occurences have been happening for millions of years. Yet, scientists have understood what causes earthquakes for only about 30 years.

Ancient peoples all over the world have explanations about these natural occurences and how they have affected their way of life. These explanations, passed on by word of mouth, are called legends.

Many American Indian legends tell about the earth and its inhabitants. These stories do not try to explain facts scientifically. Instead, they explain certain beliefs.

One story tells how the Navajos came to be. The legend says that the Navajos rose from the center of the earth through a hollow reed. The first Navajo home, or hogan, was built on this spot. The legend divides the earth into four sections. Each section has a sacred mountain and a person who guards it. Today, most Navajos live in the sacred homeland called Dinétah in Colorado and New Mexico. This area is bordered by four mountains: Blanca Peak, Francisco Peak, Mount Taylor, and Hesperus Mountain.

Another legend of the Navajo people explains the relationship between the earth and the sky. The photograph is a sandpainting of Mother Earth and Father Sky, the two halves of Navajo creation. Plants grow from Mother Earth. The stars belong to Father Sky.

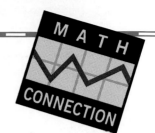

MATH CONNECTION

How much is a billion?

The earth is about 4.6 billion years old. This is such a big number that it's hard to imagine. In this activity, determine the number of containers needed to hold one billion objects.

Observe and Collect Data

1. **ACTIVITY JOURNAL** Work in groups. Select an object. Count the number of items in a container. Then estimate how many containers it will take to hold 1 billion objects. Complete the table below in your Activity Journal.

2. Add the results from at least three other groups to your table.

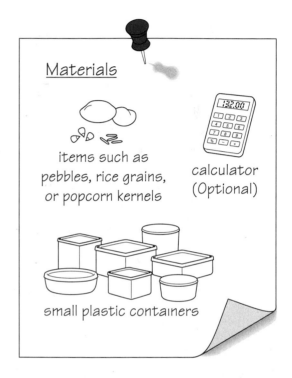

Materials

items such as pebbles, rice grains, or popcorn kernels

calculator (Optional)

small plastic containers

Draw Conclusions

1. How did your estimate of the number of containers compare with the actual number that it took? Why do you think you estimated the way you did?

2. Compare your description of one billion with those of your classmates. What do the descriptions have in common? How are they different?

3. How does your new understanding of a billion affect how you now think about the age of the earth?

Counting to a Billion

A	B	C
Number of objects in a container	Number of containers for 1 million $1,000,000/A =$	Number of containers for 1 billion $B \times 1000 =$

Looking Back

Words and Concepts

Match the description in Column A with the correct term in Column B.

Column A

1. Method used by scientists to determine the exact age of a rock
2. An impression in the shape of a once-living organism
3. The longest unit of geologic time
4. Organisms that no longer live on the earth
5. Mammals appeared in this era
6. Plants and animals first inhabited land in this era

Column B

a. Mesozoic Era
b. Radiometric dating
c. Extinct life
d. Precambrian Era
e. Fossil mold
f. Paleozoic Era

Some whale bone fossils are too big and heavy to hold. This is a small vertebra.

Applied Thinking Skills

Answer the following questions. You can use words, drawings, and diagrams in your answers.

7. Describe the organisms that lived during the early part of the Paleozoic Era. Contrast organisms with those that lived at the end of the era.
8. Explain some conditions that are necessary for fossil formation.
9. **Your World** Describe two ways you could create fossils that could provide clues about you for scientists in the future.

Show What You Know

Can you make a geologic clock?

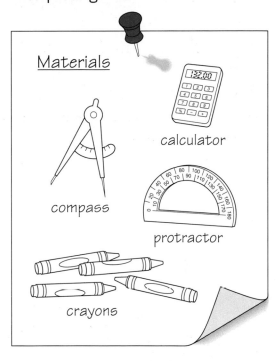

Observe and Collect Data

1. Make a circle that is divided into 24 equal segments to represent a 24-hour day. This can be approximated by dividing the circle into thirds and then halving each section three times.

2. Use the data in the table below to plot the earth's history on the 24-hour graph. Color each section.

3. Make a key that explains what each color represents.

4. Make a 24-hour circle graph that shows how you might spend a day. Include a color key.

Draw Conclusions

1. Study your clock of the earth's history. What can you say about the amount of time that life has been present on the earth?

2. Compare your clock with the geologic clock. Which activity or activities can be compared to the Precambrian Era?

3. Which activity do you spend the least amount of time doing? Which geologic era is this activity "equivalent" to?

Process Skills

Measuring, Making models, Interpreting data

Materials

calculator

compass

protractor

crayons

Unit of geologic time	Actual time in years	Time in 24-hour model
Precambrian Era	4.03 billion	20 hours, 52 minutes
Paleozoic Era	375 million	1 hour, 58 minutes
Mesozoic Era	160 million	48 minutes
Cenozoic Era	65 million	22 minutes

▲ Earth scientists investigating a fissure or ground rupture, caused by the 1989 Loma Prieta earthquake.

▲ A road and fence were displaced by the 1906 San Francisco earthquake.

Chapter 3

The Earth's Plates

Slabs made of the earth's crust and rigid upper mantle ride on the hot, semisolid part of the mantle, which has the consistency of modeling clay. As these rigid slabs move slowly across the earth's surface, mountains form. Ocean basins open and close. These movements that are taking place today also took place millions and billions of years ago. It wasn't until the 1960s that geologists were able to make these conclusions.

Throughout history, scientists have made many hypotheses, or guesses, about how our planet formed and how and why it constantly changes. Many of these hypotheses were changed as more data were collected. Our current explanation is a model called plate tectonics. The theory of **plate tectonics** states that the earth's crust and upper mantle are broken into huge slabs. These slabs, or **plates**, are joined much like the pieces of a jigsaw puzzle. There are up to 12 major plates in our earth's outer rock shell.

It is not known exactly why these plates are in constant motion and how they move slowly across the earth's surface. Scientists have speculated that the earth's internal heat causes convection currents in the semisolid mantle. The convection currents under the floating plates cause the plates to move.

SCIENCE JOURNAL

The students in the photograph are standing along the San Andreas fault. This fault separates two of the earth's plates. Think about what you have just read. Make a hypothesis about why earthquakes happen along the San Andreas fault. Write your hypothesis in your Science Journal.

Matching ground surface features to our San Andreas fault map

Can you model the earth's plates?

Process Skills

Observing, Communicating, Defining operationally

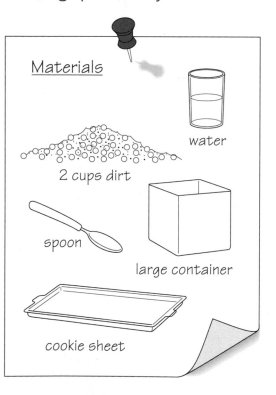

Materials

water

2 cups dirt

spoon

large container

cookie sheet

Observe and Collect Data

1. Pour the dirt into the container.
2. Add enough water to make a thick, soupy paste. Stir the mixture with the spoon until it is smooth.
3. Carefully pour the mixture into the cookie sheet. Use the spoon to spread the mixture evenly over the whole cookie sheet.

4. Put the cookie sheet in the sun or a warm place where it can dry. Choose a location where the sheet will not be disturbed.

5. After the mud has dried, study the slab to see if you can determine lines or zones of weakness. **Predict** where you think the mud slab might crack. Record your observations in your Activity Journal. Make a sketch to support your prediction. To crack the mud slab, get a partner to help you to gently twist the corners of the sheet in opposite directions.

Share Your Results

Compare and contrast your "mud puzzle" with those of at least two other pairs of students. How did your prediction of how the slab might crack compare with how the slab actually did crack? Write your observations in your Activity Journal.

Draw Conclusions

1. How is your model like the earth's tectonic plates?
2. What kinds of things about the earth's plates can't be shown with your model?

Apply What You Know

Carefully, remove all the pieces of your puzzle from the cookie sheet. Work with your partner to try to put it back together. How might this activity be like one in which scientists try to reconstruct ancient landmasses?

What evidence supports plate tectonics?

The four global maps show how the drifting continents may have moved from 500 million years ago to the present time. ▶

Be a Scientist

HANDS-ON ACTIVITY

Can you model convection currents?

1. ⚠ A convection current is movement in a fluid when hot fluid rises and cold fluid sinks. These currents are thought to drive the movements of the earth's plates. Use a clear, heat-resistant container to observe similar currents. Fill your container ³⁄₄ full of water.

2. Add ½ cup of rice or popcorn kernels to the water. Carefully bring the water to a slow boil. Observe the movements of the rice or popcorn.

3. **ACTIVITY JOURNAL** Draw a picture of your observations in your Activity Journal. How might this movement be like the movement that drives the earth's plates?

In 1912, a German scientist named Alfred Wegener proposed that landmasses had drifted across the earth to their present positions. This hypothesis was called **continental drift**. Wegener based his hypothesis on several pieces of evidence. He collected evidence from the rocks, fossils, and climates of different continents. His evidence supported his hypothesis that continents had once been joined together. He noted that the coast of eastern South America seemed to fit like a puzzle piece into the western coast of Africa. He also observed that many of the rock formations on the two continents were similar.

Another line of evidence came from fossils. Similar fossils were found in similar rocks on different continents. Also, fossils of certain organisms seemed out of place. For example, fossils of a plant called *Glossopteris* (gläs äp´tər əs) have been found on all the continents in the Southern Hemisphere. *Glossopteris* lived in temperate, humid regions. How could this plant have survived on present-day Antarctica?

Even though Wegener's argument was supported by numerous observations, most scientists rejected his hypothesis of continental drift. Why? Wegener could not explain *how* such enormous masses of land could

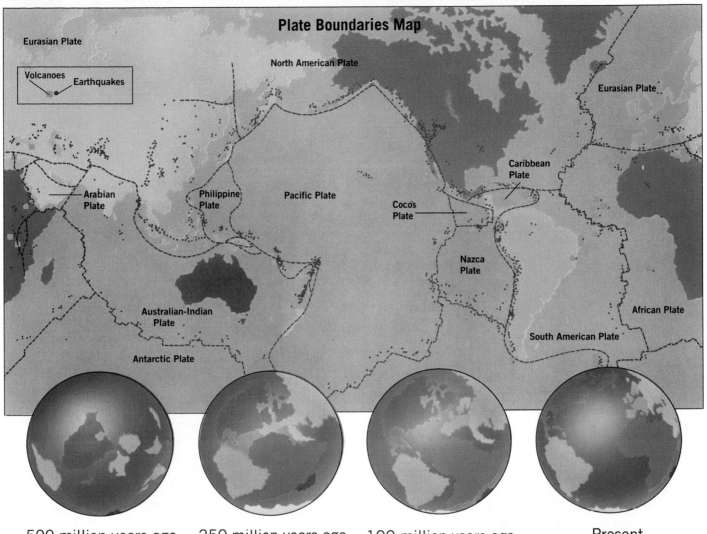

Plate Boundaries Map

Eurasian Plate

North American Plate

Eurasian Plate

Volcanoes ■ ● Earthquakes

Arabian Plate

Philippine Plate

Pacific Plate

Caribbean Plate

Coco's Plate

Nazca Plate

African Plate

Australian-Indian Plate

South American Plate

Antarctic Plate

500 million years ago   250 million years ago   100 million years ago   Present

move around. Wegener thought that the continents moved through the mantle like a plow moves through soil.

It wasn't until the early 1960s, when scientists were able to map the ocean bottoms, that evidence was gathered to support continental drift. Maps of the ocean bottom revealed that the basins were very young features. The maps also showed that near the middle of the Atlantic and Indian oceans there is a long narrow mid-ocean ridge. One

ridge system is called the Mid-Atlantic Ridge. Red-hot lava from the mantle flows from these ridges and adds new ocean floor material to the earth. Rocks closest to the ridge are younger than rocks farther from the ridge. The scientists realized that the ocean floors are spreading apart. This process of making new ocean crust is called **sea-floor spreading**, and it occurs along certain plate boundaries.

How do plates move?

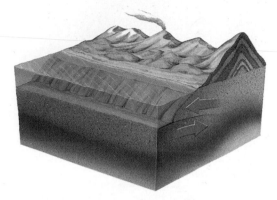

▲ Convergent boundary

▲ Divergent boundary

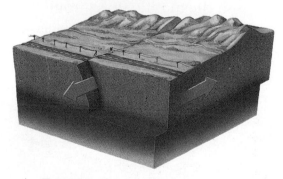

▲ Transform-fault boundary

Plates come into contact with one another at three types of boundaries. In some places, plates collide. Sometimes they separate. And sometimes plates move sideways past each other.

Places where two plates collide or come together are called **convergent boundaries.** What do you think might happen when two enormous plates of rock push against each other? Sometimes, the plates buckle and

DILEMMA

Burying Hazardous Wastes

Some people have suggested burying containers of radioactive waste at certain convergent boundaries. Their reasoning is that this dangerous material, which can cause problems if buried near the surface, will be taken deep into the earth.

Think About It Do you think this is a good idea? Why or why not? Should the containers be buried at boundaries that are colliding slowly or quickly? Why? Organize a class debate on this topic.

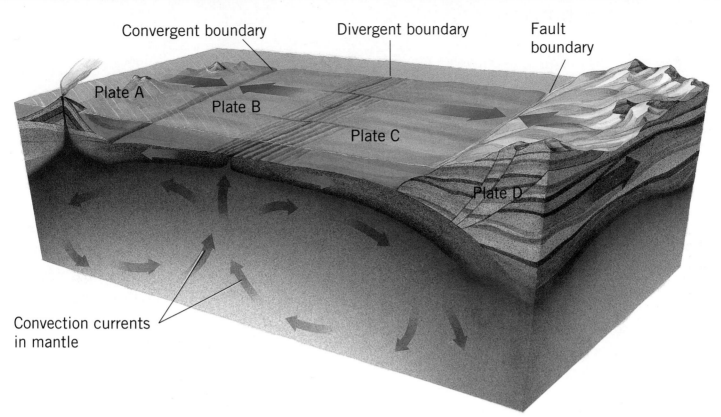

Convergent boundary

Divergent boundary

Fault boundary

Plate A

Plate B

Plate C

Plate D

Convection currents in mantle

rise to form mountains. In other cases, one plate slides beneath the other. As the lower plate sinks into the mantle, it melts. The magma that forms from this melting plate may slowly rise to produce volcanoes.

Plates move apart at **divergent boundaries.** As plates separate, magma rises to fill the gap. When the magma hardens, new ocean crust is formed. Divergent boundaries most often occur on the ocean floor along mid-ocean ridges.

Transform faults are the third type of plate boundary. At a **transform-fault boundary**, plates move horizontally past each other. The plates make contact with each other at a fault. Earthquakes are very common along these boundaries. The San Andreas fault is a transform-fault boundary.

▲ The theory of plate tectonics states that the earth's crust and upper mantle are broken into large slabs called plates. Convection currents in the mantle cause these plates to move slowly across the earth's surface. Some plates move fewer than 1.5 centimeters per year. Other plates move between 10 and 20 centimeters yearly, or about as fast as your fingernails grow.

How are you doing?

1. What is the theory of plate tectonics?
2. What is sea-floor spreading?
3. **Think** Compare and contrast convergent and divergent boundaries.
4. **Think** If continental landmasses were once joined, why don't they fit together perfectly today? How might these landmasses look 50 million years from now?

What are earthquakes?

An earthquake sends seismic waves through the earth. The point where the earthquake starts is called the **focus.** Although they can be as deep as 700 km, the focuses of most earthquakes are shallow, usually less than 100 km deep. The point on the earth's surface directly above the focus is called the **epicenter** (ep´i sent ər). Epicenters are usually in narrow zones called belts, where mountain building and volcanic activity are present. ▼

An earthquake is a trembling, a vibration, or motion of the earth. Earthquakes happen when the ground shakes suddenly and rapidly as energy that has been slowly building up in the earth's crust is released in the crust or upper mantle. Most earthquakes happen because rocks move past each other along faults. More than 900,000 earthquakes occur each year. Thousands of them occur in California, with many due to movement along the San Andreas fault. Most earthquakes aren't felt by people. Others do enormous amounts of damage.

One of the most damaging earthquakes on the San Andreas fault occurred in 1906. It struck the area around San Francisco. Scientists estimate that the San Francisco earthquake released 60 times more energy than the Loma Prieta earthquake of 1989. Fires, some of which started from broken gas lines, raged for days after the San Francisco earthquake.

Earthquakes send out energy waves in all directions. These waves are called seismic waves. Seismic waves that travel through the earth's interior are called body waves. Seismic waves that move through the earth's crust are called surface waves.

There are two kinds of body waves, P-(Primary) waves and S-(Secondary) waves. P-waves always travel faster than S-waves. Body waves help us locate the focus of an earthquake. P-waves travel through molten and solid rocks. They cause

Epicenter

Fault

Focus

Seismic waves

Be a Scientist

How do earthquake waves travel?

1. ⚠ Wear your safety goggles throughout this activity. Work with two other people. Two people in your group need to hold the ends of a coiled spring toy and stretch it to about 2 meters. While the spring is stretched, the third person squeezes together about 20 of the coils, then releases them. Switch roles so that each person can observe what happens.

2. 📓 Draw your observations in your Activity Journal. You may want to make notes.

3. Next, two people in your group hold the ends of the spring. One of them makes a quick flip of the wrist to the right to set the spring in motion. Switch roles so each person can observe what happens. Draw a picture of your observations.

4. Finally, two people hold the ends of the spring. One of them moves the spring up and down while the other person moves the spring sideways. Switch roles and record your observations.

the rock particles to be pushed together and pulled apart, which causes the ground to stretch and then compress. S-waves also travel through rocks. They cause rock particles to move at right angles to the wave movement, which causes the ground to vibrate sideways. S-waves do not travel through the outer core.

There are two kinds of surface waves. One kind of surface wave travels sideways. They cause the ground to shake from side to side, much the way a snake moves. The other surface waves have up-and-down motion and can open and close cracks in the earth. The surface waves are usually responsible for shaking the ground.

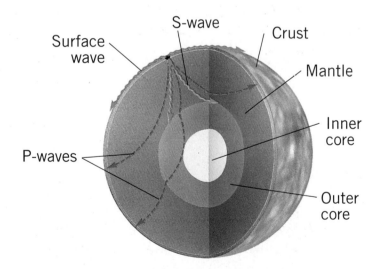

▲ The study of earthquake waves allowed scientists to divide our planet into three major layers—the crust, the mantle, and the core. How do you think scientists found out that the outer core was liquid?

How are earthquakes detected?

Earthquakes have been happening on the earth since it formed 4.6 billion years ago. These events are more common in some places than others. Look at the map on page E45. Where do most earthquakes occur? Why do you think earthquakes happen where they do?

Many earthquakes, such as those that occur along the San Andreas fault, are recorded with an instrument called a seismograph (sīz´mə graf´). A seismograph records the direction, intensity, and duration of earthquakes. One type of seismograph has a mass, which is a quanity of matter, that hangs from a support. The support is anchored in the ground. When an earthquake occurs, the mass vibrates, and movement is recorded as a zigzag line on a rotating drum.

The information recorded by a seismograph is called a seismogram. P-waves are the

Be a Scientist

Can you make a seismograph?

1. Stack several books in a pile on a cart with wheels. Anchor a ruler between the top two books. Now attach a washer and clay to a pen with rubber bands as shown in the photograph.

2. **ACTIVITY JOURNAL** Put a sheet of paper under the pen. Make sure the pen tip just touches the paper. Have your partner hold the books in place while you gently shake the cart to produce an "earthquake." What do you see on the paper?

3. Take turns producing "earthquakes." Describe how different forces produce different seismograms.

Geophysicist

Rufus Catchings is a geophysicist who conducts scientific investigations related to earthquakes, volcanoes, mineral exploration, and nuclear safety. Some geophysicists conduct studies on the temperature of rocks, electrical energy in rocks, magnetism of various rocks, and the stress and strain in rocks. This information is applied to fields of study such as mineral and oil exploration, volcano research, earthquake research, tectonic studies, and environmental studies.

" Much of my research is on understanding the San Andreas fault and other faults that pose a threat to public safety. I conduct experiments on how seismic waves travel through the earth. I also study the composition of the earth and what it is like at great depths.

"I studied mathematics, physics, electrical engineering, and earth science in college and later earned a doctorate degree. I now do research for the United States Geological Survey.

"I like my job because the type of research that I do can actually save lives. One of the best things about my job is that the whole earth is my laboratory. **"**

fastest seismic waves, so they arrive first and are recorded first. S-waves, which travel about half as fast as P-waves, arrive next. The last seismic waves to arrive and be recorded are the surface waves.

Arrival times recorded on seismographs give the distance of the earthquake from three or more recording stations. Circles are drawn to represent the distance from each station to the focus. The point where the circles intersect is the epicenter of the earthquake. ▶

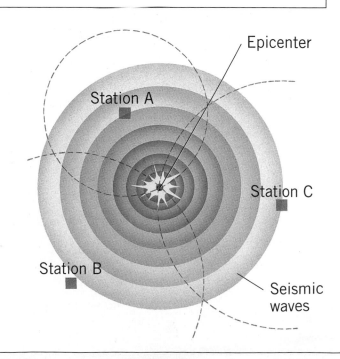

How are earthquakes measured?

Two scales measure earthquakes. Both scales use numbers to describe how strong earthquakes are.

The Mercalli scale was developed in 1902 by Giuseppe Mercalli, an Italian geologist. This scale uses Roman numerals from I to XII to describe the intensity of the physical effects of an earthquake. A gentle earthquake not felt by people is rated I. Earthquakes that produce heavy damage are rated IX. If there is total destruction, the earthquake is rated XI or XII, the highest value on the scale.

The Richter scale was developed in 1935 by Charles Richter, an American physicist. This scale ranks earthquakes with Arabic numbers according to the amount of energy released. The Richter scale is very accurate because it uses scientific instruments to measure ground motion.

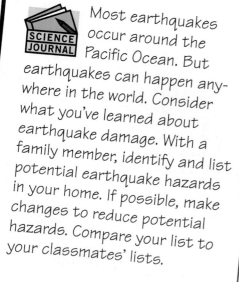 Most earthquakes occur around the Pacific Ocean. But earthquakes can happen anywhere in the world. Consider what you've learned about earthquake damage. With a family member, identify and list potential earthquake hazards in your home. If possible, make changes to reduce potential hazards. Compare your list to your classmates' lists.

 CALIFORNIA

BACK HOME

▲ Unreinforced brick walls can collapse during strong earthquakes.

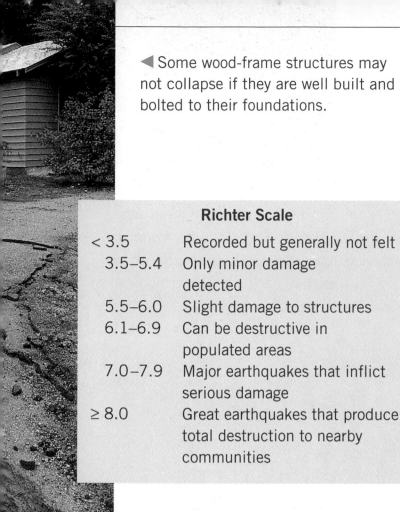

◀ Some wood-frame structures may not collapse if they are well built and bolted to their foundations.

Richter Scale

< 3.5	Recorded but generally not felt
3.5–5.4	Only minor damage detected
5.5–6.0	Slight damage to structures
6.1–6.9	Can be destructive in populated areas
7.0–7.9	Major earthquakes that inflict serious damage
≥ 8.0	Great earthquakes that produce total destruction to nearby communities

SIDE TRIP ▶

The New Madrid Fault

Most earthquakes occur along plate boundaries. One of the most intense earthquakes in the United States, however, occurred far from any plate boundary. The New Madrid fault is a system of active faults buried thousands of meters below sand and mud in Illinois, Missouri, Kentucky, Tennessee, and Arkansas. In 1811, movement along the New Madrid fault zone caused more than 2,000 shock waves. Five of these tremors would have measured 8.0 or greater on the Richter scale. Scientists predict that the next powerful earthquake along this fault system will be between the years 2000 and 2050.

▲ The vibrations produced by an earthquake can cause freeway overpasses to collapse.

How are you doing?

1. How does a seismograph work?
2. What is the Richter scale?
3. **Think** Compare and contrast seismic surface waves and seismic body waves.
4. **Think** What is the value of having two scales to measure earthquakes? How do they give you different information?

What is a volcano?

A **volcano** is a mountain that forms when lava, ashes, rocks, and melted rock material piles up and hardens. Volcanoes are found on landmasses and on ocean floors. Volcanoes, like earthquakes, are common along plate boundaries because where plates collide or

Shield volcanoes are gently sloped volcanic mountains. They usually erupt quietly and without much force. **Shield volcanoes** are made mostly of the igneous rock basalt, which results from lava flows. The Hawaiian Islands are made of five shield volcanoes that formed as the Pacific plate moved over a hot spot in the mantle. Mauna Loa on the island of Hawaii is the largest volcano on the earth.

Cinder cones are volcanoes with steep sides. They erupt with explosive force, throwing out volcanic ash and cinders, which are lava fragments. Krakatau, in Indonesia, has many small **cinder-cone** volcanoes. In 1883, it exploded and most of the mountain was blown away! The noise from the eruption could be heard in Australia. The ash was so thick it blocked the sun's light as far as 150 kilometers away.

pull apart, a vast amount of energy is released. This energy creates heat that causes the parts of the plates to melt and form magma. This magma rises toward the earth's surface to form volcanoes.

Some volcanoes form when plates drift over hot spots in the mantle. The heat from the hot spots causes the plate above to melt. As the plate continues to move, the magma rises and forms volcanoes.

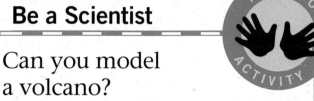

Composite cones are volcanoes made of alternating layers of volcanic rock fragments, lava, and ash. The volcanic rock and ash are ejected with great force. The lava escapes during quiet eruptions. A well-known **composite cone** is Mount Vesuvius in Italy. The composite cone shown in the photograph is Mount Shishaldin in Alaska. It is the highest peak in the Aleutian mountain range. It is nearly 3,000 meters high.

Be a Scientist

Can you model a volcano?

1. Take a sheet of blank paper and roll it into a cone. Use a piece of tape to hold the cone together. Gently fold the cone so that it lies flat.

2. On one side of your model, use colored pencils to show what the outside of a volcano might look like. On the other side of your model, show what the inside of your volcano might look like.

3.  In your Activity Journal, write the type of volcano you made and its characteristics. Show your volcano to a classmate and see if he or she can identify it.

What is Mount St. Helens?

Mount St. Helens is a composite volcano in Washington state. This mountain is a part of the Cascade Range, a chain of volcanoes that formed when the Pacific plate collided with the North American plate millions of years ago. For more than 100 years, scientists had thought that the volcano was inactive. But on May 18, 1980, the volcano spewed tons of volcanic debris into the air. What caused this eruption? How did it affect the mountain and nearby areas? Has the area around this volcano recovered from the blast?

Imagine how a shaken soda pop explodes out of its can when it is opened. Mount St. Helens also erupted as a violent explosion. This happened because the lava was thick and the water in the lava was superheated, and because of the mixture of chemicals in the lava.

▲ Earthquakes and super-heated steam in lava may have caused a bulge to form on the north slope of the volcano.

▲ Just after 8:00 a.m. on May 18, 1980, Mount St. Helens erupted. This explosion blew away the upper 550 meters of the mountain.

▲ For days after the explosion, ash fell over the region. In some places, the ash was nearly 2 meters thick.

◀ Within one year, plants such as fireweed and avalanche lilies started to grow in the volcanic ash around the mountain. Over the next decade, more plants grew in the soil. Birds, deer, elk, and insects have also returned to the area.

Shortly before the explosion, an earthquake that measured 5.1 on the Richter scale sent rocks and ice tumbling down the mountain. It is not unusual for earthquake and volcanic activity to occur at the same time. During the eruption, volcanic ash and broken rocks were ejected from the mountain through an enormous hole. The temperature of the materials and gases was probably greater than 800°C. Mudflows carried rock, ash, and trees into a river. Some of this debris dammed the river and caused nearby lakes to rise tens of meters. As a result of the blast, sixty people were killed. All the plants and animals in the vicinity were destroyed by the explosion. Yet only a year later, life returned to the area around the volcano.

Amazing!

The explosion of Mount St. Helens stripped limbs from trees 25 kilometers away and caused the trees to fall like matchsticks.

How are you doing?

1. How do volcanoes form?
2. Describe what happened to Mount St. Helens on May 18, 1980.
3. **Think** Compare and contrast the three types of volcanoes.
4. **Think** Would it have been possible for animals to return to the area around Mount St. Helens before plants? Explain.

Looking Back

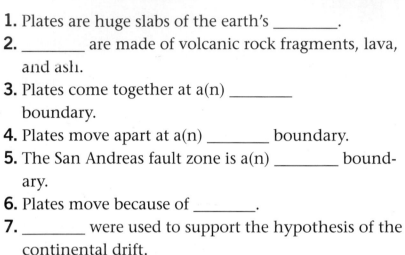

Words and Concepts

Complete the following statements.

1. Plates are huge slabs of the earth's _____.
2. _____ are made of volcanic rock fragments, lava, and ash.
3. Plates come together at a(n) _____ boundary.
4. Plates move apart at a(n) _____ boundary.
5. The San Andreas fault zone is a(n) _____ boundary.
6. Plates move because of _____.
7. _____ were used to support the hypothesis of the continental drift.

Applied Thinking Skills

Answer the following questions. You can use words, drawings, and diagrams in your answers.

8. How can the theory of plate tectonics explain how volcanoes form?
9. Explain how new oceanic crust forms.
10. **Your World** Look at the map of tectonic plates on page E45. How close do you live to the edge of a plate? Which plate? Why do you suppose people would want to live there? If you could live any place in the United States, where would you live? Explain your reasoning.

Show What You Know

Why do earthquakes occur along the San Andreas fault?

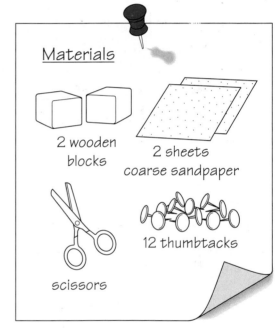

Observe and Collect Data

1. Use one sheet of sandpaper to sand one of the largest surfaces on each block.

2. Cut the other piece of sandpaper in half.

3. ⚠ Use the thumbtacks to attach half of the sandpaper to the large, unsanded side of each block. The thumbtacks should go on the sides of the blocks.

4. Hold a block in either hand and slide the smoothed surfaces against each other. Describe the movement. Slide the sandpapered sides against each other. Describe the movement in your Activity Journal.

Draw Conclusions

1. Which of your movements represents a day with no earthquakes along the San Andreas fault?

2. Which of your movements represents an earthquake along the fault?

3. Why do earthquakes occur?

4. How are you able to predict where earthquakes will occur? Can you predict when they will occur?

Process Skills
Inferring, Defining operationally, Making models

Materials

2 wooden blocks

2 sheets coarse sandpaper

scissors

12 thumbtacks

Earth Movements

Show what you have learned about the layers of the earth, the history of the earth, and plate tectonics. Work by yourself, with a partner, or in a group. Select one activity.

Model Maker Using any materials you wish, make a model of the layers of the earth. Use your model to show how plates might move, how mountains could form, or how earthquakes happen. Be sure to be as accurate as possible. Design a way to label the parts.

Journalist You are a newspaper reporter covering an earthquake. For someone who has never seen or heard of an earthquake, write a story explaining what you see and how you feel.

Songwriter Write a song about earthquakes or volcanic eruptions. Use words to describe how these events occur. Try it out on your class. How did your classmates respond to the song? Did they feel the way you thought they would?

Geologist You work for the federal government. Your job is to take people on tours of the area around the San Andreas fault. What do you tell people as they tour the area? Make a tour guidebook that can be used to follow your talk.

Science-Fiction Writer Imagine an organism that lives in the center of the earth. Write a story about how it lives. Describe its environment and what happens there. Be creative, but scientifically accurate.

Puzzle Maker Make a puzzle that tells something about the way that the continents move. You might want to include plates, earthquakes, and volcanoes. Make sure that it can be worked over and over again.

Glossary

cinder cone (sinʹdər kōn) A volcano with very steep sides that erupts with explosive force. (page E54)

composite cone (kəm päzʹit kōn) A volcano made of alternating layers of volcanic rock, lava, and ash. (page E55)

continental drift (känʹtə nentʹʹl drift) A theory that the earth's landmasses moved across the earth's surface into their present positions. (page E44)

convergent boundary (kən vərʹjənt bounʹdə rē) A place where the earth's plates come together. (page E46)

core (kôr) The innermost layer of the earth, lying below the mantle. (page E10)

crust (krust) The outermost, thinnest, and most solid layer of the earth. (page E10)

divergent boundary (dı vərʹjənt bounʹdə rē) A place where the earth's plates separate. (page E47)

epicenter (epʹi sentʹər) The point on the earth's surface that is directly above the focus of an earthquake. (page E48)

extinct (ek stiŋktʹ) No longer existing on the earth. (page E22)

focus (fōʹkəs) The place within the earth where an earthquake begins. (page E48)

fossil (fäsʹəl) The preserved remains of an ancient plant or animal. (page E26)

geologic time scale (jeʹə läjʹik tīm skāl) Units of time that divide the earth's history. (page E32)

index fossil (inʹdeksʹ fäsʹəl) A fossil used to determine the age of rocks. (page E28)

mantle (manʹtəl) The middle layer of the earth, between the crust and core. (page E10)

plate (plāt) An enormous slab of the earth's crust and rigid upper mantle. (page E40)

plate tectonics (plāt tek tänʹiks) A theory that the earth's crust and rigid upper mantle move across the earth's surface due to convection currents in the partially melted mantle. (page E40)

sea-floor spreading (sēʹflôr spredʹiŋ) Process by which new sea floor forms as tectonic plates move apart. (page E45)

shield volcano (shēld väl kāʹnō) A gently sloped mountain that erupts without much force. (page E54)

transform-fault boundary (transʹfôrm fôlt bounʹdə rē) A place where the earth's plates move horizontally past each other. (page E47)

volcano (väl kāʹnō) A mountain that forms when melted rock material piles up and hardens. (page E54)

Unit E Index

Boldface numerals denote glossary terms. Italic numerals denote illustrations.

Credits

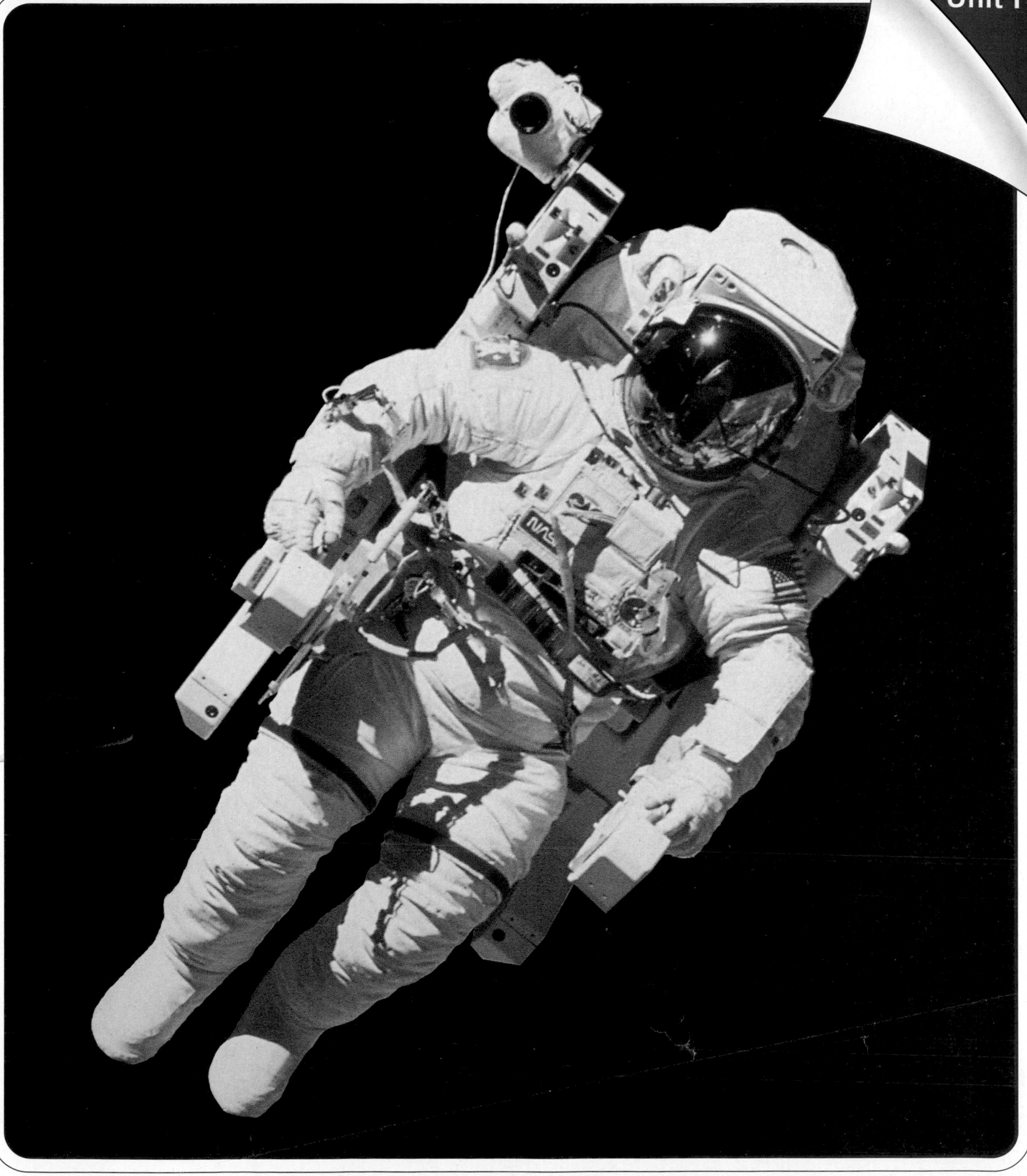

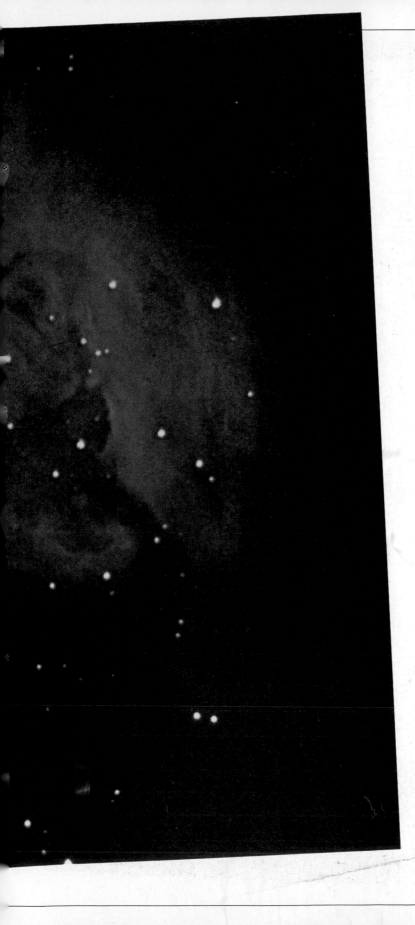

Space Probe

On April 12, 1961, a human being orbited the earth in a spacecraft for the first time. The age of space travel had begun. Since that time, people have walked on the moon and spent weeks at a time orbiting the earth in space stations.

Not all space exploration directly involves people, however. Much of what is known about the solar system has been learned from data provided by space probes without human crews. **Space probes** are spacecraft packed with instruments that collect data and send it back to earth. As you read these words, several probes are traveling in different directions toward the outer boundaries of the solar system, and maybe even beyond. From these probes, scientists hope to learn more about the solar system, the universe, and, ultimately, that very tiny part of the universe we call home—the earth.

■ What are the positions of the earth and the moon in the solar system?

■ How do we know what conditions are like on other planets in the solar system?

■ Are there other star systems in the universe similar to our solar system, where some forms of life may exist?

SPACE EXPLORATION

SPACE PROBE

Activities

Features

Chapter 1

The Solar System

Asteroid 951-Gaspra is about 19 x 12 x 11 km in size.

Would you like to explore Mars? Jupiter? Imagine that you are a crew member on a space probe that will travel to all the planets. Let's call it *Pathfinder*.

The *Pathfinder* mission is to explore the solar system. The **solar system** is made up of the sun and everything that revolves around it, including the planets, their moons, some comets, and numerous other smaller objects. The sun is, by far, the largest and most massive member of the solar system. The strong gravitational attraction between the sun and other members of the solar system holds the other members in their orbits.

As you lift off from the Kennedy Space Center in Florida, your course is set to take *Pathfinder* near the moon. The moon is different from the earth in many ways. The moon has no atmosphere or water. It is a place of extreme temperatures. Any moon location becomes broiling hot while it faces the sun and icy cold when it faces away from the sun. Nothing lives on the moon.

As you orbit the moon, the earth first disappears behind the moon and then "rises" over the edge of the moon as it comes back into view. You take a good look, because you know it will be some time before you see your home planet again.

Look around your home for the things you need to live. In your Science Journal, list the supplies you would take with you on your journey through the solar system. Also list some things that are not essential but that would make the trip more enjoyable.

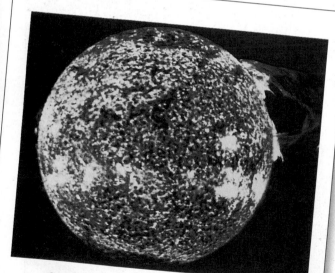

The sun, showing the largest solar flare ever recorded—588,000 km

Earth, as seen from the moon

F7

23

Explore Activity

How are shadows cast in space?

Process Skills
Communicating, Making models, Predicting

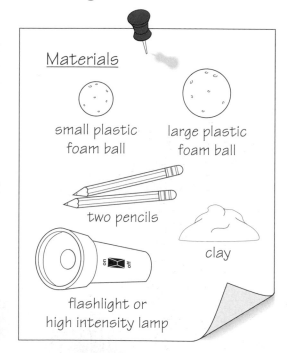

Materials

small plastic foam ball

large plastic foam ball

two pencils

clay

flashlight or high intensity lamp

Observe and Collect Data

1. Assemble the balls, pencils, and clay as shown and place them on a table. Let the larger ball represent the earth and the smaller ball represent the moon.

2. Hold the flashlight the same height from the table as the balls. Turn off the room lights and shine the light on the balls. Stand far enough back for the light to shine on both balls.

3. Gently move the moon around the earth. Keep the flashlight in the same place and observe at what position the moon casts a shadow on the earth. Then observe at what position the earth casts a shadow on the moon.

4. Now reposition the pencil holding the moon so that the moon is not in line with the earth.

5. **Predict** whether any shadows can be cast by the moon now. Move the moon around the earth to find out.

Share Your Results

1. Did all groups identify the same positions in which shadows are cast?

2. Find out which groups moved the moon higher in step 4 and which moved it lower. Was there any difference in the results?

Draw Conclusions

1. Where does the light come from that causes the earth and the moon to cast shadows?

2. Pretend that you could draw a line between the earth and the sun. When the moon travels around the earth, do you think it would touch this line sometimes, always, or never?

Apply What You Know

What would it be like at a place on the earth where the moon's shadow was cast?

Why does the moon seem to change shape?

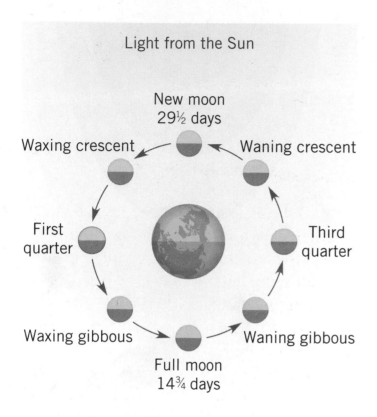

Light from the Sun

New moon
29½ days

Waxing crescent

Waning crescent

First quarter

Third quarter

Waxing gibbous

Waning gibbous

Full moon
14¾ days

The moon is a natural satellite of the earth. A **satellite** is any body in space that revolves around another body in space. A natural satellite is one that was not made by people. A satellite is held in its orbit by the force of gravity that exists between the two bodies.

It takes the moon about one month to complete one cycle around the earth. For every time it does this, the moon also rotates once. This means that the same side of the moon is always facing the earth.

As a member of the *Pathfinder* crew, you have an opportunity to observe objects in space, such as the moon, closely. But think about how the moon appears from the earth. Have you noticed that as each night passes, the moon seems to change shape?

It takes the moon approximately 29½ days to complete one cycle of phases.

New moon

Waxing crescent

First quarter

Waxing gibbous

Make a calendar showing five rows of seven boxes each. Label the boxes with the days of the week. Go outside tonight and, in today's box, draw a picture of how the moon looks. (If it's cloudy, draw what you see.) Do this every day, or every other day, for a month. At the end of 29 days, you should have a complete record of the phases of the moon.

BACK HOME

The moon revolves around the earth once every 29½ days. At one point during the month, the moon is not visible. A few days later, a sliver of it appears. Each day, the sliver grows a little larger until the moon appears round. Then each night, it looks less and less round, until it disappears again. These changing shapes are called phases of the moon.

The moon does not give off light of its own. People on earth can see the moon because it reflects light from the sun. The moon's shape never changes. It's always a sphere. Why, then, does it seem to change shape?

The changing phases are caused by the moon's revolution around the earth. Look at the diagram on the opposite page. It will help you to understand how this motion causes the moon to seem to change shape. First look at the new moon. The moon is between the sun and earth. In this position, the lighted side of the moon is facing away from the earth. From the earth, the moon shows no reflected sunlight. Therefore, you cannot see it. When do you see a full moon?

Notice that the same features on the moon's surface are always evident from earth. Why? ▼

Full moon

Waning gibbous

Third quarter

Waning crescent

What causes eclipses?

▲ During a solar eclipse, when the sun is completely hidden, the sun's corona (the atmosphere surrounding the sun) is finally visible. Do you know why?

Imagine being in space and looking at the earth through *Pathfinder's* telescope. As you gaze at your home planet, a small shadow covers part of California. There are no clouds in the sky over California that might block the sun. Then you notice that the moon has moved directly between the earth and the sun. The shadow covering part of California is cast by the moon. Down in California, the sky darkens as the moon passes in front of the sun, slowly blocking more and more of its light. An eclipse of the sun, or **solar eclipse**, is rare on the earth. Many years may pass between total eclipses of the sun at any given place on the earth.

⚠ Do not look directly at the sun to view an eclipse. Doing so can cause permanent eye injury. Use one of the special viewing techniques developed by scientists.

During a solar eclipse, only a small part of the earth is in the darkest part of the moon's shadow. ▼

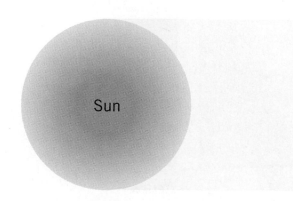

Sun

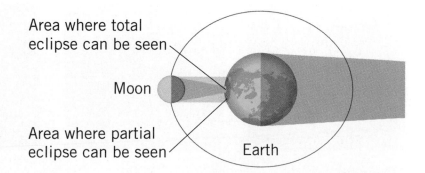

Area where total eclipse can be seen

Moon

Area where partial eclipse can be seen

Earth

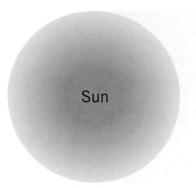

Sun

Area where lunar eclipse
can be seen

Earth

Moon

Eclipses of the moon, or **lunar eclipses**, occur more often at any particular spot on earth. One to three times a year, the moon passes through the earth's shadow.

Because the moon's orbit is tilted compared to the earth's orbit, the moon usually passes above or below the earth's shadow and the earth usually passes above or below the moon's shadow. But when they do enter each other's shadows, that's when eclipses occur.

Be a Scientist

HANDS-ON ACTIVITY

What does a lunar eclipse show?

1. Use a flashlight and a ball to represent the sun and the moon. Use a cube, a disk, and a sphere to represent possible earth shapes.

2. Cast a shadow on the moon with each object and notice the shadow's shape. Rotate each object and find out if the shape of the shadow changes.

3. 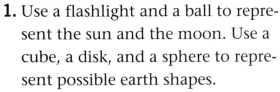 In the past, many people did not think that the earth was a sphere. In your Activity Journal, write what you would tell them based on what you have just learned.

How are you doing?

1. During which phase of the moon can a solar eclipse occur? And a lunar eclipse?

2. Why doesn't a lunar eclipse occur every month?

3. **Think** If the moon were to stop revolving around the earth, how would the moon's phases be affected?

4. **Think** When a quarter phase of the moon is visible, you see what looks like half of a circle. Why do you think the word quarter is used to describe this phase?

What are the major members of the solar system?

No real space probe mission is designed to visit the entire solar system in one journey. However, if *Pathfinder* could take you to all the planets of the solar system, your first stop might be Mercury, the planet closest to the sun. As you swung around this tiny planet, you would notice that its surface is similar to that of the moon. Instruments aboard *Pathfinder* would show that temperatures on Mercury range from 427°C on the side facing the sun to –173°C on the side away from the sun.

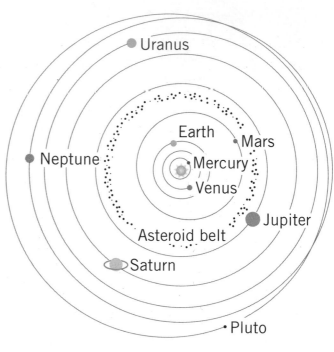

Mercury
4,878 km diameter
0.4 AU from sun

Venus
12,104 km diameter
0.7 AU from sun

Mars
6,787 km diameter
1.5 AU from sun
2 moons

Earth
12,756 km diameter
1 AU from sun
1 moon

Jupiter
142,980 km diameter
5.2 AU from sun
16 moons
at least 1 ring

Saturn
120,540 km diameter
9.5 AU from sun
at least 18 moons
10,000 rings

The next planet you would come to is Venus. You wouldn't see its surface because Venus is surrounded by a thick blanket of clouds and a dense atmosphere made up mostly of carbon dioxide. You recall that sunlight reflecting from this atmosphere makes Venus the brightest planet when viewed from the earth's surface.

On your way to Mars, you might glimpse the earth and its natural satellite, the moon. As you approached Mars, you would recognize its red color. The surface of Mars is made up largely of iron oxide, which you probably know by its more common name, rust.

Mars is the last of the four inner planets. Beyond the orbit of Mars you would pass through a wide band of rocks of varying sizes. Scientists believe that these rocks may be left over from the time the solar system formed. Once you got safely past the band of rocks, you would approach the largest of the outer planets, Jupiter, with its colored bands and Great Red Spot. Then would come Saturn, with its beautiful rings, and Uranus, with its distinct greenish color. The next planet probably would be Neptune. However, it could be Pluto because their orbits seem to overlap.

Uranus
51,120 km diameter
19.2 AU from sun
15 moons
at least 9 rings

Neptune
49,530 km diameter
30.1 AU from sun
8 moons
at least 3 rings

1 astronomical unit (abbreviated as AU) is 149.6 million kilometers. This is the average distance between the earth and the sun.

Pluto
2,300 km diameter
39.8 AU from sun
1 moon

What are the minor members of the solar system?

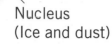

Tail
(Gas and dust)

Coma
(Gas and dust)

Head

Nucleus
(Ice and dust)

▲ Sometimes, the earth passes through an area of space containing many small pieces of orbiting debris from old comets. A higher than normal rate of visible meteors, called a meteor shower, results.

▲ A small meteorite

As *Pathfinder* moves through the solar system, crew members are observing the planets and their satellites. However, there are many smaller bodies traveling around the sun. These, too, are members of the solar system.

If you are really lucky during your journey, you will see one of the most unusual members of the solar system—a comet. A **comet** is a large chunk of ice, frozen gases, and dust that travels around the sun in a very long, oval orbit. Comets form near the outer boundaries of the solar system.

Comets are not visible from the earth until they get close to the sun. As a comet approaches the sun, the head of the comet begins to turn to gas. The gases glow, and a long tail of glowing gases streams out from the head. The comet circles the sun and returns to the outer regions of the solar system. The most famous comet in the solar system is Halley's Comet. It circles the sun once every 76 years. The last time Halley's Comet was visible from the earth was in 1986.

Asteroids (as´tər oidz´) are small rocky bodies that orbit the sun. There are thousands of asteroids in the solar system. Most of them are located in the asteroid belt, the wide band of rocks in the region between the orbits of Mars and Jupiter. The diameter of Ceres, the largest known asteroid, is about 1,000 kilometers. This is about the distance from New York City to Detroit,

Meteor Crater in Arizona

Most meteors burn up well above the earth's surface. Some are so large that they don't burn up completely. They strike the earth. Then they are called meteorites. About 5 to 50 thousand years ago, a meteorite struck the earth near what is now Winslow, Arizona. The impact produced a crater about 1.2 kilometers across and 170 meters deep, with a rim rising 60 meters above the surrounding countryside. The meteorite exploded. More than 30 tons of iron fragments found near the crater indicate that it was made up mainly of iron.

Michigan. Most asteroids are less than 1 kilometer in diameter, and some are as small as grains of sand.

The solar system also contains countless numbers of solid, rocklike objects called **meteoroids** (mēt´ē ər oidz´). Sometimes a meteoroid enters the earth's atmosphere. Friction between the air and the meteoroid heats the meteoroid and causes it to glow brightly as it speeds across the sky. The streak of light produced is called a meteor.

How are you doing?

1. Venus is a relatively small planet, yet it appears very bright when observed from the earth. Explain.
2. How are a meteoroid, a meteor, and a meteorite alike? How are they different?
3. **Think** How would you answer this question: What is the ninth planet out from the sun?
4. **Think** How is it possible that planets are also satellites?

Looking at the Earth from Different Points of View

Things are not always what they appear to be. A great deal depends on your point of view. Think about a new piece of chalk, for example. When viewed from the end, the chalk looks round; from the side, it appears rectangular. When viewed from a few meters away, the surface of the chalk appears very smooth. When viewed from up close through a hand lens, the chalk is seen to be rough and pitted.

What you can learn about the earth's surface also depends on your point of view. The pictures on this page show different viewpoints of the same kind of location—a coastline. In each case, the distance from the area being viewed is different.

 Study the pictures. In your Science Journal, tell what you can learn from the view shown in each picture that you can't learn from the other two viewpoints.

Next, select some object or place in your environment and observe it from three or more different viewpoints. You may use hand lenses and binoculars to provide different viewpoints. In your Science Journal, describe how the subject's appearance is different in each view. You may also wish to draw or photograph the subject from different viewpoints.

Data Collection and Analysis

What does an astrolabe measure?

Observe and Collect Data

1. With a partner, build an astrolabe, as shown.
2. In your Activity Journal, make a data table to record your observations. It should have columns for time, astrolabe reading, and compass reading.
3. Go out and look at the moon through the straw. Have your partner observe where the string crosses the degree scale on the astrolabe. Subtract this number from 90° to get your reading. Record this reading and the time in your data table.
4. Use the compass to find the position of the moon. Record the compass reading in the data table.
5. Repeat steps 3 and 4 every twenty minutes for two hours.

Draw Conclusions

1. In what compass direction does the moon appear to be moving?
2. How is the moon moving relative to the horizon? What is the change in degrees above the horizon between your first and last readings?

Process skills
Observing, Collecting data, Measuring

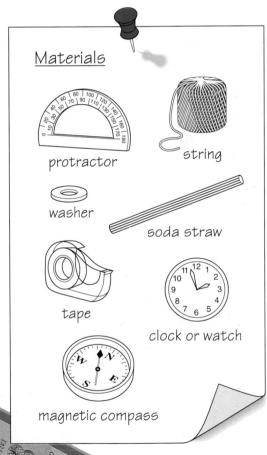

Materials

protractor

string

washer

soda straw

tape

clock or watch

magnetic compass

Looking Back

Words and Concepts

Choose the word or phrase that best completes the statement.

1. The moon is not visible from the earth during the _____ phase.
   a. full moon
   b. new moon
   c. waxing gibbous
   d. third quarter

2. The objects of the solar system are held in their orbits by _____.
   a. strings
   b. moons
   c. gravity
   d. the earth

3. The planets of the solar system revolve around _____.
   a. the earth
   b. the sun
   c. one another
   d. the moon

4. The motion that causes the changing phases of the moon is the _____.
   a. earth's rotation
   b. earth's revolution
   c. moon's rotation
   d. moon's revolution

5. The moon's shadow falls across the earth during an eclipse of _____.
   a. the sun
   b. the moon
   c. the earth
   d. all of these

6. The phase of the moon that occurs right after a full moon is the _____.
   a. first quarter
   b. waning gibbous
   c. new moon
   d. waxing crescent

Applied Thinking Skills

Answer the following questions. You can use words, drawings, or diagrams in your answers.

7. What would you have to consider in designing a spacecraft that would come close to the sun?

8. The farther a planet is from the sun, the longer it takes for that planet to make one revolution around the sun. Why do you think this is so?

9. Why is a total eclipse of the sun visible only from a small area of the surface of the earth?

10. **Your World** How many times during a year can you see a full moon? How do you know?

Show What You Know

Can you show the moon's phases?

Observe and Collect Data

1. Using string and a pencil, draw a large circle on the poster board. Use the protractor to divide the circle into eight equal sections.
2. Arrange the pencils and plastic foam balls as shown, to represent the earth and the moon. Use clay to support the model.
3. Place the earth-moon model on the circle as shown. Turn off the room lights and shine the flashlight on the model. Stand far enough away from the model for the light to shine on both balls. Imagine that you are on the earth ball. Describe the phase of the moon that is represented.
4. Move the model around the circle, section by section. Describe the phase represented at each point along the orbit.

Draw Conclusions

1. Imagine that you are on the earth part of your model and tell how the moon's shape appears to change as it moves from full moon to new moon.
2. How does the moon's shape appear to change as it moves from new moon to full moon?

Process skills
Making models, Observing, Communicating

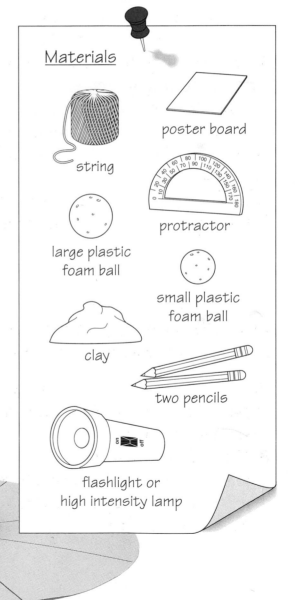

Materials

string

poster board

protractor

large plastic foam ball

small plastic foam ball

clay

two pencils

flashlight or high intensity lamp

Chapter 2

Exploring Space

▲ Radio telescopes allow us to study objects in space that are not visible through optical telescopes.

▲ **1975.** American Apollo astronauts and Soviet Soyuz cosmonauts docked their capsules together for a historic meeting in earth orbit. This photo was taken aboard the Soyuz spacecraft.

Since the beginning of recorded history, and probably before that, people have been curious about the objects they saw in the sky. For thousands of years, they could only observe with their eyes and use their imaginations to speculate about what they saw. However, many accurate records were kept, and calendars were devised based on observations of the sun and the moon.

The invention of the telescope revealed objects in space that had formerly not been visible. New information about the moon and planets taught us that the sun, not the earth, was the center of the solar system. But exploring space *from* space was still centuries away.

In order to launch a missile into space, some means had to be found to provide the force needed to overcome the earth's gravity. At the turn of the century, Konstantin Tsiolkovsky, a Russian scientist and inventor, studied the use of rockets for space travel. He applied principles developed by the Chinese almost 1,000 years earlier in which gunpowder was used to propel objects some distance through the air.

On October 4, 1957, a Soviet rocket boosted *Sputnik 1* into orbit around the earth. The earth had its first artificial satellite. Since that time, space probes have explored the outer regions of the solar system. People have been to the moon and have lived and worked in space for weeks at a time.

SCIENCE JOURNAL

What do you think it would be like to travel in space? In your Science Journal, write what you think would be the best part and the hardest part of space travel.

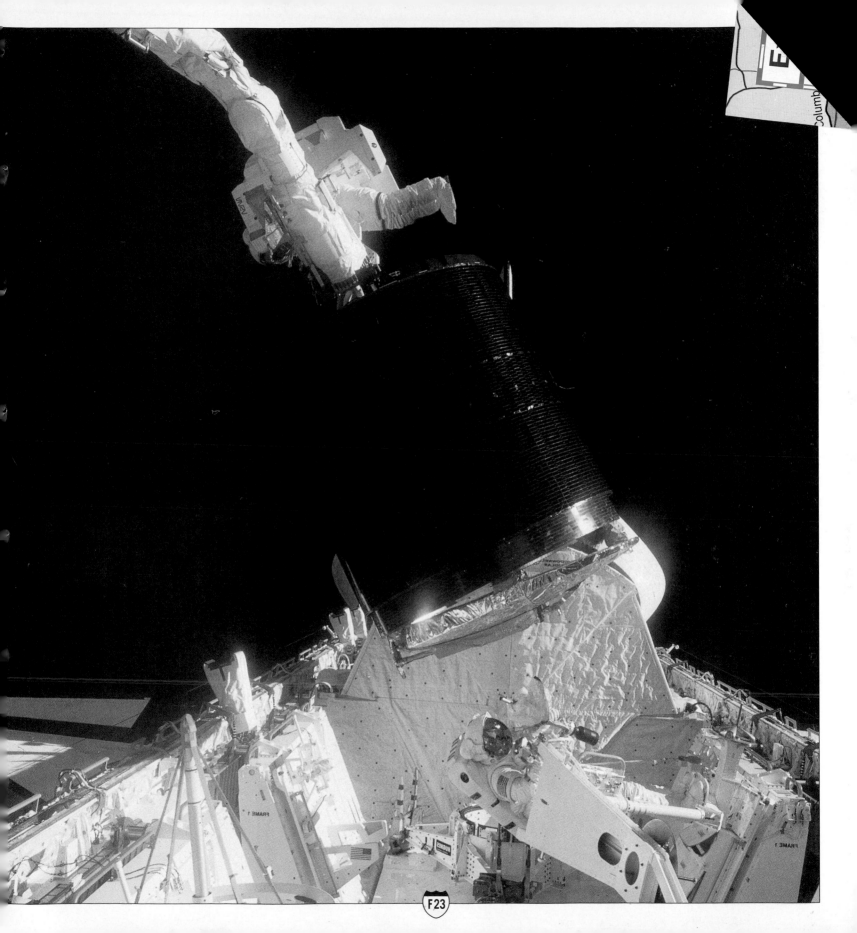

F23

xplore Activity

Can you show how a rocket works?

Process Skills

Making models, Observing, Predicting

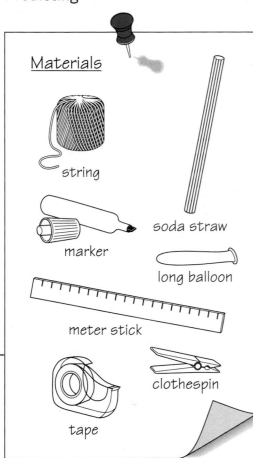

Materials

string

marker

soda straw

long balloon

meter stick

clothespin

tape

Observe and Collect Data

1. Work with a partner. Pull one end of a long piece of string through a straw. Tie the string to the backs of two chairs that are about 3 meters apart. Make sure the string is taut and level. Mark a starting point on the string with a marker.

2. Blow up the balloon. Clip the clothespin on the end so air does not escape. Tape the balloon to the straw as shown.

3. Move the straw to the starting point. Release the clothespin.

4. **ACTIVITY JOURNAL** Measure how far the balloon moves along the string and record the distance in a data table.

5. Run five trials by repeating steps 2–4 and record the results each time. Calculate the average distance traveled by the balloon.

Oregon

amento

Fresn

5

Los
annel
lands

Share Your Results

1. How do your results compare with those of other groups?
2. How might you account for the differences between groups?

Draw Conclusions

1. How does the appearance of the balloon differ at its starting and resting points?
2. What do you think causes the balloon to move forward when released?

Apply What You Know

1. **Predict** how you might increase the distance the balloon travels. Test your prediction.
2. **Predict** what might happen if you tied the string to objects of different heights. Can the balloon climb up the string? How far do you think it can travel? Test your prediction.

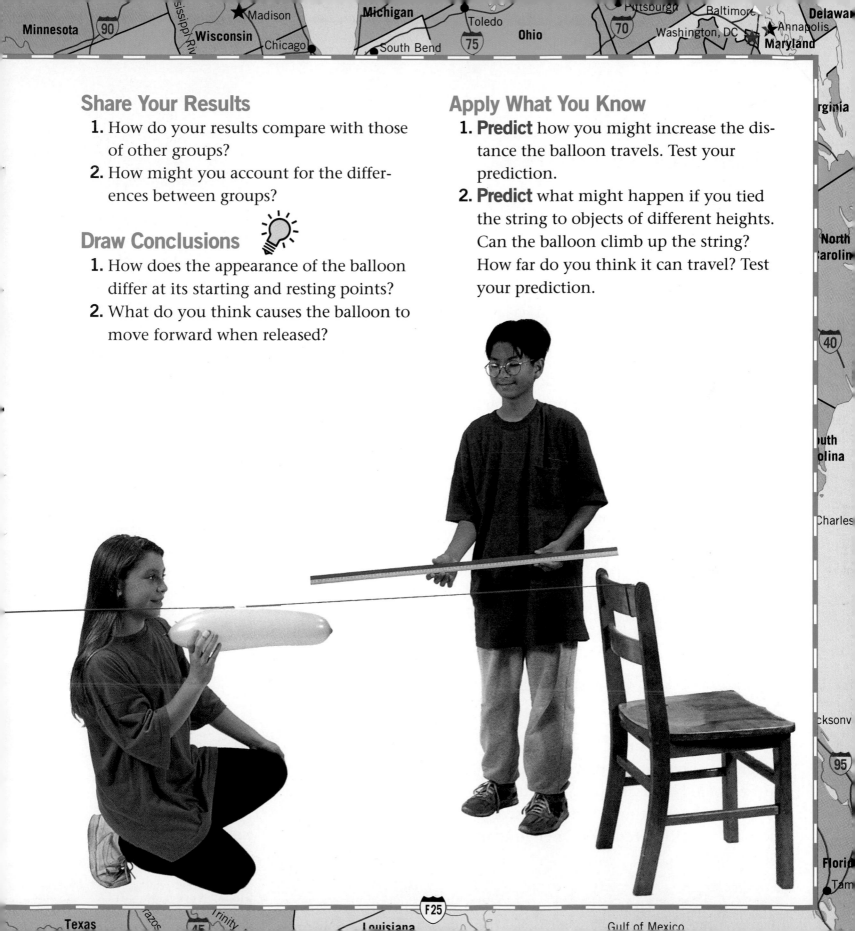

How do space missions leave the earth?

Imagine that you are strapped in your seat aboard *Pathfinder*, listening to mission control count down the seconds to ignition. Suddenly you hear a loud roar and feel the ship begin to vibrate. The powerful rocket engines are lifting *Pathfinder* from its launching pad. You have liftoff!

The principle behind the way a rocket engine works is a law of physics. For every action, there is an equal reaction in the opposite direction. If you blow up a balloon and then let it go, the balloon flies through the air. The balloon moves in one direction while air rushes out of the balloon in the opposite direction.

When rocket fuel is ignited, it burns very rapidly. Hot gases are produced, and they expand quickly, creating pressure inside the rocket engine. The pressure forces the gases to rush from the rear of the rocket. This is the action. The rocket is pushed up in the opposite direction. This is the reaction.

The force that pushes a rocket forward is called thrust. In order to launch a spacecraft into space, a rocket must be moving fast enough to escape the force of the earth's gravity. This speed is called escape velocity.

A great deal of thrust is needed to reach escape velocity. A single rocket that could generate this much thrust would be very heavy. So multistage rockets like the one shown on these pages are used. A multistage rocket is actually several rocket engines fitted one on top of the other.

1 Rocket fuel is ignited. When the fuel burns, hot gases rush out of the rear of the rocket's engine. The force produced by these gases thrusts the rocket in the opposite direction. The rocket rises from its launch pad.

2 The rocket gains speed as it goes up into the sky. When the fuel in the first stage of the rocket is used up, this stage falls away, making the rocket lighter. The engine of the second stage ignites and thrusts the rocket faster and higher.

3 When escape velocity has been reached, the second stage of the rocket falls away. The spacecraft continues on into space.

PEOPLE

SCIENCE TECHNOLOGY & SOCIETY

Robert Goddard

Robert Goddard was an American physicist whose main interest in life was rocketry. At first he experimented with rocket engines that burned solid fuels such as gunpowder. In 1926, Goddard launched the world's first liquid-fuel rocket. It was a little more than one meter high and 15 centimeters in diameter. In his lifetime, Goddard developed many of the ideas and designs that are standard in rocketry today. Although he did not live to see the beginning of the space age, his contributions made it possible.

What are orbiters?

▲ Astronaut Millie Hughes-Fulford communicates with ground controllers about samples from an experiment in the Shuttle Columbia.

An **orbiter** is anything that travels around a planet, star, or other celestial body in a regular orbit. The first step in launching an orbiter is deciding exactly where above the earth the orbit will be. How high will the orbit be? What shape will it be—circular or oval?

Once the decision is made, the rocket carrying the orbiter is launched. For the first minute or so after liftoff, the rocket carries the spacecraft straight up. Then its path curves into the proper direction for the selected orbit. Finally, the last stage of the rocket fires and gives the spacecraft the thrust it needs to go into orbit.

Once a spacecraft is in orbit, no engines are used to keep it there. Instead, the earth's gravity keeps the spacecraft in orbit by pulling down on it. The forward motion of the spacecraft keeps it from falling to the earth. It is falling, but it falls *around* the earth. Without gravity, this forward motion would cause the spacecraft to shoot off into space in a straight line.

At the present time, thousands of artificial satellites circle the earth. Each is an orbiter. As the time line below indicates, *Sputnik 1* was the first orbiter. *Sputnik 2,*

Sputnik 1
1957

First artificial
earth satellite

Explorer 6
1959

First satellite to send
back images of the earth

Yuri Gagarin
1961

First person
in space

DILEMMA

SCIENCE
TECHNOLOGY & SOCIETY

Space Garbage

As unlikely as it may sound, "space pollution" is becoming a problem! Orbiting the earth are potentially harmful materials, such as satellites that have stopped working, pieces of spacecraft, or tools dropped by astronauts while working outside their spacecraft.

Two dangers are presented by space garbage. First, some of the larger pieces may eventually slow down so much that gravity will pull them to the earth. This could cause injuries and damage. The second danger is that a spacecraft or an astronaut working in space might be struck by a piece of debris.

Think About It What can be done to avoid adding more garbage to space? Can anything be done to clean up what is already there? In your Science Journal, try to answer these questions.

also launched in 1957, was the first spacecraft to carry a live "crew." The "crew" was a dog named Laika.

The time line also shows a number of other important "firsts." Each of these events marks an important advance in space exploration. For example, *Skylab* was the first space station placed in orbit by the United States. It served as a laboratory and observatory in space. These functions have since been taken over by the space shuttle program. The chief advantage of the shuttle over earlier spacecraft is that most of it is reusable. At the end of a mission, the orbiter can be steered back to the earth and safely landed on a runway.

John Glenn
1962

Skylab
1973

Space shuttle program
1981–present

First American
to orbit the earth

First U.S.
space station

First reusable
spacecraft

How are satellites used?

There are thousands of artificial satellites that are now in orbit around the earth. These satellites have been placed in orbit by many different nations, and they serve a variety of purposes.

Some are no longer working but remain in orbit. Most, however, still serve important purposes such as those described on these two pages.

Navigation satellites transmit continuous signals to ships and airplanes. Pilots and ship captains can determine their exact locations in seconds. ▼

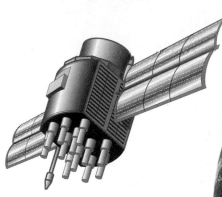

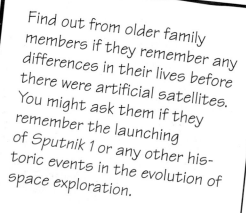

Weather satellites send pictures of weather patterns from all over the world. By studying these pictures, meteorologists can track the movement of weather systems, such as storms, and provide early warnings to people in their paths. ▶

Find out from older family members if they remember any differences in their lives before there were artificial satellites. You might ask them if they remember the launching of Sputnik 1 or any other historic events in the evolution of space exploration.

BACK HOME

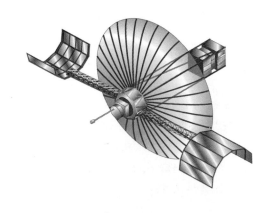

▲ Landsat satellites provide information about the earth's surface. These satellites are used for such purposes as mapping remote areas, searching for mineral deposits, and identifying sources of pollution.

◀ Scientific satellites are used to learn more about outer space. For example, the Hubble Space Telescope orbits high above the earth. Its view of outer space is not distorted by the earth's atmosphere.

◀ Communications satellites make it possible for television and radio broadcasts, telephone conversations, and other kinds of communications to be beamed around the world. The satellites serve as relay stations. They receive signals from one earth station and send them back to another earth station thousands of kilometers away.

How are you doing?

1. What is an orbiter?
2. Name three ways that we use satellites and explain the benefits of each.
3. **Think** Television and radio signals travel in straight lines. Use this fact to discuss the importance of communications satellites.
4. **Think** What are the advantages of using a multistage rocket rather than a single rocket to launch a spacecraft into orbit?

How has the moon been explored?

In 1959, the Soviet Union's *Luna 2* was the first space probe to reach the moon. On July 20, 1969, the United States landed the first people on the moon. What hard work and preparation had made these missions possible? Since much more power is needed to send a spacecraft to the moon than to put it in orbit around the earth, years were spent designing, testing, and building new, more powerful rockets.

Between 1959 and 1969, while the Soviet Union worked on its own space program, the United States did the same. The United States sent probes to the moon and received back valuable information. In 1961, Soviet cosmonaut Yuri Gagarin, and later, American astronaut Alan Shepard Jr. became the first people to travel in space. By the end of 1968, more space missions carrying astronauts had been successfully carried out. One of these missions orbited the moon without landing.

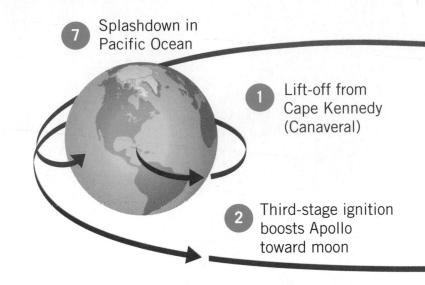

7 Splashdown in Pacific Ocean

1 Lift-off from Cape Kennedy (Canaveral)

2 Third-stage ignition boosts Apollo toward moon

▲ **1969.** After orbiting the moon, two astronauts crawled into the lunar module. The lunar module separated from the command module and landed on the moon's surface.

Luna 2
1959

First probe to land on the moon

Apollo 8
1968

Astronauts first orbit the moon

Apollo 11
1969

Astronauts first land on the moon

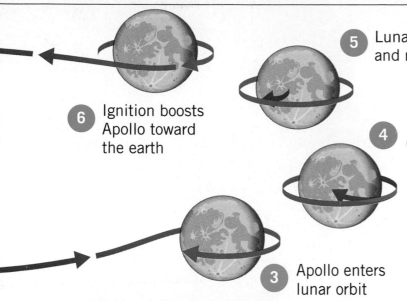

5 Lunar module lifts off moon and returns to Command module

6 Ignition boosts Apollo toward the earth

4 Lunar module separates from Command module and lands on moon

3 Apollo enters lunar orbit

In 1969, *Apollo 11* carried three astronauts to the moon. Two of them—Neil Armstrong and Edwin Aldrin Jr.—were transported to the moon's surface in a lunar module, while Michael Collins remained aboard the spacecraft, which orbited the moon. Armstrong and Aldrin explored the area around their landing site on foot, then returned to their spacecraft in the lunar module, and headed for home.

On later missions, astronauts traveled across the lunar surface in a special vehicle called a lunar rover. On all missions, astronauts brought back samples of moon rocks and soil for analysis.

▲ **1971.** Some astronauts rode over the surface of the moon in a lunar rover. The rover had compartments in which the astronauts could store samples of moon soil and moon rocks.

Apollo 15
1971

Astronauts first drive lunar rover on the moon

Apollo 17
1972

The last Apollo mission

HANDS-ON ACTIVITY

Be a Scientist

Can you see the moon's features?

1. Use binoculars or a telescope to observe the moon. Do this when the moon is in various phases.
2. During which phases are features such as craters more easily seen? Why do you think it is easier to see such features during these phases?

How have the inner planets been explored?

On November 28, 1964, *Mariner 4* became the first spacecraft to send back to earth photographs of Mars from distances much closer to the planet than had ever been possible before. Since that time, six other planets have been explored by space probes. Of the inner planets, Mercury has been photographed and studied by *Mariner 10*, and spacecraft have landed on Venus and Mars.

A few space-craft have penetrated the thick clouds and landed on Venus. They sent back information about the planet's surface before being destroyed by the heat and atmospheric pressure. ▲

▲ This plateau on Venus is about the size of Australia and rises 8.2 km at its highest point. Information about it was gathered by several *Pioneer* probes that entered the atmosphere of Venus.

Mariner 4
1965

First flyby
of Mars

Venera 7
1970

First probe to
send back information
from the surface of Venus

Mariner 9
1971

First probe
to orbit Mars

▲ *Viking* landers from the United States collected soil samples from Mars and analyzed them for signs of life, either past or present. None was found. But it was discovered that the Martian sky is pink.

◀ *Mariner 10* flew by Mercury in 1974 and 1975. NASA had saved expense and fuel by using Venus's gravitational pull as a slingshot to get *Mariner 10* to the planet. Once there, cameras and other instruments on board this probe sent back pictures of Mercury's surface and information about conditions on the planet.

Mariner 10
1973

First flyby
of Mercury

Viking 1
1976

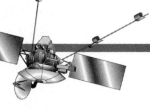

First landing
on Mars

Magellan
1990

Made detailed
radar map of Venus

How have the outer planets been explored?

The planets beyond the asteroid belt are known as the outer planets. With the exception of Pluto, these planets differ in two main ways from the inner planets. They are much larger than the inner planets, and their densities are much lower. *Voyager 1* and *2* both flew close to both Jupiter and Saturn, while *Voyager 2* also passed close to Uranus and Neptune. Only Pluto has not been visited by a space probe from the earth.

Pioneer 11 and the *Voyager* flybys provided detailed looks at Saturn's system of thousands of rings. Some of these rings can be seen with a small telescope, but additional rings were discovered by *Pioneer 11*. Saturn also has at least 18 moons, 11 of which were discovered by *Voyager 1*. ▶

▲ Jupiter's Great Red Spot is a huge whirling storm in the planet's atmosphere. The four largest moons were photographed by *Voyager 1* and *2*. The moon Io (ī′ō), shown here, was found to have many active volcanoes.

Pioneer 10
1973

First flyby
of Jupiter

Pioneer 11
1979

First flyby
of Saturn

Voyager 2
1986

First flyby
of Uranus

SCIENCE TECHNOLOGY & SOCIETY

Useful Space Program Discoveries

Thanks to space exploration, our world has gained numerous new products and processes that help us lead healthier and more comfortable lives.

The fields of medicine and scientific research have benefited from our greatly improved skill in computerized image processing. High-efficiency solar hot water heaters, sunglasses that protect our eyes from the damaging ultraviolet rays of the sun, faster designs for racing sailboats, insulated clothing that can withstand wide extremes of temperature, satellite images useful to archaeologists in finding new historical sites, and energy efficient building techniques are all related to the innovations and discoveries made during work on our space exploration programs.

◀ Because of its great distance from the earth, information about Neptune was fairly sketchy until it was visited by *Voyager 2* in August 1989. This probe provided astronomers with data about the planet's faint rings, its eight satellites, its period of rotation, and its magnetic field.

Voyager 2
1989

First flyby
of Neptune

Galileo
1995 (planned)

Plans to
drop probe into
atmosphere of Jupiter

How are you doing?

1. What makes the exploration of the moon unique?
2. What were the functions of the lunar module and the lunar rover?
3. **Think** Why was it necessary to use a lander to gather information about the surface of Venus?
4. **Think** Why hasn't Pluto been explored by a space probe?

Back in the Beforetime

Tales of the California Indians. Retold by Jane Louise Curry

This story, called "Coyote Rides a Star," is an American Indian legend.

. . . Coyote . . . spied the stars glittering in the dark sky above. A shooting star streaked overhead.

"Hai! How beautiful!" Coyote exclaimed. And suddenly he knew what he wanted most in the world to do.

"I want to ride on a star," said he. "Even Mouse and Measuring Worm, the least of the animal people, can walk around on the earth. I, Coyote, should have a better way of going. And I shall! I shall take a journey on a star."

So Coyote climbed to the top of the nearest hill, lifted his nose to the sky, and howled up at the Evening Star. "Hai, Bright Star!" he called. "Come down here to me. I am going to take a ride on your back."

But the Evening Star did not obey. It barely blinked as it moved along its sky path. . . .

Coyote would not be put off. Each day at nightfall he returned and howled and yowled, whined and whispered and blustered and begged until at last Evening Star grew tired of listening.

"Enough, enough!" it said one night in a voice more sharp than silvery. "Jump on before I change my mind."

Evening Star slid down the sky, barely slowing as it skimmed past the hilltop, and then soared upward once more. Coyote gave a great jump, catching hold with his front paws, and almost slid off. "Hai, yi, yi!" he cried, but the sound whirled away in the star-wind. Evening Star flew so fast that poor Coyote could not haul himself up to crouch on its back. It took all of his strength just to hold on.

Evening Star flew up and up and up, and then north over lands of ice and snow. The sharp star-wind grew bitter cold. Coyote's paws grew cold, then stiff, then numb, until he could hold on no longer. Letting go, he fell, head over feet over tail, back to earth.

He was a long time falling. Ten snows passed, some say. And when he came at last to earth, his landing was so hard that he was—say some—flattened out as thin as an acorn cake. Certainly, from that day to this he has been thin.

And every day to this day, he climbs at nightfall to the top of the nearest hill and scolds the Evening Star.

Think About Your Reading

1. What do you think is the moral of this legend?
2. How did Coyote get what he wanted? Think of a time you persuaded someone to give you what you wanted. Compare and contrast Coyote's methods and your own.

Inferring Reread the description of Evening Star. Find out about the movements of the stars and planets at your library. Which star or planet do you think is being described in this legend? Give reasons for your answer.

Where to Read More

Roy A. Gallant, *The Constellations: How They Came to Be* (Four Winds Press, 1991)
Learn what ancient peoples saw when they looked up at the stars.

Looking Back

Words and Concepts

Choose the word or phrase that best completes the statement.

1. The first artificial satellite of the earth was _____.
   a. the moon
   b. the space shuttle
   c. *Sputnik 1*
   d. *Apollo 1*
2. When hot gases push out of the back of a rocket, the rocket moves _____.
   a. backward
   b. to the left
   c. to the right
   d. forward
3. Escape velocity is the speed needed for an object to _____.
   a. land on the moon
   b. escape into space
   c. return to the earth
   d. return from the moon
4. The part of a space shuttle that glides back to the earth and lands like an airplane is the _____.
   a. orbiter
   b. external fuel engines
   c. main engines
   d. booster rockets
5. Live television shows are sent around the world by _____.
   a. the Hubble Space Telescope
   b. Landsat satellites
   c. communications satellites
   d. navigation satellites
6. The only object in the solar system that has been explored by astronauts is _____.
   a. Mars
   b. Jupiter
   c. Venus
   d. the earth's moon

Applied Thinking Skills

Answer the following questions. You can use words, drawings, or diagrams in your answers.

7. How is an inflated balloon like a rocket?
8. If gravity could be "turned off," what would happen to the earth's satellites? What would happen to the planets?
9. You look at Jupiter and see all sorts of shiny objects around it. Over the next month, you look at Jupiter and discover that four of the shiny objects keep appearing and disappearing but are always near Jupiter. What conclusions might you reach about these objects?
10. **Your World** Describe four ways that artificial satellites might affect your life in the next year.

Show What You Know

What spacecraft have explored the solar system?

Observe and Collect Data

1. Use tagboard to make labels for the sun, the nine planets of the solar system, and the earth's moon.
2. Tape the label for the sun to the back wall of your classroom.
3. Use string and tape to hang the other labels from the ceiling. To do this, place them at the following distances from the "sun": Mercury, 6 centimeters; Venus, 11 centimeters; Earth, 15 centimeters; Mars, 23 centimeters; Jupiter, 78 centimeters; Saturn, 143 centimeters; Uranus, 287 centimeters; Neptune, 449 centimeters; Pluto, 589 centimeters. Tape the earth's moon right next to the earth.
4. Make drawings of spacecraft that have visited the various objects in the solar system. Cut out the drawings and hang them from the labels of the planets they visited.

Draw Conclusions

1. To what scale, approximately, were the distances in your model constructed? HINT: To find out, you have to divide the actual distance in millions of kilometers by the distance used in the model.
2. Did you draw the spacecraft to the same scale? Why or why not?

Process Skills

Making models, Measuring, Communicating

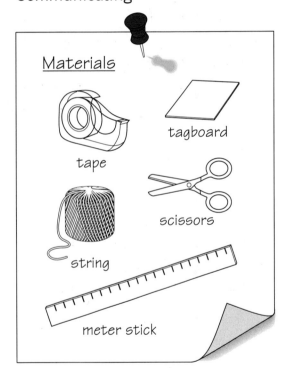

Materials

tape

tagboard

scissors

string

meter stick

Chapter 3

The Universe

Imagine that it has been fifteen years since *Pathfinder* lifted off from its launch pad at the Kennedy Space Center. You have arrived at the outer boundary of the solar system. Your mission is complete, and it's time to head for home.

As the captain sets *Pathfinder* on its course toward the earth, you wonder what it would be like to venture beyond the solar system into deep space. However, traveling at your present speed of 40,000 kilometers per hour, it would take more than 100,000 years to reach the nearest star, Proxima Centauri!

You gaze out *Pathfinder*'s window at the stars. You know that there are billions and billions of these glowing bodies, many of them larger and brighter and hotter than the sun. Think about all the billions of stars in the universe. In your Science Journal, write whether you think that some forms of life exist somewhere in the universe other than on the earth. Explain your reasoning.

Explore Activity

How can you make a star viewer?

Process Skills

Making models, Classifying, Communicating

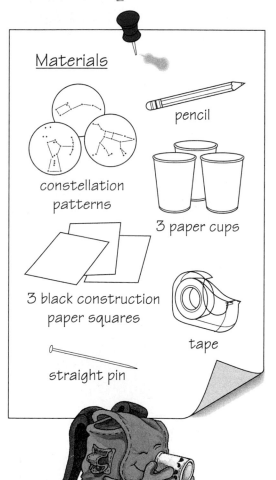

Materials

pencil

constellation patterns

3 paper cups

3 black construction paper squares

tape

straight pin

Observe and Collect Data

1. Photocopy the constellation patterns on page F45, cut the circles out, and set them aside.

2. ⚠ Trace the open end of one cup to make a circle in the middle of each black square. Lay each constellation pattern on one black circle. Use the pin to poke a hole through each dot in the pattern and the black paper under it.

3. Punch a hole in the middle of the bottom of each cup with a pencil. Turn each cup upside down on top of one black square and carefully tape the square to the cup. Don't leave any space to let light in.

4. Point the cup toward a light source and look through the hole in the bottom of the cup to see a constellation.

Share Your Results

1. How well could other groups identify the constellations you made?

2. Try to think of other objects or shapes that the star patterns look like.

Draw Conclusions

Although we now have scientific information about the stars, people continue to tell
the old stories about constellations. Why do
you think this is so?

Apply What You Know

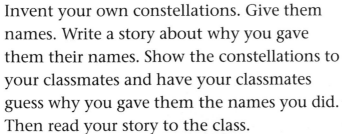

Invent your own constellations. Give them
names. Write a story about why you gave
them their names. Show the constellations to
your classmates and have your classmates
guess why you gave them the names you did.
Then read your story to the class.

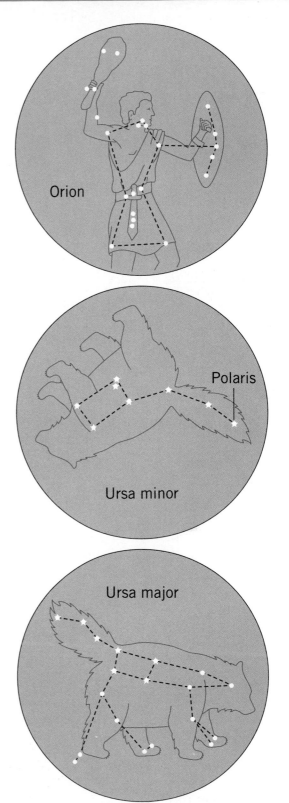

Orion

Ursa minor

Polaris

Ursa major

What is a star?

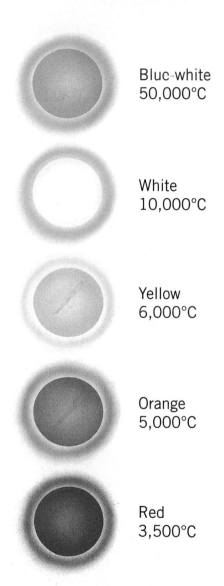

Blue-white
50,000°C

White
10,000°C

Yellow
6,000°C

Orange
5,000°C

Red
3,500°C

▲ The color of a star depends on the temperature at its surface. The hottest stars are blue-white; the coolest are red.

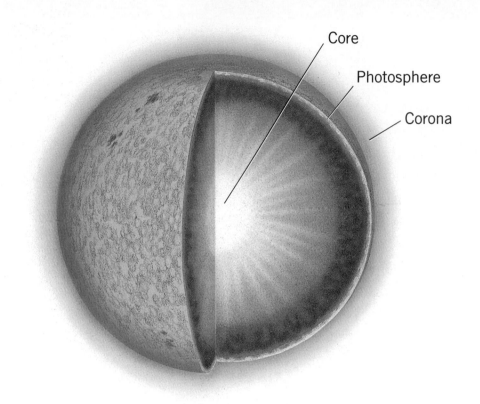

Core

Photosphere

Corona

A **star** is a huge mass of glowing matter. All stars are "energy machines." They give off tremendous amounts of heat and light. Think about the sun. It is so large that more than 100 earths could fit across its diameter and its mass equals about 333,000 earths. Although the sun is 150 million kilometers away, the sun's energy supports life on the earth.

The energy given off by a star is produced by nuclear reactions that take place deep inside the star. These reactions involve hydrogen nuclei that are moving at great speeds. Because of the tremendous heat and pressure inside a star, hydrogen nuclei that collide with one another often stick together. They fuse, forming helium nuclei. These nuclear-fusion reactions release huge amounts of energy. The energy is in the form of heat and light.

There may be more than 200 billion billion stars in the universe. And half of these stars may be larger,

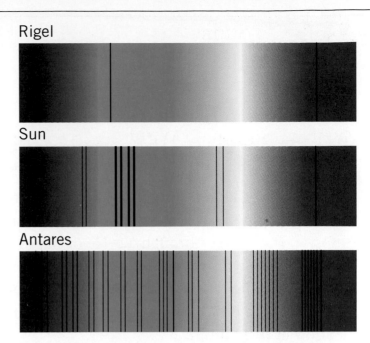

Rigel

Sun

Antares

▲ The light from every star produces a unique spectrum, which tells something about its temperature and composition. The lines in the spectrum represent elements found in the star.

brighter, and hotter than our sun! Although all stars produce heat and light, they vary in size, temperature, color, composition, and brightness. As you can see from the diagram on page F46, the color of a star is related to its temperature.

On a clear, moonless night you can see thousands of stars. If you have ever looked up on such a night, you probably noticed that stars vary in brightness, or **magnitude**. Temperature and size affect how bright a star really is: this is called actual (or absolute) magnitude. Distance affects how bright a star appears when viewed from the earth. A dim star that is closer to the earth may seem brighter than a bright star that is much farther away. This is called apparent magnitude.

Stars also vary in composition. To find out what stars are made of, scientists use a spectroscope. A spectroscope is a device used to analyze light. It separates light into patterns of lines called *spectra* (singular *spectrum*). Spectra are like "fingerprints" of the elements. When an element is heated or burned, it produces its own unique spectrum. The light from a star can be separated into spectra to find out what elements make up the star.

Amazing!

It has been calculated that the sun produces enough energy each second to supply the United States with all the electricity it needs for 13 million years.

What is the life cycle of a star?

Stars are not living things. They do not carry out the life functions that identify something as "alive." However, stars do go through a cycle of stages similar to that associated with living things. Stars are born, they age, and they die. The sun is a fairly young star. It was born about five billion years ago and will remain stable for another five billion.

Protostar

A star begins as a vast cloud of gas and dust. Nearby particles are pulled together by gravity into a huge mass. The mass contracts, causing a dramatic increase in its temperature.

HISTORY

A Supernova

On July 4, 1054, a brilliant light flashed in the sky. This light was so bright that it was visible 24 hours a day for the next 23 days. This rare event was witnessed by people in various places on earth. Records of it have been found in China, the Middle East, and North America, where Anasazi people recorded the event in the petroglyph shown here. It is now known that the light was produced by a supernova, a gigantic explosion of a star. The matter shot out from that supernova can still be seen spreading across the sky. It is called the Crab Nebula (neb´yə lə).

Nebulae like the Crab Nebula provide the matter from which new stars are formed.

SCIENCE TECHNOLOGY & SOCIETY

Star

When the temperature gets high enough for nuclear fusion to take place, a star is "born." A star lives as long as fusion reactions continue. The star becomes stable when the force of fusion pushing out is in balance with the force of gravity pulling in.

Red giant and Red supergiant

When a star uses up most of its hydrogen, it expands greatly and cools. Stars larger than the sun become red supergiants.

Supernova

When its fuel is used up, a red supergiant suddenly collapses and explodes as a supernova. Dust and gases from the explosion may produce a nebula from which new protostars form. Following a supernova, the core of a massive star may become a neutron star or a black hole.

Neutron stars

A neutron star is very small and incredibly dense, and it spins rapidly. If it gives off short bursts of energy as it spins, it is called a pulsar.

White dwarf and Nova

When all its fuel is used up, a red giant collapses under its own gravity and heats up to become a white dwarf. Sometimes material from a nearby star causes a white dwarf to flare suddenly and then fade over a few months. This is called a nova.

Black dwarf

When a white dwarf no longer radiates energy, it dies and becomes a cold, dense mass. As it gives off no light, it is called a black dwarf. This is how life ends for most stars.

Black holes

The cores of the *most* massive stars become so dense that they are thought to become "black holes." The gravity of a black hole is so great that light cannot escape from it.

What is a constellation?

Through the centuries, people of many cultures have connected certain stars with imaginary lines to make pictures in their minds. These groups of stars, which seem to form a pattern or picture, are known as **constellations**.

Be a Scientist

How can the North Star help people?

People long ago discovered something special about Polaris, or the North Star. They learned that it always remained in the same place in the sky, while other stars near it seemed to change their positions. The Pawnees called Polaris "The Star That Does Not Walk Around."

Using the star chart to help you, locate Polaris and some other bright star. Note their relative positions in the sky. A few hours later, check their positions again. What do you observe? How can knowing that Polaris is always in the same location help to save a person's life?

The sky does not look the same from all parts of the earth. The star chart on page F51 shows some well-known constellations visible to people in the Northern Hemisphere. However, people in the Southern Hemisphere look out at a different part of the sky. So they see different stars and constellations.

Another factor that affects the appearance of the sky is the movement of the earth in its orbit around the sun. Think about how far the earth moves in six months. The earth's position in space in early July is directly across its orbit from its position six months later, in early January. So because the earth moves, people look out at different parts of the night sky and therefore at different constellations at different times of the year.

Look again at the star chart and find the star Polaris (pō lar´ is) in the center of the chart. Polaris is also known as the North Star because it is directly over the north pole of the earth's axis. Now find the constellation Ursa Major, which means "Big Bear." Seven stars of this constellation make up the Big Dipper. You can always locate Polaris by extending an imaginary line through the two end stars of the dipper's bowl. Can you locate Cassiopeia on the other side of Polaris from the Big Dipper?

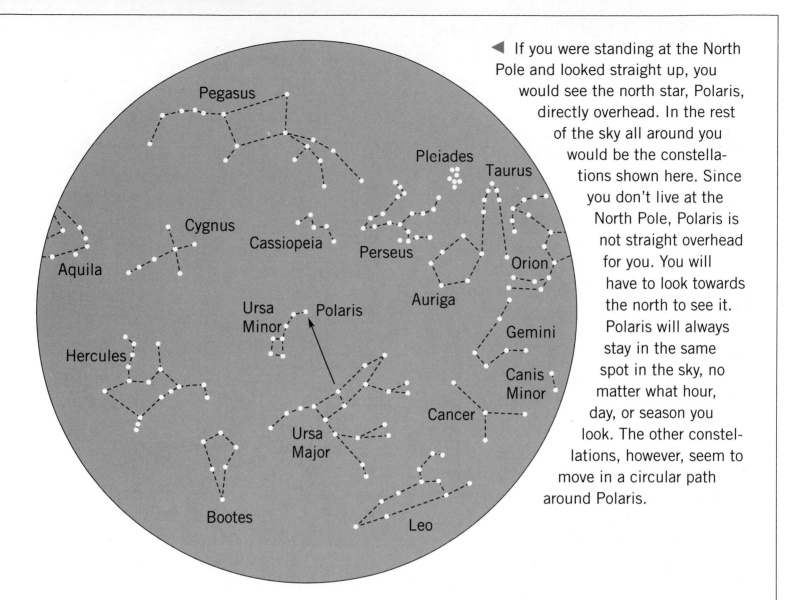

Pegasus

Pleiades

Taurus

Cygnus

Cassiopeia

Perseus

Orion

Aquila

Auriga

Ursa Minor   Polaris

Hercules

Gemini

Canis Minor

Cancer

Ursa Major

Bootes

Leo

◀ If you were standing at the North Pole and looked straight up, you would see the north star, Polaris, directly overhead. In the rest of the sky all around you would be the constellations shown here. Since you don't live at the North Pole, Polaris is not straight overhead for you. You will have to look towards the north to see it. Polaris will always stay in the same spot in the sky, no matter what hour, day, or season you look. The other constellations, however, seem to move in a circular path around Polaris.

Modern astronomers recognize 88 constellations. Since the late 1920s, the boundaries of constellations have been used to map the sky. Amateur astonomers often use constellations to describe the locations of different planets. The planets are not actually in the constellations. They are simply passing in front of them, as you might pass in front of a group of distant trees.

How are you doing?

1. What is a protostar?
2. What is a constellation?
3. **Think** What are the chances that the life of our sun will one day end in a supernova? Explain your answer.
4. **Think** What conditions are necessary for a star to be born?

What is a galaxy?

Without a telescope, you can see a few thousand points of light in the night sky. Except for the planets, almost all of these are individual stars that are part of the Milky Way galaxy. A **galaxy** is a huge system, or family, of stars. The Milky Way galaxy consists of between 100 and 200 billion stars. Our sun is one of those stars.

Our solar system makes up a very tiny part of the Milky Way. Are there other solar systems in our galaxy? Do any of the billions of stars have planets revolving around them? And if so, do any of those planets support some form of life? No one knows yet.

In addition to individual stars, the Milky Way galaxy contains clusters of stars, nebulae, and vast quantities of gas and dust. In fact, until the 1920s, astronomers thought that all

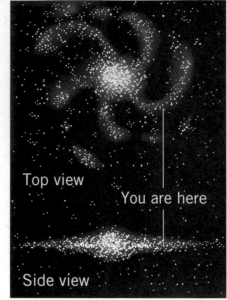

Top view

You are here

Side view

the matter in the universe was contained in the Milky Way. Today we know that the Milky Way is only one of billions of galaxies. As shown in the pictures below, galaxies exist in a variety of shapes. The Milky Way has a spiral shape.

When you look at the night sky in summer, you see what looks like a thick band of stars stretching across the sky. Our galaxy was

Elliptical galaxy

Irregular galaxy

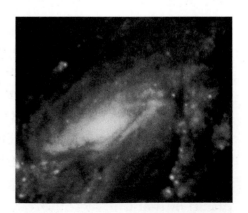

Spiral galaxy

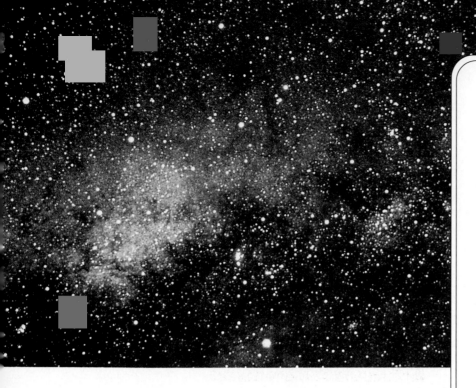

SIDE TRIP →

The Planetarium

Many large cities have planetariums. Inside a planetarium building is a complex instrument, also called a planetarium. This instrument contains many projectors that can produce pictures of the sky on the walls and ceiling of a domed room. The pictures can show the sky as it is today or as it was any time in the past. It can show the movements of the planets, the passage of a star from its birth to its death, galaxies whirling in space, and even some of the ways the universe may have started. A planetarium is a great place to explore the mysteries of space.

named for the whitish appearance of this band. What you are seeing is a side view of part of the Milky Way. The solar system is located in one of the spiral arms near the edge of the galaxy. In summer you can observe the main body of the galaxy, which is thick with stars.

Distances between galaxies, or even between individual stars within a galaxy, are very great. For example, the nearest galaxy to the Milky Way is 20 billion billion kilometers away. If you were to write this number out, how many zeros would you have to add?

Working with such large numbers is awkward, so when dealing with these distances, scientists use a unit called a light-year. A **light-year,** abbreviated as LY, is the distance light travels in one year. One light-year is equal to 9.46 trillion kilometers, or 9,460,000,000,000 kilometers! At this speed,

light reflecting from the moon takes slightly more than one second to reach the earth!

The distance from the Milky Way galaxy to the Andromeda galaxy is about 2 million light-years. This means that when you look at that galaxy, you are not seeing what it looks like today. You are seeing how it looked 2 million years ago! That's because the light you see began its journey 2 million years ago and is just now reaching the earth. If a star in that galaxy exploded in a supernova today, the explosion would not be visible from the earth for 2 million years.

How did the universe begin?

In 1929, an American astronomer named Edwin Hubble suggested a startling hypothesis. Hubble said that the universe was expanding. All the galaxies were moving apart at incredible rates of speed.

If Hubble's idea is right, and most scientists agree that it is, everything in the universe must once have been squeezed together in a single mass. Some event, probably a gigantic explosion, blew the mass apart. This is the most widely accepted theory for the beginning of the universe. Scientists call it the big bang theory.

According to the big bang theory, the galaxies are still moving away from one another as a result of the force of the explosion. Based on the speeds at which the galaxies are traveling, scientists estimate that the explosion occurred between 15 and 20 billion years ago.

Following the big bang, it is thought that the gases that were released began to collect into gigantic blobs. These blobs gradually became organized into the systems we now call galaxies.

The oldest objects in the universe are thought to be quasars (kwā′zärz′). A **quasar** is a starlike object that gives off tremendous amounts of energy. Quasars are among the

Be a Scientist

Can you show an expanding universe?

Use a balloon and a marker to make and study a model of Hubble's hypothesis. Draw dots on the flat balloon and then blow the balloon up. Remember, the model represents an expanding universe. Work with your model to answer the following questions: How does the distance between galaxies change as time passes? As time passes, do the galaxies move apart faster or slower?

Scientific Illustrator

Scientific illustrations should not be confused with scientific art. Lynette Cook does scientific illustration. For her work she needs to draw or paint what she sees *accurately* because scientific illustration requires showing things as they exist in nature. She may use only minimal personal or artistic interpretation, balancing an artistic quality in her work with scientific accuracy.

66 For astronomical illustration, I study NASA photographs or visit earth sites that are thought to be similar to places on other planets. Sometimes I work with geologists, space scientists, astronomers, astrophysicists, and science writers to get information.

"I use traditional drawing and painting media for my illustrations, but some astronomical illustrators create their art using personal computers. Either way, the goal is to help people understand the subject. I was always interested in both science and art, and now I've found a way to combine them both. It's wonderful to be able to work at something you enjoy.**99**

least understood objects in the universe. Although they seem much too small to be galaxies, quasars release more energy than 100 galaxies combined. Quasars appear to be the oldest objects in the universe because they have traveled farthest since the big bang.

Another question facing astronomers is what will happen to the universe. Will it continue to expand forever? Or will something occur to make all the matter come together again in a "big crunch"? It will be a long time before these questions are answered, if, indeed, they ever are.

What might future space exploration include?

Beginning in the 1960s, astronomers set out on a new journey of inquiry. Unlike Columbus 500 years earlier, these "explorers" were not searching for a shortcut to distant lands. Rather, they were searching for signs of intelligent life elsewhere in our galaxy.

The search does not involve people traveling through space. In fact, no travel is involved. The "looking" is being done with radio telescopes. These are very large dish-shaped instruments that can receive radio signals from deep space. The telescopes are aimed at 800 stars in the Milky Way, all within 100 light-years of the earth.

In 1992, scientists in the United States, Argentina, Australia, Russia, and India began monitoring 14 million broadcast channels. For 10 years, computers connected to the telescopes will be programmed to identify signals that have a pattern unlike those made by nonliving objects in space. If any intelligent life forms are out there and are sending messages, the chances are very good that one of these telescopes will receive them.

Astronomers are not only trying to receive messages, however. In 1974, a message was *sent* from Earth, describing our planet. Traveling at the speed of light, it will take 24,000 years to reach the cluster of stars at

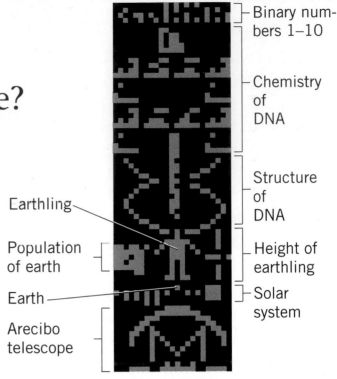

Labels (top to bottom, right side): Binary numbers 1–10 · Chemistry of DNA · Structure of DNA · Height of earthling · Solar system

Labels (left side): Earthling · Population of earth · Earth · Arecibo telescope

▲ The above drawing is a picture representation of the binary message (made up of zeros and ones) sent out from the radio telescope at Arecibo, Puerto Rico, in 1974. Its purpose was to tell other intelligent life in the universe about our planet. The message was also sent in English.

which it was aimed, so even if it is received and deciphered, an answer will not reach the earth until at least 48,000 years after our message was sent!

In addition to the radio search, other space adventures are possible. Space probes now hurtling toward outer space will be relaying information back to the earth for some time. A new probe, perhaps carrying a human crew, is another possibility.

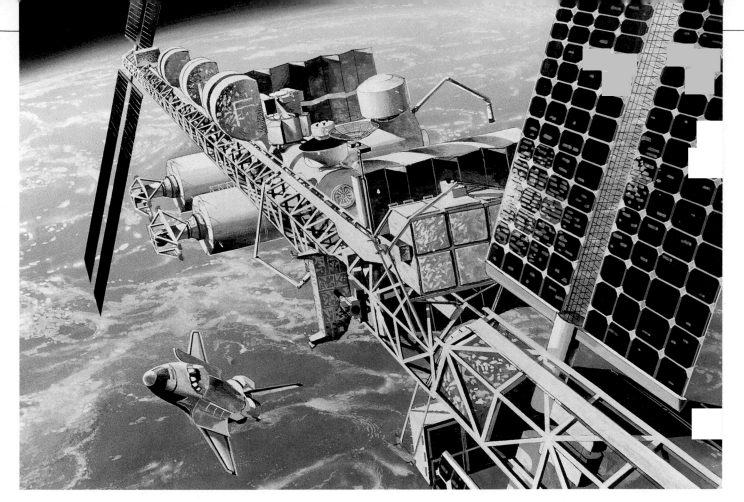

▲ Four to eight astronauts will live in Space Station Freedom for six months at a time, doing research leading to an improved quality of life on earth and to leadership in space science and exploration.

For years, scientists have talked about and planned for the creation of a space station. If such a station is built, it could be used as a space observatory and laboratory. It also might be used as a launch site for flight missions to outer parts of the solar system and beyond. One thing is certain. When speculating about our future in space, the sky's the limit.

How are you doing?

1. What does a light-year measure?
2. Briefly describe the big bang theory.
3. **Think** If scientists discover objects in the universe beyond the quasars, will those objects probably be older or younger than quasars? How do you know?
4. **Think** If you were in charge of preparing a recording to be sent into space, what information would you include about the earth and its living things?

Looking Back

Words and Concepts

Complete the following statements.

1. A star gives off its own heat and _____.
2. To measure distance in the universe, scientists use a unit of measure called the _____.
3. Groups of stars that form patterns when viewed from the earth are called _____.
4. You could determine compass directions if you could locate a star called _____.
5. A system, or family, of stars is called a(n) _____.
6. The brightest and most distant objects in the universe are _____.

Applied Thinking Skills

Answer the following questions. You can use words, drawings, or diagrams in your answers.

7. If you saw an object in the sky that over a few months moved from one constellation to another, what might you conclude the object was? Why?
8. How is a black hole like the drain in a sink?
9. One model of the universe shows the galaxies as spots on a balloon that is being inflated. Based on this model, what generalization can you make about the universe?
10. **Your World** In what ways might your life change if scientists were able to communicate with intelligent beings on other worlds?

Show What You Know

How can you use a star chart?

Observe and Collect Data

1. Look at the star chart on page F51 and study the caption. Also notice the arrow that begins at two stars in the Big Dipper in Ursa Major and points to Polaris, the North Star. Make a photocopy of the chart.
2. At about 9:00 p.m., go outdoors and face north. Compare the sky with what you see on the chart.
3. Find the Big Dipper in the sky. Use the two dipper stars to imagine the arrow pointing to Polaris. Now position your chart so it shows the Big Dipper and Polaris in the same positions as they are in the sky.
4. Finally, try to locate the other constellations in the positions indicated on the chart.

Process Skills

Observing, Reading a diagram

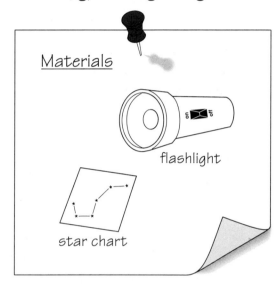

Materials

flashlight

star chart

Draw Conclusions

1. Which stars are easiest to find? Why?
2. Which constellations are easiest to find? Why?

Space Exploration

Show what you know about the universe. Work by yourself, with a partner, or in a group. Select one activity.

Music Archivist You have been asked to choose some musical selections to put on a probe heading for the stars. If an extraterrestrial ever finds the probe, this music should reveal something about our planet. What would you choose? Why?

Model Builder Using materials you can buy inexpensively or can find around your home, build a model of *Pathfinder* or of *Voyager 1*. If you build *Pathfinder,* use your imagination to build the model. If you build *Voyager 1,* go to a library and find books that describe and show pictures of this spacecraft. Be sure to identify the spacecraft's parts and explain their role.

Historian What is Stonehenge? Use a local or school library to find out more about this ancient place. Prepare a talk to give to your class. Support your talk with copies of photographs, drawings, or models of Stonehenge. Tell how Stonehenge relates to what you have learned in the unit.

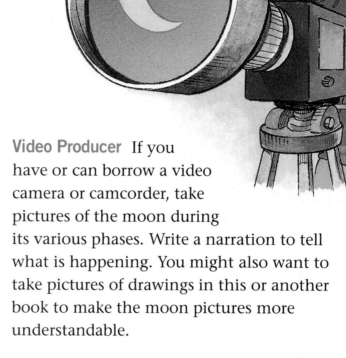

Video Producer If you have or can borrow a video camera or camcorder, take pictures of the moon during its various phases. Write a narration to tell what is happening. You might also want to take pictures of drawings in this or another book to make the moon pictures more understandable.

Mythologist Do some research about star myths from different cultures and choose one you especially like. Rewrite it in your own words. Or, if you like, tell the story to a group of your friends, the way these stories were told long ago.

Environmentalist The earth, like a spacecraft, provides us with life-support systems. Describe these systems and tell how they can be protected.

Glossary

asteroid (as´tər oid´)   A small, rocky body that orbits the sun. (page F16)

comet (käm´it)   A large chunk of ice, frozen gases, and dust that travels around the sun in a very long, oval orbit. (page F16)

constellation (kän´stə lā´shən)   A group of stars that seem to form a pattern, or picture. (page F50)

galaxy (gal´ək sē)   A huge system, or family, of stars. (page F52)

light-year (līt´ yir´)   The distance that light travels in one year; a unit used to measure distance between stars or galaxies. (page F53)

lunar eclipse (lo͞o´nər i klips´)   An eclipse of the moon; occurs when the earth's shadow falls on the moon. (page F13)

magnitude (mag´nə to͞od´)   The brightness of a star. (page F47)

meteoroid (mēt´ē ər oid´)   A solid, rock-like object that is found throughout the solar system. (page F17)

orbiter (ôr´bit ər)   Any spacecraft that travels around the earth in a regular orbit. (page F28)

quasar (kwā´zär´)   A very bright starlike object. (page F54)

satellite (sat´´l īt´)   Any body in space that orbits around another body in space. (page F10)

solar eclipse (sō´lər i klips´)   An eclipse of the sun; occurs when the moon's shadow falls on the earth's surface. (page F12)

solar system (sō´lər sis´təm)   The sun and everything that revolves around it. (page F6)

space probe (spās´ prōb´)   A spacecraft packed with instruments that gathers information and sends it back to earth. (page F3)

star (stär´)   A huge mass of glowing gas. (page F46)

Unit F Index

Boldface numerals denote glossary terms. Italic numerals denote illustrations.

Credits

Photographs

1 NASA; 2–3 U.S. Naval Observatory; 4L NASA; 4TR Jim Ballard/AllStock; 5 Ken Karp*; 6–7 NASA; 9 Elliott Smith*; 10–11 Lick Observatory/University of California; 12 Richard A. Keen/Hansen Planetarium/U.S. Naval Observatory; 16B Geoffrey Nilsen Photography*; 16T National Optical Astronomy Observatories; 17 Tom Bean/AllStock; 18B NASA; 18C Larry Lipsky/Tom Stack & Associates; 18TC Ken Karp*; 18TR Kevin Schafer-Martha Hill/Tom Stack & Associates; 19 GHP Studio*; 21 GHP Studio*; 22B NASA; 22T Stephen Frisch*; 23 NASA; 25 Elliott Smith*; 26–36 NASA; 42–43 Copyright 1961 by California Institute of Technology and Carnegie Institution of Washington; 45 Elliott Smith*; 52–53 Astrostock* Sanford; 52BC U.S. Naval Observatory; 52BL The Kitt Peak National Observatory; 52BR Hansen Planetarium/U.S. Naval Observatory; 55 Anne Dowie*; 57 NASA; 58 Royal Observatory, Edinburgh; 59 Stephen Frisch*

Special thanks to Mike Gentry, NASA Lyndon Baines Johnson Space Center; Malcolm X Elementary School, Berkeley, California; Franklin Year-Round School, Oakland, California; Carl B. Munck Elementary School, Oakland, California; Hintil Ku Ka Child Care Center, Oakland, California.

*Photographed expressly for Addison-Wesley Publishing Company, Inc.

Illustrations

Jacque Auger 14B, 15, 16–17, 34–35, 36-37, 46, 48–49, 54
Nea Bisek 8T, 19, 21, 24L, 41, 44T, 59
Illustrious, Inc. 4, 10, 12, 13, 14T, 28, 29, 30, 31, 32–33, 34B, 35B, 36B, 37B, 45, 51, 52, 56
Jane McCreary 8B, 24B, 44B, 47
Larry Pearson 38–39
Randy Vertoustraete 60–61

Text

14, 15 Based on data from *Observer's Handbook 1993,* The Royal Astronomical Society of Canada. By permission of Dr. Roy Bishop.

38–39 Jane Louise Curry, *Back in the Beforetime* (New York: Margaret K. McElderry Books, Macmillan Publishing Co., 1987). Text copyright © 1987 by Jane Louise Curry. Reprinted with permission of Margaret K. McElderry Books, an imprint of Macmillan Publishing Company.

Party Time!

EXPLOSION!
drug free
YOUTH to YOUTH

A book
is a present
you can
open again
and again

my choice
drug free!

SECOND

THEATRE 50

THE AMUSEMENT PARK
ADMIT ONE
GOOD FOR DAY OF PURCHASE ONLY
0095487

10

...ay, is Mr. McPherson's...
...k a Social Studies quiz...
...ng that I did really well...
...hope I did because that test...
...for about one-fourth of...
...ocial Studies grade—F or this...

...built something that will...
...fountain pens upright...
...ll of the ink will flow...
...the cartrige instead...
...tip when I'm not...
...lly cuts down on...
...a lot of writing...
...enjoy Wizards, I...
...ally nice of you...
...What do you...
...way? I skulk about...
...you tomorrow.

			Wedne...
			1
5 Party	6	7 soccer Practice	8
12	13	14	15

In Your World

It is the end of the school day. Students pour out of their classrooms. Some wait for buses. Others ride bikes or walk home. You make your way to the park for soccer practice.

You hurry along by walking faster and taking longer steps. Your heart beats, and blood pumps through your body. With your eyes, you see people and objects as you zig-zag to avoid them. And your brain thinks about the school day and soccer practice.

Your body must adjust to changing conditions so everything works together. Your body adjusts whether you are running during the day or sleeping at night. How does your body coordinate and adjust to the many activities that keep you alive and help you respond to your world?

- How does your nervous system coordinate your body's activities?

- How does your endocrine system control your body's activities?

- What choices can you make to keep your body healthy?

CONTROL SYSTEMS

Talking about changes

Activities

Features

Chapter 1

Nervous System

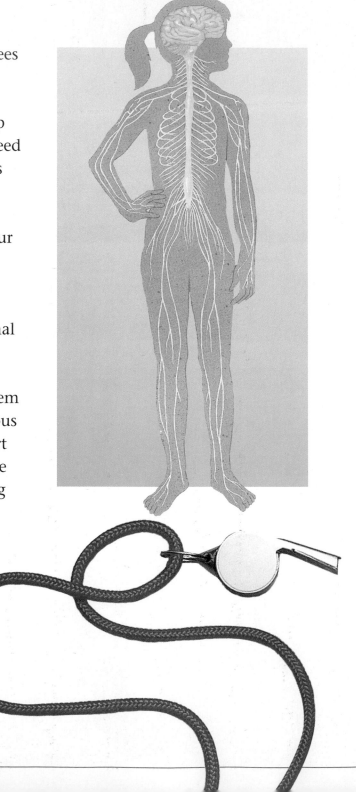

Jogging in place, you think, *Knees, higher!* Your knees go higher as you bounce up and down. You can hear and feel your feet hit the ground.

Many things happen in your body as you warm up for soccer practice. When your muscles move, they need more oxygen. You breathe faster, and your heart beats faster to pump oxygen-rich blood to your muscles.

Breathing and blood circulation are automatic. However, some activities, such as deciding to raise your knees, involve thinking and making conscious decisions. What coordinates all of these activities?

The **nervous system** is your body's control and communication system. It consists of your brain, spinal cord, and nerves. Most of your actions, and many of your body's functions, are controlled by this system.

To help keep your body working, the nervous system sends and receives messages. For example, your nervous system is sending a message when it signals your heart to beat faster. Hearing and feeling your feet hitting the ground are examples of your nervous system receiving messages. What other examples of messages in your nervous system can you think of?

Your brain receives messages about the environment through your five senses. In your Science Journal, name two senses that might give your brain the information you need to play soccer. List one example of information that each of these senses could provide.

Playing goalie takes practice and good reactions.

Warming up during soccer practice

What factors affect reaction time?

Process Skills

Measuring, Collecting data, Hypothesizing

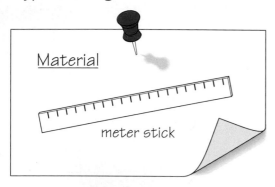

Material

meter stick

Observe and Collect Data

1. In your Activity Journal, copy the data table. Then have your partner hold a meter stick vertically in one hand near the middle of the stick. Next, point the 0-centimeter mark toward the floor and the 100-centimeter mark toward the ceiling.

2. Place your thumb and forefinger around the meter stick at the zero mark, leaving about 1 centimeter of space between each finger and the meter stick. If necessary, have your partner raise the meter stick so that you don't have to bend over.

3. Your partner will let go of the meter stick without warning you. Catch the meter stick between your thumb and forefinger. Note the centimeter reading at which you caught the meter stick and record this value.

Measuring My Reaction Time

Name	Trial	Eyes Opened or Closed?	Measurement (cm)

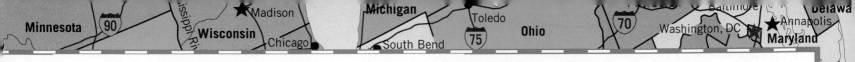

4. Repeat this procedure four times, recording the centimeter reading each time. Switch roles with your partner and repeat the procedure.

5. **Predict** what will happen when you do the activity with your eyes closed. Try this with your partner saying, "Now!" when he or she releases the meter stick. Record the centimeter reading each time.

Share Your Results

1. Compare your data with those obtained when your partner caught the meter stick. How close are the results?

2. Compare your data with those of other groups. What similarities and differences do you note?

Draw Conclusions

1. How is your reaction time being measured in this activity?

2. How was reaction time affected when you closed your eyes? Why do you think this occurred?

3. How do you think the message that the meter stick had been dropped got from your eyes or ears to your fingers?

Apply What You Know

1. How might your reaction time be affected if you were tired?

2. How might drugs affect a person's reaction time?

What are the parts of the nervous system?

Soccer is a fast-moving game. It requires quick reactions and good coordination. Your nervous system allows you to make the decisions you need to play, and it helps direct your actions.

The main parts of the nervous system are the brain, spinal cord, and nerves. The brain and spinal cord make up the central nervous system. The nerves extend throughout your body and carry messages.

To play soccer well, players must work as a team. In the same way, your brain, spinal cord, and nerves act as a team to help your body function. Your brain is the command center. The spinal cord allows messages to travel between your brain and your body. The nerves deliver messages. Think *Move!*, and a signal leaves your brain and travels through your spinal cord to a nerve that reaches a muscle. Your leg moves.

The largest part of the brain is the **cerebrum** (ser´ə brəm). The cerebrum controls the movements of muscles that allow you to walk, run, talk, and do other activities. Messages about what you see, hear, smell, taste, and touch are interpreted in the cerebrum. Thinking, learning, and memory are functions controlled by the cerebrum. As you

It takes teamwork to play soccer.

watch your opponents and consider how to score, your cerebrum is in action.

The **cerebellum** (ser´ə bel´əm) is located at the back of the brain. The cerebellum controls balance and coordination. When you bend your knee and swing your foot at the ball, your cerebellum directs your muscles to work together so that a smooth kick is made.

The brain stem controls basic bodily functions. For example, the brain stem controls your breathing and heartbeat. These activities are regulated automatically, without your direct control or awareness.

The spinal cord is like a telephone cable. Messages that travel between the brain and the nerves in other parts of your body move along the spinal cord.

Your brain is divided into three regions—the cerebrum, the cerebellum, and the brain stem. The brain and spinal cord make up your central nervous system.

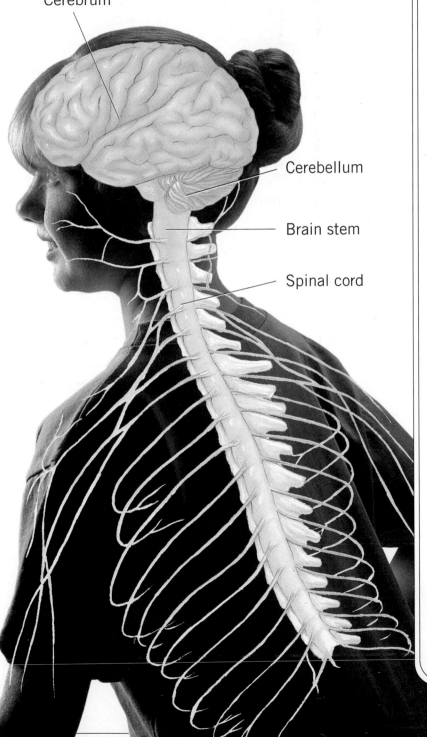

Cerebrum

Cerebellum

Brain stem

Spinal cord

CULTURAL CONNECTION

Acupuncture Soothes Pain

Pain is a message carried by the nervous system. Some medicines can relieve pain. Acupuncture can also treat pain.

Acupuncture (ak´yo͞o puŋk´chər) is a medical procedure developed in China more than 5,000 years ago. It involves inserting needles at various locations in the body to relieve pain and to treat diseases. In 1959, Chinese doctors began using acupuncture during surgery instead of anesthetics.

How does acupuncture stop pain? No one knows for sure. Some researchers think that acupuncture prevents messages from being delivered to the pain centers in the brain.

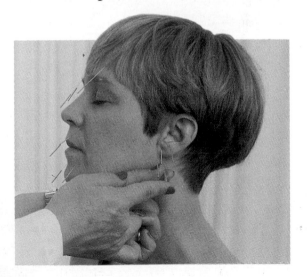

What paths do messages follow in the nervous system?

The whistle sounds. Action on the field stops. You trot to the sidelines for instructions from your coach. "Nice job!" he says. "But I want you to pass the ball more often. You've got to depend on your teammates."

Your brain and spinal cord are referred to as your central nervous system. Nerves extend from your spinal cord to the rest of your body. Nerve cells have branches, or extensions, coming from the cell body. Nerve cells receive messages, called nerve impulses, through short nerve branches. The nerve impulses travel through the cell body and then along the long nerve branches.

The message travels along the long part of the nerve cell, and a chemical is released at the other end. The ends of the next nerve cell pick up the chemical message. The message continues from one nerve cell to the next. ▼

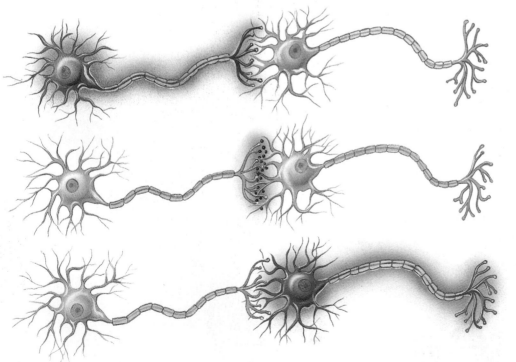

Message moves from neuron's long end.

Chemical is given off at the end of the neuron. Chemical spreads across short end of the next neuron.

Chemical transfers message. Message continues.

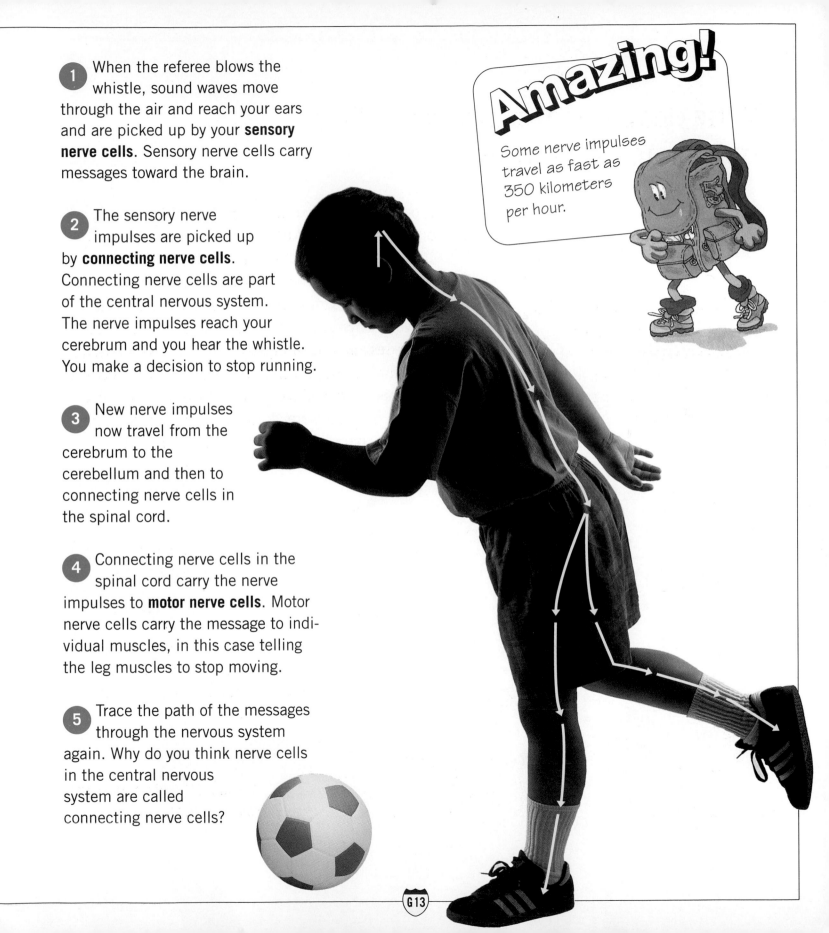

1. When the referee blows the whistle, sound waves move through the air and reach your ears and are picked up by your **sensory nerve cells**. Sensory nerve cells carry messages toward the brain.

2. The sensory nerve impulses are picked up by **connecting nerve cells**. Connecting nerve cells are part of the central nervous system. The nerve impulses reach your cerebrum and you hear the whistle. You make a decision to stop running.

3. New nerve impulses now travel from the cerebrum to the cerebellum and then to connecting nerve cells in the spinal cord.

4. Connecting nerve cells in the spinal cord carry the nerve impulses to **motor nerve cells**. Motor nerve cells carry the message to individual muscles, in this case telling the leg muscles to stop moving.

5. Trace the path of the messages through the nervous system again. Why do you think nerve cells in the central nervous system are called connecting nerve cells?

Amazing!

Some nerve impulses travel as fast as 350 kilometers per hour.

How does the nervous system receive messages?

While you eat an orange, your brain can receive many other kinds of messages at the same time. ▼

It is half time. As you are snacking on an orange, walking around, and talking about the game, your nervous system is receiving many messages. You hear voices. The orange smells sharp and tastes sweet. Your clothing looks colorful and bright. You take this all in through your senses.

Your senses are special parts of the nervous system. Your eyes, ears, nose, and tongue are called sense organs. What messages from outside the body does each of these organs receive? Your skin is also a sense organ. It responds to heat, cold, pressure, and pain.

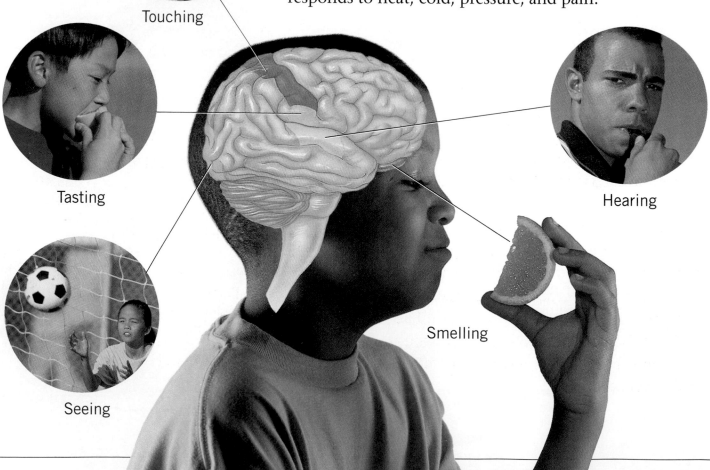

Touching

Tasting

Seeing

Hearing

Smelling

Be a Scientist

How sensitive are people to odors?

1. Your teacher will give you a small cup containing a sample of matter that gives off an odor. Then your teacher will assign a blindfolded student to be your partner. Do not let your partner know who you are.

2. Let your partner sniff the sample in your container. Then take your container and stand with the other students who are holding containers. The blindfolded students will remove their blindfolds and try to find their mystery partners, based on the odors from the samples that they are holding. When partners have been found, change roles and repeat the activity.

3. How is the cerebrum involved in this activity? Which samples seemed to make it easier to find the mystery partner? Which samples seemed less effective in identifying the mystery partner?

In each sense organ there are special sensory nerve cells that can detect certain things in your environment. For example, sensory nerve cells in your eyes detect light. These nerve cells do not respond to sound, taste, or odors. In your ears, sensory nerve cells respond only to vibrations caused by sound waves.

A sense organ responds by sending nerve impulses to the central nervous system. These impulses are directed to connecting nerve cells in the cerebrum. You see, hear, taste, smell, and feel with your brain. But without the sense organs, the brain would have no way of knowing what was going on in the outside world.

How are you doing?

1. What's the function of the nervous system?
2. Make a sketch to show nerve impulse paths when you walk into the kitchen and smell food.
3. **Think** Paralysis is a condition in which a person's muscles can't move. Explain what might cause muscle paralysis.
4. **Think** Your tongue can distinguish four taste sensations: sweet, salty, bitter, and sour. What other sense organ helps you recognize flavors?

How do drugs affect the nervous system?

It is important to understand how drugs affect your body. Without good information, you can't make good decisions. ▶

You and some friends have formed a student drug-education committee. You start the first meeting by asking, "What are drugs?"

"Drugs are chemicals that can affect your body," says one friend. She goes on to say that she saw a TV program that said that some drugs are found in foods or beverages. Coffee and cola contain a drug called caffeine. Drugs that are used to treat pain or disease, such as aspirin, are called medicines.

Someone holds up a poster that shows a cup of coffee and a cigarette. A student

HISTORY

Medicines from Plants

Before modern science, medicine cabinets were often gardens, fields, or forests. People found plants from which they made teas, powders, or ointments to cure ailments.

One such plant is the purple foxglove, also called digitalis (dij´i tal´is). Since the thirteenth century it has been used as a source of medicine.

The leaves of the purple foxglove contain a chemical that can help control heart rates. This chemical is still used in some drugs that treat heart failure caused by clogged or hardened arteries. Drugs developed from foxglove also decrease extra fluid that collects in tissues. However, the leaves of the purple foxglove are poisonous if they are given in the wrong dosages.

wonders what caffeine in coffee and the nicotine found in cigarettes have in common. They are stimulants. These drugs speed up the activity of the nervous system. Cocaine and crack cocaine are dangerous stimulants that can cause heart attacks.

Other drugs are depressants. A depressant slows the activity of the nervous system. Alcohol is a depressant. It slows reaction time and keeps a person from thinking clearly.

Narcotics, such as heroin, slow the nervous system. For this reason, they are used to relieve pain. Narcotics are often injected with a needle. Disease can be spread when a person with a disease shares a needle with another person.

Drugs such as marijuana (mar´i wä´nə) are hallucinogens (hə lōō´si nə jənz). Users may hear, see, and feel things that are not there. Marijuana can damage brain cells and affect memory. LSD, another hallucinogen, may cause long-lasting mental disorders.

One of the committee members wants to know about steroids because these drugs have been in the news recently. There are many different types of steroids. Some reduce swelling or relieve allergies. These steroids are sometimes prescribed by doctors.

Other steroids can increase the size and strength of your muscles. Some people take steroids to look stronger or to improve their performance in sports. But these steroids can kill you because they can damage your heart, liver, and kidneys. They also can stunt your growth. Muscle-enhancing steroids are injected. Many people who take steroids share needles and risk spreading diseases.

When your meeting ends, you realize that you already know a lot about drugs, but there is still much to learn.

What can happen when drugs are abused?

You and other committee members are meeting with a drug counselor who has agreed to be an advisor to the committee. You want to get some questions answered.

"What is drug abuse?" is the first question. "Is it the use of illegal drugs?" The counselor tells you that drug abuse is the misuse of any drug. People who take illegal drugs, such as heroin and LSD, are drug abusers. But legal drugs can also be abused. Alcohol, for example, is legal for adults, but it is often abused. Taking more medicine than is prescribed is also drug abuse.

"What is drug addiction?" is the next question. The counselor tells you that after people take drugs for a while, their bodies depend on the drug. With some drugs, addicts are nervous and feel pain if they stop taking the drug. With other drugs, an addict's mind doesn't feel at ease unless the drug is taken. Many people are addicted to drugs. Smokers are addicted to the nicotine in cigarettes. They become nervous, tense, and depressed when they stop smoking. Some people who drink alcohol become addicted to it. Narcotics are very addictive to people.

With this class of drugs, the user needs more and more each time to be able to feel the effects of the drugs.

"How can I avoid becoming a drug abuser?" is the last question. "By educating yourself and others," is the counselor's answer. A person chooses whether or not to use drugs. Knowing how drugs can affect your health helps you to make good choices and stay healthy.

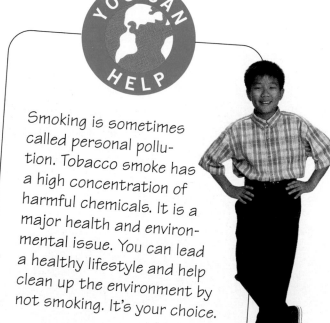

Smoking is sometimes called personal pollution. Tobacco smoke has a high concentration of harmful chemicals. It is a major health and environmental issue. You can lead a healthy lifestyle and help clean up the environment by not smoking. It's your choice.

DILEMMA

Saying No to Alcohol

Your best friend greets you at the door, "Hi! I'm glad you came." As you walk into the house, you are surprised to find some of your friends passing around a can of beer.

"My parents aren't home," says your friend. "Loosen up and have some beer with us."

You have to decide what to do. You know it's all right not to drink, but you need some way to say no. You know it is your choice.

Think About It How would you handle a situation such as this? In your Science Journal, make a list of ways that you could say no to drugs or alcohol. Ask a parent, teacher, or other adult for some suggestions.

How are medicines and legal drugs abused?

Medicine is the topic for today's class discussion. Yesterday, the school counselor asked each student to bring in an empty medicine package selected with a parent's help. You brought in a cold tablets' package.

On the package is a description of what the medicine does. There are also instructions about how much to take and how often. You are amazed at how much more information there is. A paragraph labeled "Warnings" tells about possible side effects: "may cause drowsiness … may cause excitability … use with caution when driving."

A second paragraph warns you not to use the medicine "if you have any of the following conditions" and lists more than ten medical conditions that could cause problems if this medicine is taken. Another warning tells you not to use the product if you are taking certain other medicines.

All medicines and drugs have such warnings. But some people ignore the warnings. They take more of the medicine than they should or they take the medicine more often than they're supposed to.

Diet pills, sleeping pills, and pills to make you less sleepy can be bought without a prescription. These pills contain powerful drugs. Both diet pills and pills to perk you up contain stimulants. Sleeping pills contain depressants. These drugs are often abused.

The label on a prescription drug names the person who is to take the medicine. Sometimes a person shares a prescription drug with someone who seems to have a similar condition. But the condition may not be the same as that of the person for whom the drug was prescribed. A person who uses someone else's prescription is taking a risk.

Also, a drug label has a date on it. Past that date, the medicine should not be used. Some people keep old medicines and use them past the date on the label. These drugs may change chemically and could become useless or dangerous. Taking such a drug might even make a medical problem worse.

◀ Medicines can have side effects when taken with other medicines. Follow directions carefully and do not mix medications without your doctor's consent.

⚠️ Discuss with your family members the reasons why drugs have dates on them. Also discuss the possible dangers of using them after the dates listed. Decide the best way to get rid of these outdated medicines. Compare your family's possible solutions with your classmates.

BACK HOME

How are you doing?

1. Compare stimulants and depressants.
2. What are the differences between drug abuse and drug addiction?
3. **Think** Hallucinogens seem to be similar to some natural chemicals in the brain. These chemicals help to transmit signals between nerve cells. How might this similarity explain the effects of hallucinogens on the brain?
4. **Think** Why do you think it is dangerous to take medicine prescribed for someone else?

The Willow Tree

What do you see when you see a tree? Look at the tree in the picture on this page. Do you know what kind it is? American Indians did. They also knew that by chewing its bark, people could relieve headaches, some stomach disorders, and minor pains.

This tree is a willow. Its bark contains salicin (sal´ə sin), a chemical that is used to make the main ingredient in aspirin.

Willow trees grow all over the world. The flowers of willow trees produce honey. Artisans use the willow's spindly branches to make wicker furniture and baskets. Dutch shoe-makers use its wood to make soles for clogs. And glove makers use a chemical from its bark to turn hide into leather. Even cricket bats are made with willow wood. Cricket is a British game played with a leather ball and flat bat.

Examine a tree. What do you see? What would you see if you were a bird, a squirrel, an artist, a medical researcher, a furniture maker, or a beetle?

Data Collection and Analysis

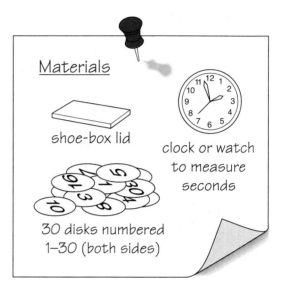

Does learning affect reaction time?

Observe and Collect Data

1. In your Activity Journal, make a copy of the data table. Then, place the disks in the shoe-box lid in number order in three rows, ten disks to a row.

2. Use the watch to time how long it takes your partner to touch each disk in number order. Record the time.

3. Mix up the disks so that they are no longer in number order, but still in three rows of ten. Time your partner as he or she touches the disks in number order. Record the time.

4. Have your partner touch the disks five more times. Record all of your data. Switch roles with your partner and repeat the activity.

5. Make a graph of the data for the six times the disks were not in order.

Materials

shoe-box lid

clock or watch to measure seconds

30 disks numbered 1–30 (both sides)

Draw Conclusions

1. How did the time it took to touch the disks in number order compare with the time it took to touch the disks when they were not in number order?

2. How would you explain any differences in time?

3. Did repeating the activity have any effect on reaction time? What data support your answer?

Measuring My Learned Reaction Time

Name	Trial	Time

Looking Back

Words and Concepts

Read each statement. If a statement is true, write *true* as your answer. If a statement is false, change the underlined word or phrase to make the statement true.

1. Thinking, learning, and memory are functions of the <u>cerebellum</u>.
2. <u>Sensory</u> nerve cells carry nerve impulses toward the central nervous system.
3. The nerve pathway of a reflex is from a sensory nerve cell, to a connecting nerve cell in the <u>spinal cord</u>, and then to a motor nerve cell.
4. <u>Narcotics</u> speed up the activity of the nervous system.
5. <u>Drug abuse</u> involves the use of illegal drugs and the misuse of legal drugs.
6. Basic body activities, such as regulation of breathing and heart rate, are controlled by the <u>cerebrum</u>.

Applied Thinking Skills

Answer the following questions. You can use words, drawings, and diagrams in your answers.

7. Compare the functions of the brain, spinal cord, and nerves. How are they alike? How are they different?
8. Why do you think it is not safe to ride in a car with a driver who has been drinking alcohol?
9. Make a chart that shows four classes of drugs, their effects, and some examples.
10. **Your World** You have just caught a ball. Describe the pathway of messages through the nervous system that made this possible.

Practice, practice, practice makes perfect!

Show What You Know

What is the nervous system?

Observe and Collect Data

1. Lie down on the paper and have your partner draw an outline of your body on the paper.
2. Use crayons to draw and label the brain and spinal cord in the outline.
3. Use the colored yarn to show how sensory nerve cells, motor nerve cells, and connecting nerve cells carry messages throughout the body. Use tape to connect the different types of nerve cells. Include nerve cells in the arms and legs.
4. Use yarn to show sensory nerve cells leading from the eyes and ears to the brain.

Draw Conclusions

1. Use your model to show the pathway of messages through the nervous system during a reflex action.
2. Use your model to demonstrate how a sound can cause you to move your legs.
3. How might damage to the spinal cord cause a person to be unable to move his or her legs?

Process Skill
Making models

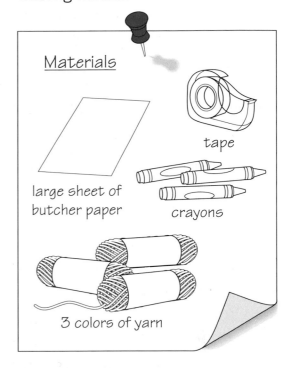

Materials

large sheet of butcher paper

tape

crayons

3 colors of yarn

Chapter 2

Endocrine System

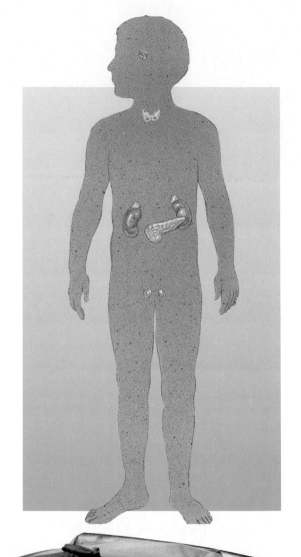

You catch up with some friends between classes. Recently, you have observed that one of your friends has changed. Sometimes he is bursting with energy. Sometimes he is quiet and moody. So many of your friends are changing. And you are noticing and feeling some changes in yourself, too.

Of course, you've been changing since you were born. You've been growing all the time. But now your body is beginning to change in other ways. These changes mark the beginning of puberty (pyo͞o′bər tē), the time when your reproductive organs mature and begin to function. Your growth rate increases during puberty. You outgrow clothing quickly. You have new interests that begin to replace your old ones.

Puberty occurs during the period of life called adolescence (ad′l es′′ns). Adolescence is a bridge between childhood and adulthood. Many of the changes that occur during adolescence are caused by chemicals that begin to be released in the body. These chemicals are released by glands that make up the endocrine system.

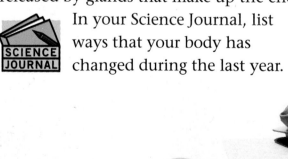

In your Science Journal, list ways that your body has changed during the last year.

Explore Activity

What's important to you?

Process Skills
Collecting data, Interpreting data, Making a graph

Observe and Collect Data

1. Use the following attitude survey to determine some of your interests and concerns. Decide how much you value each trait.

My Interests and Concerns

Trait	Very Important	Somewhat Important	Not Important
Athletic ability			
Artistic ability			
Good health			
Good grades			
Close friends			
Appearance			
Sense of humor			
Popularity			
Leadership			
Independence			
Approval of friends			
Approval of parents			

2. In your Activity Journal, copy this data table and fill it in for yourself.

3. **Predict** what you think will be the most important traits for your friends. Interview them and record their responses.

Share Your Results

Compare your interests and concerns with your friends'. How are they alike or different?

Draw Conclusions

1. What traits do you most want to have?
2. What traits do you value most in your friends?
3. Do you want to have the same traits that you value in your friends?

Apply What You Know

How are your interests and concerns today different from those you had when you were younger?

What activities of the body are controlled by chemicals?

As you eat lunch, you are aware that some of your classmates seem different. They seem to have changed. You also realize that their interests have changed. You and your friends talk about different topics. Some of you are going through some changes associated with adolescence.

Adolescence is a time when your body and your interests change. Many of the physical changes are caused, in part, by the release of chemicals called hormones (hôr′mōnz′).

Hormones are chemical messengers that control many of your body's activities. Hormones control reproduction, your growth and development, and how your body uses nutrients and responds to stress. Often a hormone will affect a specific organ or group of cells. But some hormones affect many organs and cells.

Most hormones are released by organs called glands. Glands are located throughout your body. Certain glands release hormones directly into the blood. These are called endocrine glands. Other glands deliver chemicals through tubes called ducts. Your oil glands deliver oil to your skin through ducts. The oil glands are not endocrine glands.

How have your tastes in clothing, movies, and music changed as you have grown older? Look around your home for evidence of such changes. For example, is there music that you once liked, but now seldom listen to? Also, find out how your tastes in these areas are similar to and different from those of your parents. Record your findings in your Science Journal.

BACK HOME

◄ Your endocrine system consists of glands that release substances into your blood. These substances have an effect on your behavior, emotions, and personality.

Remember, endocrine glands release hormones directly into the blood. Because endocrine glands don't have ducts, they are sometimes called "ductless glands."

Endocrine glands and hormones make up your endocrine system. Like the nervous system, the **endocrine** (en´dō krin´) **system** is one of the body's control and communications systems. Many body functions are carefully monitored by your endocrine system. This system even affects how tall you are and how fast you grow.

Some endocrine glands, such as the parathyroid (par´ə thī´roid´) glands, release only one hormone. This hormone helps regulate the amount of calcium in your blood. You need calcium for the growth of bones and for other body functions. Other endocrine glands release many hormones. For instance, the adrenal (ə drē´nəl) glands release more than thirty different hormones. The adrenal hormones help your body respond to stress and illness.

Some glands began making and releasing hormones in your body before you were born. During adolescence, the production of certain hormones increases. Many of them are responsible for the changes that happen as you become a young adult.

What are the functions of endocrine glands?

Recall that the nervous system regulates body activities through nerve impulses that travel along nerve cells. The endocrine system regulates body activities by releasing hormones into the blood. The blood carries the hormones to the organs and tissues.

The **pancreas** (pan´krē əs) makes and releases a hormone called insulin (in´se lin). Insulin causes the cells of the body to absorb sugar from the blood. This sugar is used by the cells to obtain energy.

The **adrenal glands** make adrenaline (ə dren´ə lin´). This hormone increases the heart rate and breathing rate, which prepares the body to react to dangers and emergencies. The adrenal glands also produce and release hormones that help the body to fight stressful conditions, such as disease and tiredness.

The **ovaries** (ō´və rēz), the reproductive organs in females, produce egg cells. The ovaries also produce female sex hormones.

The **pituitary** (pi tōō´ə ter´ē) **gland** is located near the base of the brain. This small gland releases many hormones. One is the growth hormone. The pituitary is called the "master gland" because some of its hormones control the activity of other endocrine glands.

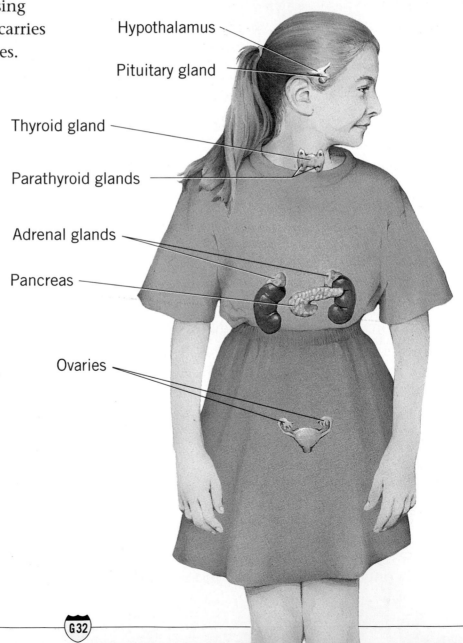

Hypothalamus

Pituitary gland

Thyroid gland

Parathyroid glands

Adrenal glands

Pancreas

Ovaries

The **hypothalamus** (hī´pō thal´ə məs) contains both nerve cells and endocrine tissue. The hypothalamus controls the production and release of pituitary hormones. In some cases, nerve impulses from the brain stimulate the hypothalamus to produce the hormones that affect the pituitary gland. In this way the hypothalamus acts as a link between the nervous and endocrine systems.

Hypothalamus

Pituitary gland

Thyroid gland

Parathyroid glands

Adrenal glands

Pancreas

Testes

The **thyroid** (thī´roid) **gland** produces a hormone that controls how fast energy is released from sugar in cells. This hormone also works with growth hormones to control the growth of organs and tissues.

A hormone from the **parathyroid glands** helps to regulate the amount of calcium in the blood and bones. Calcium is needed for the growth of bones.

The **testes** (tes´tēz), the reproductive organs in males, produce sperm cells. The testes also produce male sex hormones.

How are you doing?

1. Why is the pituitary gland considered the master gland of the endocrine system?
2. How does your hypothalamus link your central nervous system with your endocrine system?
3. **Think** Compare and contrast how your nervous and endocrine systems send messages to various parts of your body.
4. **Think** Producing too much or too little of certain hormones might affect your energy level. Explain how.

How do the endocrine glands affect you during adolescence?

Getting pimples is a sign that your body is changing. That change is associated with adolescence. Adolescence begins when your pituitary gland signals your reproductive endocrine glands to produce sex hormones.

During adolescence, the increase in production of sex hormones causes physical changes. Sex hormones affect the growth of the body. These physical changes are part of the process of growing into an adult.

In females, egg cells in the ovaries begin to mature and be released about every month. In addition, breasts begin to develop. In males, the production of sperm cells begins in the testes. In addition, muscles increase in size and facial hair begins to grow.

Adolescence can be a difficult time, raising concerns about changing bodies. One concern is pimples, or acne (ak´ne). Acne usually appears on the face, chest, and upper back.

Acne occurs because the pituitary gland releases a hormone that signals your oil glands to produce more oil. The excess oil blocks the pores in the skin, and bacteria grow in the blocked pores.

You can help control acne by washing your skin with warm water and soap several times a day. You can also try acne medicine, which can be found in drugstores.

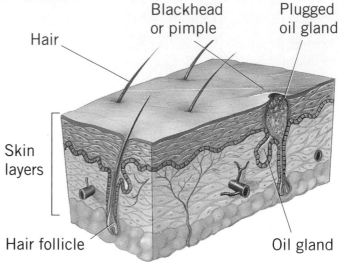

▲ There are oil glands in the skin. They open into follicles, which are small cavities from which hair grows. Oil keeps hair and skin from drying out.

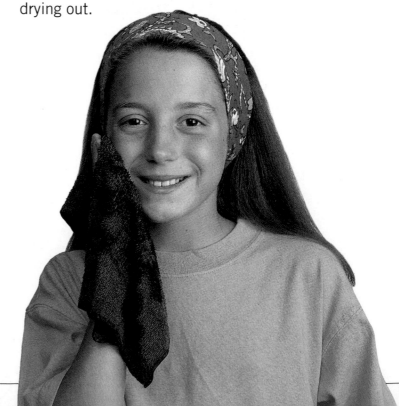

Coming of Age

Recall that adolescence is seen as the period of change from childhood to adulthood. Teenagers have greater independence than younger children. They begin making more of more of their own choices. Socializing with the opposite sex becomes more common. Adolescents share certain interests, such as music and clothing styles.

In some cases, more formal ceremonies mark the "coming of age." In some religions, a ceremony indicates that the young person now assumes responsibility for his or her religious life.

Adolescents of some cultures must show that they are ready to be accepted as adults. There may be a test of skills that an adult should have. Such a ceremonial test is an important part of being accepted by the society.

Some American Indian girls celebrate this period of change. A shaman, or spiritual leader, conducts a ceremony. The shaman gives her instructions about the responsibilities of adulthood. An eagle feather is put into her hair to show her new status. Then there is a great feast for everyone.

The bar mitzvah ceremony is for Jewish boys and the bat mitzvah is for Jewish girls. These ceremonies are a formal recognition and celebration of new responsibilities associated with young adulthood.

Adolescents in many cultures undergo rites of passage to show that they are ready to become adults.

What can happen when endocrine glands don't function properly?

One of your friends has an endocrine disorder called diabetes (dī´ə bēt´ēz´). With diabetes, the pancreas does not produce enough of the hormone insulin. Sugar stays in the blood instead of entering cells. Without sugar, cells do not get enough energy and a person feels weak. So much sugar builds up in the blood that the kidneys begin to excrete it in the urine.

Diabetes is serious, yet it can be treated. Some people control diabetes by staying on a special diet. Others, like your friend, have insulin injections each day. This insulin takes the place of insulin that the pancreas doesn't make.

The table below lists various endocrine disorders and describes their effects on the body. One endocrine disorder occurs when the thyroid gland doesn't produce enough of its hormone. As a result, the release of

▲ This digital tester allows people with diabetes to check their blood sugar level. Some individuals with diabetes maintain their blood sugar level by eating the right foods. Others take insulin and watch their diet. People with diabetes can lead normal lives.

Gland	Disorder	Description
Pancreas	Diabetes	Cells unable to use sugar properly
Pituitary	Dwarfism	Below-normal growth
Pituitary	Gigantism	Above-normal growth
Thyroid	Goiter	Enlarged thyroid and neck
Thyroid	Hyperactivity	Weight loss and nervousness
Thyroid	Hypothyroidism	Tiredness, sensitivity to cold

energy from sugar is slowed. People with this disorder are usually tired and they are sensitive to cold temperatures. All body activities are slowed. One way this condition can be treated is with medicine containing the thyroid hormone.

The thyroid needs iodine to function properly. If a person does not have enough iodine in their diet, the thyroid won't make enough of its hormone. Body activities are slowed, and the thyroid gland becomes swollen. This condition is called a goiter.

Sometimes the thyroid gland makes too much of its hormone. In this case, a person becomes overactive, nervous, and sensitive to heat. This disorder can be treated by taking medication. Sometimes, part of the thyroid gland has to be removed or destroyed.

As might be expected, too little or too much growth hormone from the pituitary gland can affect how tall a person will grow. It is now possible to treat young people whose pituitary glands make too little growth hormone.

Be a Scientist

What is a simple test for detecting diabetes?

1. A person with untreated diabetes excretes sugar in his or her urine. A test can diagnose diabetes. Imagine that five cups contain urine from five patients. Use Tes-tape® to find the individual who is likely to be diabetic.

2. Which cup contained "urine" from a person with diabetes? Why might this person excrete sugar in urine?

How are you doing?

1. What endocrine gland triggers changes during adolescence?
2. What is diabetes, and how is it treated?
3. **Think** When you eat too much sugar, you may at first feel energetic, but then you may feel tired. Explain the role of insulin in this reaction.
4. **Think** A person with an overactive thyroid might have an increased appetite. However, that person loses weight. Using what you know, explain the weight loss.

The Summer of the Swans

by Betsy Byars

*This is an excerpt from a book in which
Charlie, who has a mental disability, is missing. His sister Sara and her friend
Mary are looking for him.*

(Sara said,) ". . .
You're slowing me up on this search."

"Well, if I'm slowing you up so much, then maybe I'll just go on home."

"That suits me fine."

They looked at each other without speaking. Between them the radio began announcing: "Volunteers are needed in the Cass area in the search for young Charlie Godfrey, who disappeared from his home sometime during the night. A search of the Cheat woods will begin at three o'clock this afternoon."

Mary said, "Oh, I'll keep looking. I'll try to walk faster."

Sara shrugged, turned, and started walking up the hill, followed by Mary. They came to the old fence that once separated the pasture from the woods. Sara walked slowly beside the fence. "Charlie!" she called.

"Would he come if he heard you, do you think?"

Sara nodded. "But if they get a hundred people out there clomping through the woods and hollering, he's not going to come. He'll be too scared. I know him."

"I don't see how you can be so sure he came up this way."

"I just know. There's something about me that makes me understand Charlie. It's like I know how he feels about things. Like sometimes I'll be walking down the street and I'll pass the jeweler's and I'll think that if Charlie were here he would want to stand right there and look at those watches all afternoon and I know right where he'd stand and how he'd put his hands up on the glass and how his face would look. And yesterday I knew he was going to love the swans so much that he wasn't ever going to want to leave. I know how he feels."

"You just think you do."

"No. I *know*. I was thinking about the sky one night and I was looking up at the stars and I was thinking about how the sky goes on and on forever, and I couldn't understand it no matter how long I thought, and finally I got kind of nauseated and right then I started thinking, Well, this is how Charlie feels about some things. . ."

Think About Your Reading
1. How do you think someone would feel if a sibling were lost? List five adjectives to describe the feelings.
2. Write a few sentences that summarize how Sara thinks it feels to be Charlie.

Collecting data Find out the procedures in your community for finding lost children. Make a chart to show all the actions taken.

Where to Read More
Jill Krementz, *How It Feels to Fight for Your Life* (Little, Brown and Company, 1989)
Fourteen kids tell what it's like to cope with diseases such as diabetes, cancer, and epilepsy.

Looking Back

Words and Concepts

Complete the following statements.

1. Endocrine glands release hormones directly into the _____.

2. The rate at which energy is released from sugars is controlled by a hormone from the _____ gland.

3. During periods of danger or excitement, the heart rate and breathing rate may increase due to the release of the hormone _____.

4. The blocking of pores by excess oil produced in the skin contributes to the condition called _____.

5. A hormone disorder that involves too little insulin is _____.

6. Hormones from the _____ gland regulate the activity of many other endocrine glands.

Applied Thinking Skills

Answer the following questions. You can use words, drawings, and diagrams in your answers.

7. During times of stress, the hypothalamus links the nervous and endocrine systems. Explain how this happens. Explain the roles of the other endocrine glands that may be involved in a response to stress.

8. The pituitary gland releases a hormone that causes the thyroid gland to make and release hormones when there is a low level of thyroid hormone in the blood. A low level of thyroid hormone in the blood is sensed by the hypothalamus, not by the pituitary gland. Make a drawing that shows how these three glands work together to regulate the amount of thyroid hormone in the blood.

9. Identify endocrine glands that are associated with the changes that occur during adolescence. Describe their roles.

10. **Your World** Why do you think your classmates are changing at different rates?

Show What You Know

What is the endocrine system?

Observe and Collect Data

1. Work in pairs. One partner lies on the butcher paper while the other partner traces the outlines of the body.
2. Use construction paper to make life-size cutouts of the endocrine glands. Color the models. Use the following size comparisons for your cutouts: The pituitary gland is about the size of a large pea; the thyroid is about the size of a baseball card; the parathyroids are about the size of a small pea; the adrenals are each the size of a domino; and the pancreas is about the size of a hot dog.
3. Glue the glands into the correct locations.
4. Outside of the body outline, list the names and functions of all the endocrine glands.
5. Use yarn to connect each gland to its name and function.

Draw Conclusions

1. How are the glands that make up the endocrine system similar?
2. How do endocrine hormones reach the organs that they affect?
3. Why are endocrine glands and the hormones they produce considered a system?

Process Skill
Making models

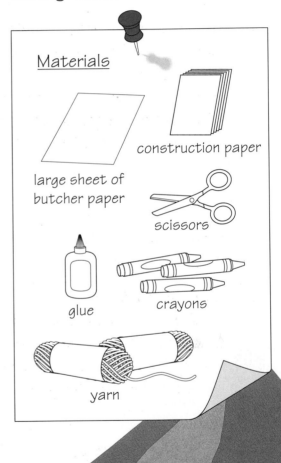

Materials

large sheet of butcher paper

construction paper

scissors

glue

crayons

yarn

Staying Healthy

You are feeling great today, so you and a few friends decide to see a movie. Just two weeks ago, you couldn't have gone to a movie. You had a fever and a sore throat. The doctor said that you had strep throat. You had heard of strep—it's a kind of bacterium.

The doctor gave you an antibiotic (an´tī bī ät´ik) to take for ten days. An antibiotic is a medicine that fights a bacterial infection. The medicine worked. The sore throat was gone in a few days, and the fever disappeared even sooner. When you went back to the doctor for a checkup, the throat infection was gone. So here you are, healthy, waiting to get tickets.

You wonder where, or how, you got sick. Maybe you caught the infection in a crowded place such as this theater. You wonder how medicines, such as antibiotics, help make you better.

 Some people don't get sick as often as others. But we all get sick sometimes because we are exposed to disease-causing organisms every day. In your Science Journal, describe the times you were sick during the past year. Also write what you know about the cause of each sickness and how it was treated. Do you seem to get some kinds of illnesses more often than others? If so, what factors might be involved?

On our way to see a Saturday movie

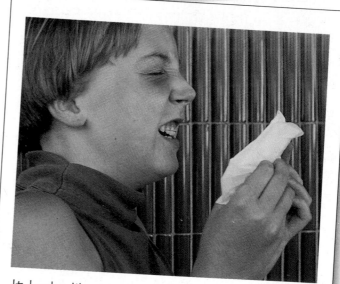
It looks like she still has a cold!

How are germs spread?

Process Skills

Observing, Making models, Inferring

Materials

flour

water

soap

container

4 sheets of dark construction paper

paper towels

hand lens

Observe and Collect Data

1. Work in groups of four. Number four sheets of dark construction paper and draw a large circle in the middle of each sheet. Pour some flour into a container.

2. The first student dusts one hand with flour and touches sheet 1 in the middle of the circle. The second student flattens his or her hand against the middle of sheet 1 and then touches sheet 2.

3. The third student touches sheet 2 and then touches sheet 3.

4. The fourth student touches sheet 1, then washes and dries his or her hands. Now he or she touches sheet 4.

5. Observe the four sheets of paper. Then use the hand lens to observe them again.

Share Your Results

Look at the papers of several other groups after they have completed the activity. How do their results compare with your results?

Draw Conclusions

1. Suppose that the flour in this activity represents germs that cause disease, and the circle on the construction paper represents a table top that many people often touch. What has happened as a result of your contact with this table top?
2. Was there any evidence of germs on the fourth piece of paper?
3. How did washing your hands affect passing on the "germs"?

Apply What You Know

Why is it a good practice to wash clothing and bed linens used by someone who has a disease caused by germs?

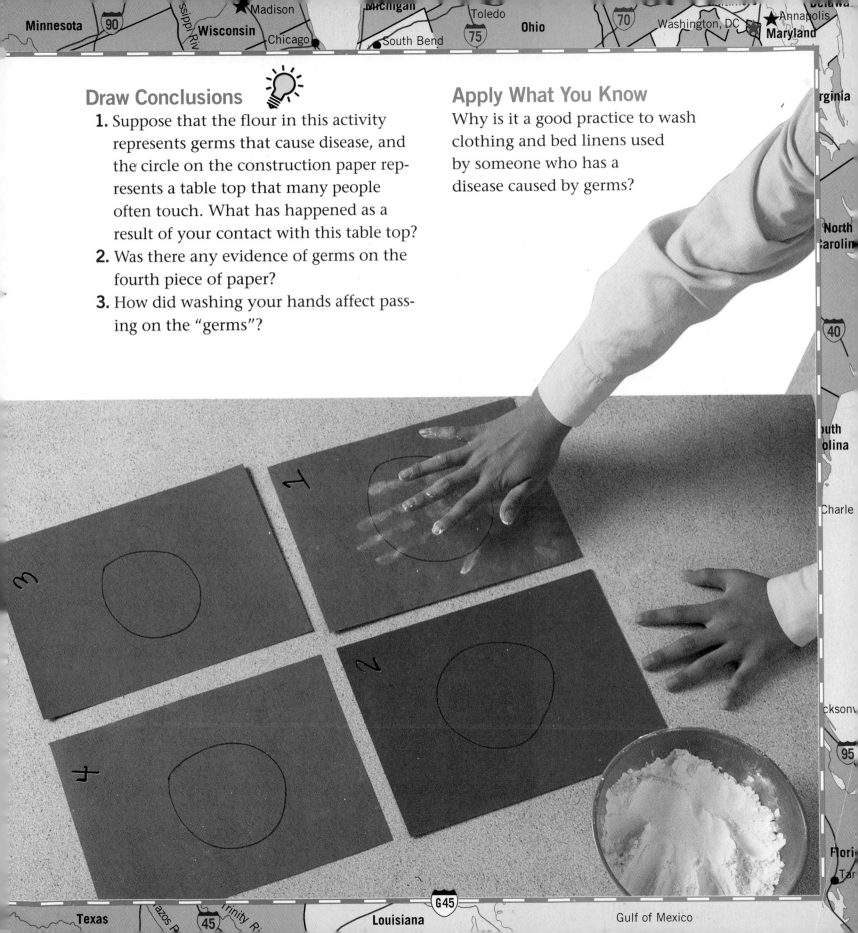

What are infectious diseases?

Be a Scientist

What makes a fungus grow?

1. To understand how a fungus grows, moisten a small piece of bread. Place the moist bread inside a plastic bag. Leave the bag open for about an hour. Make sure that the bread stays moist.

2. Put the plastic bag in a dark place. Check it every day and record your observations in your Activity Journal.

3. Where did the mold come from? What conditions are necessary for the bread mold to grow? Bread mold and athlete's foot fungus are very similar. What conditions might make athlete's foot fungus get worse? How might you catch this fungus?

The movie theater is crowded. Some people seem to have colds. You've just had a sore throat and fever, and you don't want to get sick again. You know that certain diseases are passed from person to person. But exactly what gets passed? And how is it passed?

Diseases caused by viruses or bacteria that invade the body are called infectious diseases. The common cold, flu, measles, and strep throat are infectious diseases.

Many infectious diseases are caused by viruses. Viruses are particles made up of protein and genes. Other infectious diseases are caused by bacteria and protists. Bacteria are simple, one-celled organisms that are found in all environments. Many protists are one-

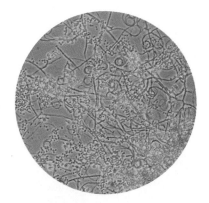

▲ Some fungi, such as the fungus that causes athlete's foot, feed on living things.

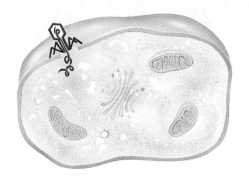

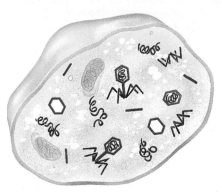

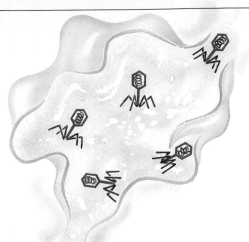

1 Virus enters living cell.

2 Virus multiplies inside cell.

3 Virus leaves body cell when it bursts.

celled organisms also. We refer to disease-causing viruses, bacteria, and protists as germs.

Viruses cause disease by invading cells in your body. Once inside the cells, the viruses reproduce. Eventually, the cells release more viruses that invade more cells.

Bacteria cause disease by releasing toxins or poisons. These toxins kill body cells. Protists cause disease by releasing toxins or by invading cells. Malaria is caused by a protist that invades and destroys red blood cells. It is spread by mosquitoes. When a mosquito bites a person with malaria, some of the protists enter the mosquito. When the mosquito bites another person, the protists enter that person's blood.

Viruses, bacteria, and protists can be spread when a person with a cold sneezes into the air. Another person may breathe in a virus and get a cold.

▲ Viruses can cause diseases.

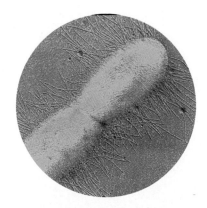

▲ Bacteria are both helpful and harmful. Harmful bacteria produce toxins, which can cause sickness.

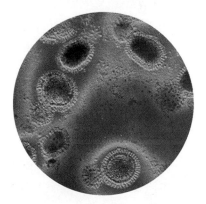

▲ Many protists are one-celled organisms.

What is your body's defense system?

With your world teeming with germs, why aren't you sick more often? It is because your body has defenses.

This system of defense is your **immune system.** The immune system includes chemicals called antibodies (an´ti bäd´ēz). They are special proteins that help kill invading microbes. Microbes are organisms such as fungi, bacteria, and viruses. They are also called germs.

Your immune system includes white blood cells too. One type of white blood cell eats bacteria and viruses. Other white blood cells, called T cells, help make antibodies.

When an invader enters your body, the microbe-eating white blood cells are the first to arrive on the scene. The T cells can recognize the shape of a molecule on the invading cell. This molecule is called an antigen (an´tə jən) and it makes the invading cell different from other types of cells. It triggers the immune system to make antibodies.

The T cells take the information about the invader's antigen back to the lymph nodes (limf nōdz). The lymph nodes are part of your immune system. You have lymph nodes in your neck, under your arms, and in other parts of your body.

1 Abnormal cell identified.

2 Helper T cell assists killer T cells to multiply.

3 Killer T cell attaches to abnormal cell.

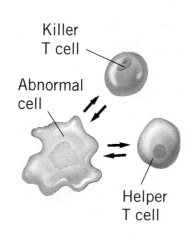

Killer T cell

Abnormal cell

Helper T cell

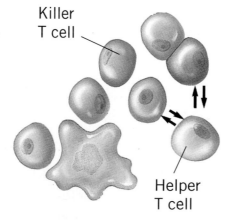

Killer T cell

Helper T cell

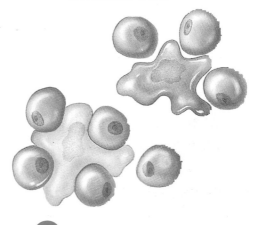

4 Abnormal cell destroyed.

In the lymph nodes there is a third type of white blood cell called a B cell. B cells use information from the T cells about the invader's antigen. Then the B cells make antibodies that can recognize the invader's antigen. Both B and T cells make memory cells that remember the shape of the antigen in case the invader attacks again.

Sometimes your immune system can kill invading microbes before they make you sick. At other times, you become ill until your immune system can make enough antibodies to kill the microbes.

Your immune system sometimes cannot overcome all infections. That's why doctors have developed vaccines (vak sēnz´) that help prevent some diseases. Many vaccines are made from killed or weakened microbes.

When you get a vaccination, a small amount of the dead or weakened virus or bacteria is injected. This small amount won't make you sick. Instead, it tricks your immune system into going into action. Your body makes antibodies against the weakened or dead microbes. It also makes memory cells. If you ever come into contact with the real microbes, your body is ready to fight the infection before it can make you ill.

Salk and Sabin

In 1916, a mysterious illness caused children to suffer from fevers, chills, sore throats, and vomiting. Some developed paralysis (pə ral´ə sis), a condition in which some muscles cannot move. Some children died.

The mysterious disease was called polio, an infectious disease of the central nervous system. It is caused by a virus that attacks the spinal cord and brain.

In 1953, Dr. Jonas Salk announced the development of an injectable polio vaccine. He had found a way to weaken the polio virus so that it would trigger the production of antibodies without causing the disease. Dr. Albert Sabin later developed a polio vaccine.

How can diseases affect the body's defenses?

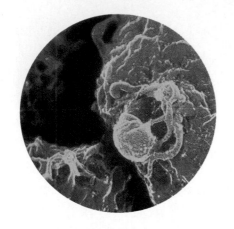

▲ HIV, the virus that causes AIDS, attacks the T cells. The T cells help coordinate the immune system's response to infection.

Today, a doctor who studies the immune system is visiting your class to talk about AIDS. She tells you, "AIDS stands for Acquired Immune Deficiency Syndrome. It is a viral disease of the immune system. AIDS is caused by a virus called the Human Immuno-deficiency Virus, or HIV.

"HIV attacks a type of T cell called a helper T cell," the doctor says. "Some people with AIDS have almost no helper T cells in their blood. Remember, the T cells help other cells in the immune system do their jobs. HIV also attacks other parts of the immune system."

Most people with HIV infection will develop AIDS. And people with AIDS develop many infections. These

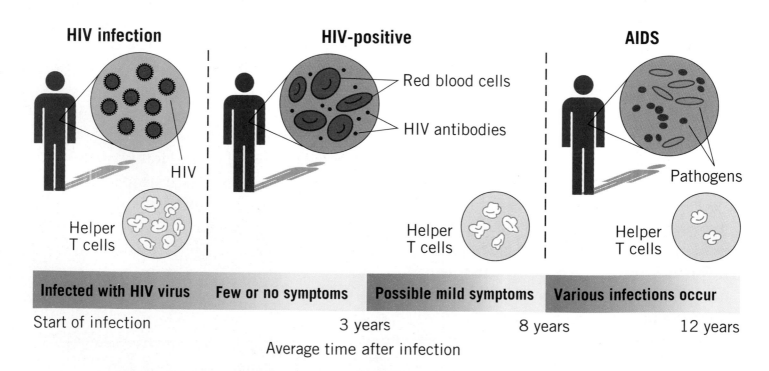

infections are called "opportunistic" infections because they attack when the defense system is weak. People with AIDS often die from infections, such as pneumonia, that healthy individuals might survive.

"When HIV enters the body, it hides inside normal cells," says the doctor. "This is why people can have HIV for years without showing symptoms of AIDS. They can spread HIV to other people without knowing it."

The doctor goes on to say that the only way a person can get HIV is through the exchange of infected body fluids. Some people have gotten HIV infection through blood transfusions. But since 1985, donated blood has been tested for HIV, thus making the blood supply much safer.

"You cannot get AIDS by giving blood," the doctor says. "You also cannot get AIDS by hugging, kissing, shaking hands, using public toilets, or sharing food or utensils."

The doctor points out that there is no cure for HIV or AIDS. At present, scientists are working on a vaccine against HIV.

▲ The AIDS quilt is a memorial to people who have died from AIDS. It is now larger than a football field. Unfortunately, names are still being added to the quilt.

How are you doing?

1. How does the immune system fight disease?
2. How do vaccines help prevent disease?
3. **Think** How might an immune system without T cells respond to the flu virus?
4. **Think** Researchers have developed drugs that block the actions of bacteria. But some bacteria become resistant to drugs. How might the virus or bacteria become resistant to a drug?

What are noninfectious diseases?

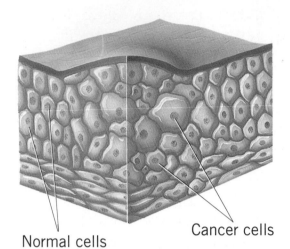

Normal cells

Cancer cells

▲ Cancer cells are runaway cells. They divide more often than normal cells. Eventually they crowd out healthy cells.

You and your friends are going swimming. But first, one friend needs to buy some sunscreen.

"What do you need that for?" you ask.

"To keep from getting a sunburn and maybe skin cancer," your friend answers.

"You're not going to catch cancer from anyone at the pool," you say.

"Of course not. You can't catch cancer from another person. But you can get skin cancer from too much exposure to the sun. This lotion contains a sunscreen."

Many diseases, like cancer, cannot be passed from person to person. These types of diseases are noninfectious diseases.

Your friend tells you that cancer is the uncontrolled growth of cells. Some cancer cells travel through the blood and begin new cancer sites in other parts of the body. If not treated, cancer is usually fatal.

There are many different types of cancer. Lung cancer is one of the most common cancers. Most lung cancer is caused from smoking cigarettes.

Many factors may contribute to causing cancer. Some people get cancer from exposure to chemicals or radiation. People with weakened immune systems may get certain types of cancers.

Ask an adult what they think are some warning signs of cancer. Compare your answers to your classmates' answers. How many did your class come up with?

BACK HOME

Many cancers can be prevented. About 90 percent of all skin cancers can be avoided if people use sunscreen or stay out of direct sunlight. Cancers caused by tobacco use can be prevented by avoiding tobacco.

Doctors can successfully treat some cancers. But there is a better chance for a cure if the cancer is detected early. That is why everyone should visit their doctor regularly for a checkup.

Sickle-cell disease is another type of non-infectious disease. Sickle-cell disease is a painful disease that can be fatal.

People with sickle-cell disease inherit two genes that cause the red cells to become sickle- or crescent-shaped. The disease is most common among people of African ancestry. People who inherit one gene for sickle-cell disease and one gene for normal red blood cells do not get the disease. But these people can pass the sickle-cell gene on to their children.

There is no cure for sickle-cell disease. However, in 1993 researchers discovered a treatment for the disease. The Food and Drug Administration has not yet approved the drug, but scientists report that it has shown promising results in patients who tested the treatment.

Be a Scientist

How are sunscreens rated?

Read sunscreen labels to find out how much protection they give against ultraviolet rays. In your Activity Journal, make a chart that shows ratings and how much protection each product gives. Then compare the protection ratings.

How are sunscreens rated for ultraviolet protection? Which level of protection would you suggest for someone who is exposed to the sun almost every day?

▲ Sickle-cell disease is an inherited disorder that causes the red blood cells to become sickle-shaped instead of round. Sickled cells carry less oxygen than normal cells. They also get clogged in small veins.

How do environmental conditions cause diseases?

Can air, water, or food in your environment make you sick? It depends on what's in your environment.

Many people get water from underground wells or reservoirs. Both sources are usually safe. However, there can be problems with some water supplies. For example, pollutants can get into underground water systems, making the water unsafe to drink.

Lead is a poisonous metal that can pollute water. Some older homes have lead pipes. Lead from the pipes dissolves in water, especially if the water stands in the pipes. Water can be tested for lead content. If lead is present, run the water before using it. Always use cold tap water for cooking because hot water carries more lead than cold water.

▲ Your air might not be as clean as you think. Be careful about exercising outdoors if you live in an area with a lot of air pollution.

▲ People who live with smokers, but don't smoke themselves, have a greater chance of getting lung cancer than people who live with nonsmokers.

YOU CAN HELP

Exhaust from cars is the main cause of smog in most cities. Using public transportation or riding a bicycle rather than riding in a car can cut down on pollution.

Lead paint also can pose health risks. If this kind of paint chips, young children may eat the chips or inhale dust from the paint. In fact, anyone can inhale the dust. Lead attacks the central nervous system and can cause serious health problems. Lead paint should be removed only by professionals.

There are many other things in your environment that can make you sick. Some farmers use synthetic pesticides and fertilizers which can pollute the environment. Some of the toxins might remain on the crops. Thoroughly wash or peel fruit and vegetables before you eat them.

Did you know that you can get lung cancer associated with cigarette smoking even if you don't smoke? Studies show that passive smoking is potentially dangerous. Passive smoking is inhaling the fumes from another person's cigarette. Also, the children of smokers have a greater chance of suffering from respiratory illnesses.

Cigarette smoke is not the only source of indoor air pollution. Chemical fumes can escape from building materials, carpets, and draperies. Spray deodorants, hair sprays, cleaners, varnishes, paints, and insecticides also are sources of indoor air pollution.

A Polluted City

Has your community ever had a smog alert? Some city governments issue smog alerts when there is so much pollution in the air that it is unsafe to exercise outdoors.

Smog can irritate your eyes and make you feel short of breath. Elderly people, young children, and people with health problems should be very careful when there is heavy smog.

Most smog in cities comes from car exhaust. Smog also comes from industrial plants such as steel mills, refineries, and utility companies.

Ozone, a form of oxygen, is found in the upper atmosphere. When it is produced close to the ground, it contributes to pollution. Carbon monoxide, a poisonous gas, and other chemicals also add to pollution.

What is a healthful lifestyle?

▲ Exercise is good for your body and your mind. A healthful lifestyle includes exercise at least three times a week.

Every day you make choices. Many of these choices can influence your health. Eating too many fatty foods contributes to heart disease and cancer. Doctors recommend that you limit the amount of fat in your diet. They also recommend that you eat plenty of grains, fruits, and vegetables. By choosing wisely, you can enjoy a variety of foods that contribute to good health.

In the past, many people lit a cigarette after dinner. But now many of them have given up smoking. They chose to do this for their health as well as the health of their families. You will be deciding whether to smoke in the future. What will you choose?

Exercise is another way to choose good health. The heart muscle, in particular, is helped by exercise.

Stress is tension or nervousness that can result from worrying about something. Stress can make you feel uncomfortable. It might affect your health. It can contribute to heart disease or stomach problems. Some stress symptoms are a rapid heartbeat, shallow

◄ You can choose good health by eating a variety of foods. Eat plenty of vegetables, fruits, and grains, and cut down on fat.

Public-Health Nurse

Public-health nurses are concerned with the health of communities or families. They give instruction on health topics, disease prevention, nutrition, and child-care. They may study the spread of diseases or plan vaccination or education programs to stop disease.

❝ My name is Eunice Rojas and I am a public-health nurse. I visit families who have health problems and find them appropriate care. Sometimes I visit patients in their homes. Also, I may teach prenatal classes or AIDS prevention to groups who have different health concerns.

"Public-health nurses have completed four years of college. Some attend school longer for advanced degrees. Public-health nursing assistants have completed college courses and have on-the-job training.

"Public-health nurses help communities all over the world. During college, I did volunteer work in Central America. This experience increased my interest in disease prevention and awareness of health problems. I enjoy teaching and learning from the different cultures I meet.❞

breathing, sweaty palms, nausea, diarrhea, and muscle tightness.

When you experience stress, it sometimes helps to talk with someone. You can also try taking a few deep breaths to relax.

Be careful of what you eat when under stress, because some foods can make the symptoms worse. Foods and beverages that are high in sugar or caffeine can make you feel more nervous.

How are you doing?

1. What is cancer?
2. Name three sources of indoor pollution.
3. **Think** How might living in a house with a smoker affect a nonsmoker's health? Explain your reasoning.
4. **Think** Some of the symptoms of sickle-cell disease are weakness, shortness of breath, and pain in the limbs. Explain what causes these symptoms.

Looking Back

Words and Concepts

Choose the answer that best completes the sentence.

1. Infectious diseases may be caused by
   _____.
   a. viruses   c. protists
   b. bacteria   d. all of the above

2. A preparation that contains weakened or dead disease agents and provides immunity to a disease is called a(n) _____.
   a. vaccine   c. antibiotic
   b. B cell   d. antigen

3. In the immune system, cells that make antibodies are called _____.
   a. antigens   c. Q cells
   b. B cells   d. anticells

4. The virus that causes AIDS is known to attack _____.
   a. the lungs   c. B cells
   b. memory cells   d. the immune system

5. A disease that involves the uncontrolled growth of cells is _____.
   a. AIDS   c. cancer
   b. malaria   d. heart disease

6. Lead in paint or water can damage
   _____.
   a. blood vessels that supply the heart muscle
   b. memory cells in the immune system
   c. lung tissue
   d. the central nervous system

Applied Thinking Skills

Answer the following questions. You can use words, drawings, and diagrams in your answers.

7. Explain the difference between a vaccine and an antibiotic.
8. Make a sketch that shows how the immune system responds to infection.
9. What is an infectious disease? Give at least two examples of an infectious disease and a noninfectious disease.
10. **Your World** Identify some changes that you can make in your life to reduce your chances of developing cancer.

Here we are discussing some choices we can make.

Show What You Know

What do students know about diseases?

Observe and Collect Data

1.  In your Activity Journal, make up a survey form to help find out what students know about diseases. Your form should include questions about the cause of diseases, how they affect the body, the ways these can be transmitted to others, how they are treated, and how they can be prevented.

2. Use your survey form to interview ten students about their knowledge of diseases. Record their answers.

3. Make a data sheet to help evaluate the students' answers. For example, the data sheet might indicate the number of students who know the cause of a certain disease and the number who don't, and so on.

Process Skills
Communicating, Collecting data, Making a graph

Draw Conclusions

1. Make bar graphs of the class data, showing the number of students who were able to answer each question correctly.

2. How would you rate the students' knowledge about diseases in general?

3. Were there some things about diseases that students seemed to know less about than others? Identify these areas.

4. What comments or suggestions would you make concerning education about diseases?

Control Systems

Show what you have learned about the nervous system, the endocrine system, and staying healthy. Work by yourself, with a partner, or in a group. Select one activity.

Sculptor Use clay or some other material to make a model of the brain. The three main parts of the brain should be identifiable. Use library resources to help you make your model as accurate as possible.

Odor Researcher Plan a test to find out if people are able to identify some odors more easily than others. Use a variety of materials in your test and be sure to record your data. Prepare a report based on your data.

Feature Writer Research the history of tobacco and cigarettes. Find out when tobacco smoking became popular and how health findings have affected its popularity. Write a magazine article based on your research.

Psychologist Find out if people identify certain emotions or moods with music. Make a tape that has six or seven different types of music. Play each selection for someone and ask what mood or emotion the selection conveys. Repeat your study with a number of people. Be sure to record your data. Draw conclusions based on your data.

Director Plan a skit that shows how nervous impulses travel from the senses to the central nervous system and then to the muscles. Audition students for parts, and then rehearse and perform the skit.

Health Interviewer Prepare a health survey to find out whether childhood infectious diseases, such as measles, mumps, and chicken pox, are more or less common now than in the past. You must interview at least two groups of people—adults over 50 years of age and youngsters (or parents with youngsters) about your age. Give an oral report to the class about your findings.

Glossary

adrenal gland (ə drē´nəl gland)   An endocrine gland that prepares the body to react to stress. (page G32)

cerebellum (ser´ə bel´əm)   The part of the brain that controls the coordination of the muscles and balance. (page G10)

cerebrum (ser´ə brəm)   The part of the brain that controls thought and voluntary muscular movement.(page G10)

connecting nerve cell (kə nekt´iŋ nərv sel)   A cell that carries impulses from sensory nerve cells to motor nerve cells. (page G13)

endocrine system (en´dō krin´ sis´təm)   A system of glands that produce hormones, which help control the body's functions. The hormones are released directly into the blood. (page G31)

hypothalamus (hī´pō thal´əməs)   An organ that contains both nerve cells and endocrine tissue. It helps regulate the levels of hormones. (page G33)

immune system (im myōōn´ sis´təm)   The cells and glands that fight invading microbes and defend the body against infectious diseases. (page G48)

motor nerve cell (mōt´ər nərv sel)   A nerve cell that carries impulses from the central nervous system to muscles and organs. (page G13)

nervous system (nər´vəs sis´təm)   One of the body's systems for communication and control of the body. (page G6)

ovary (ō´və rē)   An endocrine gland and female reproductive organ. (page G32)

pancreas (pan´krē əs)   An endocrine gland that controls blood-sugar levels through the production of insulin. (page G32)

parathyroid gland (par´ə thī´roid´ gland)   An endocrine gland that regulates the amount of calcium in bones and blood. (page G33)

pituitary gland (pi tōō´ə ter´ē gland)   An endocrine gland that releases growth hormone and triggers the activity of other endocrine glands. (page G32)

sensory nerve cell (sen´sər ē nərv sel)   Nerve cell that carries impulses from sense organs to the central nervous system. (page G13)

testes (tes´tēz´)   Endocrine glands and male reproductive organs. (page G33)

thyroid gland (thī´roid gland)   An endocrine gland that produces a hormone that controls how fast energy is released from sugar in cells. (page G33)

Unit G Index

Boldface numerals denote glossary terms. Italic numerals denote illustrations.

Credits

Photographs

2–3 Ed Elberfeld/Third Coast Stock Source; 11R Will Ryan/The Stock Market; 14LC Renee Lynn; 16 Wardene Weisser/Bruce Coleman Inc.; 18BL Owen Franken/Stock, Boston; 22B Peter Vandermark/Stock, Boston; 35B Stephen Trimble/DRK Photo; 35T Miro Vintoniv/Stock, Boston; 36 B. Daemmrich/The Image Works; 46 London Scientific Films/OSF/Earth Scenes; 47 CNRI/Science Photo Library/Photo Researchers; 50 Bill Longcore/CDC Science Source/Photo Researchers; 51 Alon Reininger/Contact Press Images/The Stock Market; 53 Science Source/Photo Researchers; 54BL W. Van Eick/Third Coast Stock Source; 54T Wayne Eastep/The Stock Market; 55 Daniel S. Brody/Stock, Boston; 56T David Madison; 57 Anne Dowie*; Elliott Smith* 9, 29, 49; GHP Studio* 1, 4BR, 4BL, 6B, 13L, 18BR, 18T, 25–26, 41, 42B, 56B, 59; Ken Karp* 5, 11L, 14C, 19, 22T, 34, 45, 54R; Ken Lax* 40; Tim Davis* 1(insets), 4TR, 7, 10, 14BL, 14R, 14T, 17, 20, 24, 27, 30–31, 42C, 42T, 43, 58

Special thanks to Malcolm X Elementary School, Berkeley, California; Franklin Year-Round School, Oakland, California; Carl B. Munck Elementary School, Oakland, California; Hintil Ku Ka Child Care Center, Oakland, California.

*Photographed expressly for Addison-Wesley Publishing Company, Inc.

Illustrations

Nea Bisek 8T, 23T, 25, 41, 44T
Marilyn Kreiger 13B
Jane McCreary 8C, 13T, 28B, 44B
Laurie O'Keefe 6, 11, 14, 26

Patrice Rossi 12, 34, 47, 48, 52
Scott Snow 38–39
Randy Vergoustraete 60–61
Nina Wallace 50
Cyndie Wooley 32, 33

Text

38–39 Betsy Byars, *The Summer of the Swans* (New York: Viking Penguin, 1970). Copyright ©1970 by Betsy Byars. Used by permission of Viking Penguin, a division of Penguin Books USA Inc.

This land is your land
This land is my land,
From California
to the New York island,
From the redwood forest
to the Gulf Stream waters,
This land was made
for you and me.

USA

Imagine that the school year has ended and you are spending your vacation traveling all across the United States. Along the way, you'll see many parts of the **environment**, all the conditions around us that affect our lives. Where will you go first?

Perhaps, like many vacationers, you will visit Yellowstone National Park. In 1872, President Ulysses S. Grant signed a law that made Yellowstone the first national park. With this law, the United States began the process of preserving its natural treasures.

Your vacation will take you to many parts of the United States, including the Florida Everglades; the Texas highways; and the city of Los Angeles, California. As you visit these places, think about ways people affect the environment. The food we eat, the vehicles we drive, and the products we make help determine how all species will live.

■ Why are our land resources important and how can we keep them healthy?

■ Why are our living species important and how can we protect them?

■ What pollutes our air and water and what can we do to reduce pollution?

THE ENVIRONMENT

Moose populations decreased when Europeans settled North America.

Hazardous wastes need to be collected separately from garbage.

Activities

Features

Chapter 1

Land Resources

Virginia

Kansas

Healthy soil is a treasure that should be protected. ▼

If your vacation travel plans include an airplane trip across the United States, you will see a vast, flat area called the Great Plains. Much of this area looks like the photograph shown here. The land looks like an old-fashioned patchwork quilt, and each block of the "quilt" is a farm field.

The land is one of the United States' greatest resources. Do you like cornflakes or corn muffins? Do you like bread, crackers, or pasta? The corn, wheat, and other grains used to make these foods are grown on the farmland of the Great Plains. Grain grown here is also used to feed the cattle, pigs, and chickens that people eat.

SCIENCE JOURNAL What did you eat for lunch yesterday? In your Science Journal, list and identify foods that came from corn or wheat or from animals that were fed these grains.

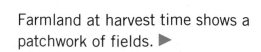

Farmland at harvest time shows a patchwork of fields. ▶

Tilling the soil

Explore Activity

What can you find in soil?

HANDS-ON
ACTIVITY

Process Skills
Predicting, Observing,
Collecting data

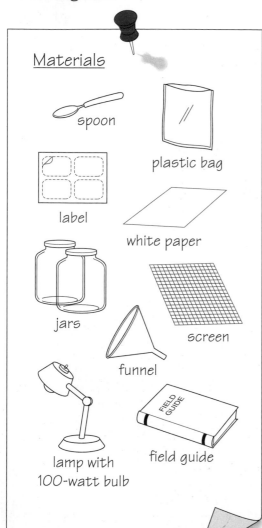

Materials

spoon

plastic bag

label

white paper

jars

screen

funnel

lamp with
100-watt bulb

field guide

FIELD
GUIDE

Observe and Collect Data

1. Collect a soil sample from a square about 3 centimeters on a side and about 5 centimeters deep. Be sure you have permission to dig in that spot.

2. Place the soil sample in the plastic bag. Make a label that tells where you collected the sample, whether the soil was darker on top than at the bottom, whether the soil was dry or damp, and if it was especially hot or cold. Stick the label on the bag.

3. **Predict** three things you expect to find when you examine the soil.

4. [ACTIVITY JOURNAL] In your Activity Journal, record the information you wrote on the label when you collected the soil. Then spread out the soil on the white paper. Check whether the soil is sandy or rocky. Look for earthworms and other larger soil animals. Use a field guide to identify what you find. Examine any plant materials that you find in the soil. Record all of these findings in your Activity Journal.

5. To separate smaller animals from the soil, place the screen over the funnel and the funnel in a jar. Scoop the soil into the funnel while another student shines the light onto the soil. Place the different animals you find in different jars. Use the field guide to identify them.

Share Your Results

Compare your findings with those of another group. How do the organisms in soil communities vary in different places?

Draw Conclusions

1. What role did the light play in separating animals from the soil?

2. How do plant materials and living things interact in the soil community?

Apply What You Know

Do you think that the kinds of organisms found in a soil community will change after a long dry period or a period of heavy rain? Explain your answer.

Why is soil management important?

Many people who live in Kansas and other states in the Great Plains are farmers. These people depend on one of the earth's most important resources—soil. Farmers in Kansas grow wheat, corn, and other grains, but these crops are not the only living things in the soil.

Be a Scientist

How can soils differ?

1. Use a cup or can to fill two containers with potting soil. In the first container, leave the soil loose. In the second container, pack the soil down. Add grass seed to both containers. Add enough water to make the soil damp but not soggy.

2. Place the containers on a sunny windowsill. Spray both plantings with water as needed to keep the top of the soil moist.

3. Observe what happens over two weeks. Record your observations in your Activity Journal. In which container does the grass grow better? Why?

Soil contains plant materials and organisms. It is a complex ecosystem made up of living, once-living, and nonliving things. At least 300 million small invertebrates such as insects and worms may inhabit one hectare (about 2½ acres) of rich soil on the Great Plains.

There are about 70,000 different types of soil in the world. Soil is a renewable resource, but the process of soil formation requires time. It can take 50 to 100 years for a depth of one centimeter of soil to form. Soil can be destroyed in a fraction of that time. Its minerals and organic nutrients can be lost. Depending on local conditions, that soil may never be replaced.

Nutrient depletion (nōō′trē ənt dē plē′shən) is the loss of nutrients and minerals from soil. This occurs as cycles that replace soil nutrients are disrupted. Soil can lose its nutrients in a number of ways. Sometimes nature itself is the cause. But human beings often play a part too. For instance, if the same crops are grown in the

◄ Typical grassland topsoil is rich in nutrients. The subsoil below it provides water and oxygen for deep-rooted plants. Below that is a layer of clay or inorganic minerals.

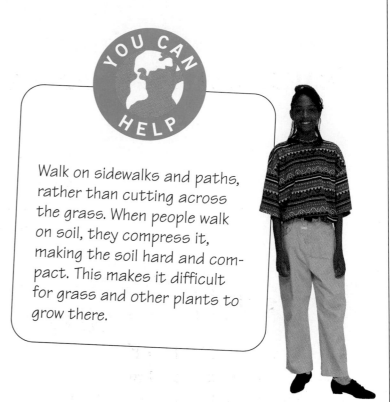

YOU CAN HELP

Walk on sidewalks and paths, rather than cutting across the grass. When people walk on soil, they compress it, making the soil hard and compact. This makes it difficult for grass and other plants to grow there.

same place year after year, the nutrients used by that crop can completely disappear from the soil. Sometimes, to keep growing more and more crops, people add chemical fertilizers. These may help the crops grow but harm the soil and the living things in it. People also sometimes add pesticides—chemicals meant to kill insects and other animals that can harm the crops. But pesticides can also kill animals that help build and enrich soil through natural cycles. In this lesson, you will learn how people are beginning to use new techniques in farming in order to better conserve their soil.

How can we maintain healthy soil?

▲ Spreading liquid manure on farm-land adds nutrients to the soil in forms that plants can easily absorb.

▲ Soy and corn grow in a field con-taining the remains of the previous crop. These remains act as green manure and keep weed growth down.

More and more farmers are now trying to use fewer chemicals and more soil-saving techniques. The use of farming methods that preserve soil is called **regenerative** (ri jen´ər ə tiv) **agriculture.** One new method being tried is **organic** (ôr gan´ik) **farming,** which means farming without the use of chemical fertilizers and pesticides.

Organic farming uses natural fertilizers, such as com-post. Compost is the rotted remains of plant material. It may also contain some manure, or animal waste. On many organic farms, the remains of plants are plowed back into the soil after the harvest. These plants are called green manure. The materials from the plants enrich the soil and help it to hold moisture. They also keep the soil soft and loose, which makes it easier for the roots of new plants to grow in the soil.

Organic farming avoids the use of pesticides by find-ing other ways to kill insects. For example, traps or natural enemies can be used to control insect pests.

Organic farming techniques require a large amount of human effort. On large farms, some of these tech-niques would be very expensive. But because chemicals are expensive, too, some farmers are combining the methods of organic farming with other soil-saving tech-niques.

Regenerative agriculture also includes the practice of crop rotation, which means growing different crops in each row or field each year. Planting the same crops in the same field every year uses up certain nutrients. Since

The Dust Bowl

Before the 1890s, the Great Plains were covered by prairie grasses. The long roots of these grasses held the soil in place. Then farmers removed the prairie grasses and planted crops. These new plants had shallow roots, which could not hold the soil well. After harvest, the plants were removed, and the farmers plowed up the land. Only bare soil covered the land in the months before the next crops were planted.

As long as the land received enough rainfall, little soil was lost due to erosion. During dry years, however, the topsoil became so dry that it could be blown away in the wind. After several years of drought in the 1930s, large amounts of soil were blown away. This erosion destroyed many farms. In some areas, the air was so thick with dust that there was darkness at midday. For many years after this event, people referred to the Great Plains region as the Dust Bowl.

different plants use different nutrients, crop rotation gives the soil time to replace nutrients through natural cycles.

Another technique involves planting seeds in raised ridges. In between the ridges is green manure. This layer of plant matter reduces the amount of weed growth. This, in turn, reduces the number of times a farmer must drive a tractor through the field to dig up weeds, a practice that causes the soil to become hard and compacted.

How are you doing?

1. What causes nutrient depletion?
2. How is organic farming different from other kinds of farming?
3. **Think** In some areas, farmers burn the remains of crops in the fields, instead of plowing them under. Why might this be a good idea? What are some problems with this practice?
4. **Think** How does planting different crops each year in the same field decrease soil damage?

Why are forests important?

Next, your summer trip takes you to Shenandoah National Park in Virginia. The park includes a river valley and tree-covered hills and mountains. You might think this forest and others like it are important because of their value as recreation areas. But there are more important reasons that we should ensure that forests continue to thrive.

The forests of the world help maintain the fertility of the soil and protect it from erosion. Tree roots form a weblike pattern that holds soil in place and helps prevent rainwater from washing the soil away. Forests also provide a home for many animals and plants. For instance, trees and other plants provide food and shelter to the animals that live there. Forests also help supply the oxygen you breathe and even have an effect on climate, not just locally, but to some extent around the world. These are the "natural" reasons that we need forests.

In addition, many forests are used as sources of products that people need. Paper, lumber, rubber, and turpentine are some of the many products of forests. In the United States, wood is mostly used for building materials and paper, but in some parts of the world, wood is the main energy source.

If too many trees in a forest are removed, wildlife habitat is lost.

A Tropical Rain Forest

The earth's tropical rain forests are an important resource. These forests are home to 50 to 80 percent of species of living things on the earth. Tropical rain forests also play a key role in regulating the earth's climate. They absorb carbon dioxide and release oxygen. In this way, the tropical rain forests help maintain a world climate that is cool enough for people and other living things.

 Unfortunately, people have logged rain forests so quickly that much of this resource has been destroyed. Millions of hectares of tropical rain forest have already been cut down or burned for farms and cattle ranches. Fortunately, many people are working hard to create sections of rain forest called reserves, where the trees may not be completely removed. Rain forest products such as rubber and nuts are harvested in a way that allows people to earn a living while keeping native species alive. By buying these products, people around the world can help save the tropical rain forests.

▲ Forested areas like this absorb and store rainwater and are called **watershed** areas. If the trees are cleared, soil is eroded, and rainwater runs off instead of being absorbed by the ground.

Keep track of the wood and paper products that you use in one day. In your Science Journal, record these products and the approximate amount of each that you use. Then identify two or more changes you can make to help reduce the demand for timber.

BACK HOME

How can people manage forests?

Although forests are renewable resources, growth of trees, like soil formation, takes time. Ten to thirty years are required to form an established pine forest. A mature hardwood forest takes seventy or more years to develop. Effective management is therefore crucial to preserving our forests.

Large forest fires char the soil, destroy all living trees, and cause many animals to die. Less damage is done by ground fires, which burn mostly dead branches on the forest floor but do not burn the forest. These small fires release nutrients into the soil, improve wildlife habitat, and help prevent destructive fires by burning off small amounts of natural fuel. The ecological benefits of periodic ground fires outweigh the risks, so they are

DILEMMA

Logging in United States Forests

Some timber companies would like to increase the amount of logging they do in national forests. They say that the country's supply of wood is getting smaller, so the costs of houses, paper, and furniture are going up. These companies also point out that many loggers will lose their jobs if the principle of sustainable yield is continued.

Environmentalists say that abandoning sustainable yield would affect more than trees. They point out that heavy cutting of forests in the Pacific Northwest has already contributed to the decline of several species, including the spotted owl.

Think About It Do you think that sustainable yield should be abandoned? Write a letter to a member of Congress or another government official to state your opinion.

used for forest management in some areas.

The way we choose to harvest trees can also be used as a management technique. In the past, many privately owned forests were harvested by removing all trees from an area. After this clear-cutting, new trees were sometimes planted. But because clear-cutting promotes erosion and harms wildlife by removing its habitat, techniques for tree harvesting are changing. Clear-cutting is being replaced by selective logging, the removal of only some of the trees in an area. The uncut trees prevent erosion, make seeds so that new trees can grow, and continue to provide a natural habitat for local wildlife.

Since 1960, lumbering has been allowed in certain national forests, which are managed according to the principle of **sustainable yield**. This means that commercial harvesting of trees does not occur faster than the forest can replace trees.

Be a Scientist

Can you manage land?

Get permission to walk around your schoolyard. Identify a section of the schoolyard that needs care. If there is litter in the area, pick it up and throw it away.

Decide what is the best way to manage the land area you selected. You might want to make and hang a bird feeder from a pole or tree. You may decide to plant seeds or seedlings, flowers, and shrubs or trees.

In your Activity Journal, write how soil, people, insects, and birds can benefit from the changes that you made in the schoolyard.

How are you doing?

1. How do forests help the environment?
2. What is sustainable yield?
3. **Think** Give one ecological reason and one economic reason against harvesting forests faster than they can renew themselves.
4. **Think** What are some ways that people can avoid starting forest fires?

Earth Prayers

Message from
Chief Seattle

The excerpt on the following page is a message from an American Indian about the environment and living in harmony with the earth. It is from a speech given in the 1850s by Chief Seattle, a leader of the Northwest Indian Nations. Chief Seattle's exact words are lost to history. But a listener, moved by Seattle's eloquence, took notes and later wrote down what he remembered of the speech. Since then, Chief Seattle's message has been adapted by many different writers. It has become a touchstone for people concerned with the environment. Although the words may have changed somewhat, Chief Seattle's message continues to inspire people. What do you think?

You must teach your children that

the ground beneath their feet

is the ashes of our ancestors.

So that they will respect the land,

tell your children that the Earth

is rich with the lives of our kin.

Teach your children what we have

taught our children,

that the Earth is our mother.

Whatever befalls the Earth

befalls the children of the Earth.

If we spit upon the ground

we spit upon ourselves.

This we know.

The Earth does not belong to us,

we belong to the Earth.

This we know.

All things are connected

like the blood that unites one family.

All things are connected.

Whatever befalls the Earth

befalls the children of the Earth.

We did not weave the web of life;

We are merely a strand in it.

Whatever we do to the web,

we do to ourselves.

Chief Seattle, Duwamish

Think About Your Reading

1. What do you think Chief Seattle means when he says, "If we spit upon the ground, we spit upon ourselves"? Do you agree with him?

2. Who do you think was Chief Seattle's audience when he gave this speech? Tell why you think so.

Diagramming Show in a diagram what Chief Seattle might mean by the "web of life." In the middle of your diagram, draw a tree struck by lightning. In the rest of the diagram, show how this event might affect other things in nature.

Where to Read More

Thane Maynard, *Saving Endangered Mammals: A Field Guide to Some of the Earth's Rarest Mammals* (Franklin Watts, 1992)
Learn about endangered animals and what we need to do to save them.

Looking Back

Words and Concepts

Complete the following statements.

1. All the conditions around us that affect our lives make up the _____.
2. The loss of nutrients and minerals from soil is called _____.
3. _____ is the use of farming methods that preserve soil.
4. _____ is a method of farming that avoids the use of chemicals.
5. _____ are chemicals used to kill insects and other pests.
6. Harvesting trees no faster than forests can replace them is called _____.

Applied Thinking Skills

Answer the following questions. You can use words, drawings, and diagrams in your answer.

7. Why is green manure easier for farmers to use than compost?
8. Why do you suppose more and more people are starting to think about forest conservation?
9. What kind of timber harvesting is shown here? What might happen if there were heavy rains?
10. **Your World** What techniques of organic farming might you use in your backyard garden?

Show What You Know

Can you tell how healthy soil is?

Observe and Collect Data

1. Your teacher will direct you to several areas where you may dig.
2. Using the shovel or trowel, examine the soil in each area. Avoid harming plants or their roots. Gently replace the soil that you remove.
3. In your Activity Journal, make note of the places where the soil is eroded or compacted.
4. If there is a sports field with base or yard lines marked on it in your schoolyard, try to infer the effect of the lines on the soil.

Draw Conclusions

1. Compare the soils that you observed. Where is the soil least healthy? What is causing the soil to be in poor condition?
2. Where is the soil most healthy? Explain why this area has healthy soil.

Process Skills
Observing, Inferring, Communicating

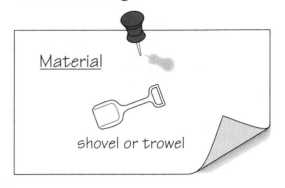

Material

shovel or trowel

Chapter 2

Living Things

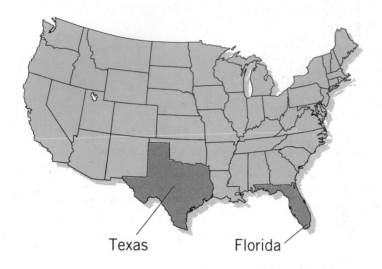

Texas   Florida

Wood storks in the Florida Everglades

The next stop on your trip is the Everglades in southern Florida. These unique wetlands are the natural habitat of plants such as saw grass and cypress trees, animals such as alligators, panthers, cormorants, and wood storks.

Many people live in South Florida and this growing population has looked to the Everglades to meet its water needs. Unfortunately, people have taken water from the Everglades without regard for the natural water cycle or the needs of other species that depend on this habitat. As people have used the water of the Everglades, many species have decreased in number, including wildlife preserved in the national park at the southernmost part of the Everglades.

In addition to water, people in South Florida need homes and farms. Construction has already taken away much of the habitat of native species. As construction continues, more species are threatened.

What can be done to meet the needs of South Florida's human population without destroying the fragile ecosystem on which humans and other species depend? Write your ideas in your Science Journal.

Controversial dredging for a development at the edge of the Everglades

90 ★ Montana Helena Billings ● 94 Yellowstone South Dakota

Columb

Orego

ramento

Fresn

5

Los
hannel
slands

Explore Activity

Can you make an ecosystem?

Process Skills

Making models, Observing, Inferring

Materials

container

spray bottle

screen

soil

sand

charcoal

plants

gravel

Observe and Collect Data

1. Decide whether you want to make a moist or dry land ecosystem. Use a natural habitat near your home, or materials provided by your teacher, to collect living and nonliving things for the ecosystem you choose.

2. For a pond ecosystem, build up layers of gravel, charcoal, and soil in your container as shown. For a land ecosystem, start with one layer of charcoal and add a second layer of mixed sand and soil.

3. Add to your container the plant and animal materials that you collected. Use a screen to cover the top.

4. Put the ecosystem in a well-lighted place.

5. Add water by gently spraying the ecosystem as needed.

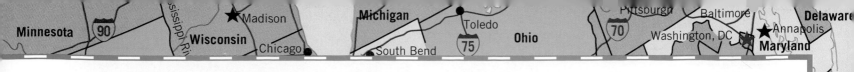

Share Your Results

Compare the living and nonliving things in the ecosystems that different groups made.

Draw Conclusions

How does your ecosystem meet the needs of living things?

Apply What You Know

1. What would happen if you removed all nonliving things from the ecosystem?
2. What would happen if you added a plant or animal species from a different type of ecosystem to the one you made?

Why do species become endangered or extinct?

The Everglades are home to the Florida panther. This area is the only place in the world that this cat lives. Because of changes in the Everglades, the population of Florida panthers was only about 50 in 1993.

When the population of a species is so small that the species might disappear from the earth, the species is said to be **endangered**. When a species has completely disappeared from the earth, the species is **extinct**. The Florida panther is endangered and very close to becoming extinct.

Natural extinction occurs because of climate changes and other natural causes. But the most common cause of extinction today

Be a Scientist

Can endangered species be saved?

1. Make four columns in your Activity Journal. In the first column, list four commercially hunted endangered species. In the second column, list the product for which each species is killed. In the third column, give an example of how this product is used.

   In the fourth column, suggest an alternative resource that people could use to meet the same need.

2. Compare your chart with those of your classmates. Did you list the same alternative resources? If not, how did your lists differ?

MINDS-ON ACTIVITY

Dredge and fill marsh development on Florida's Gulf Coast

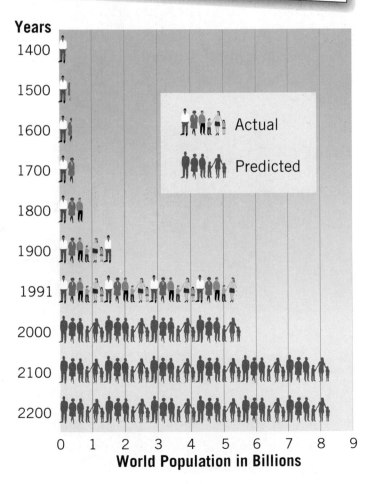

Years

1400	
1500	
1600	Actual
1700	Predicted
1800	
1900	
1991	
2000	
2100	
2200	

0 1 2 3 4 5 6 7 8 9
World Population in Billions

▲ The human population has increased at a much faster rate since 1900.

◀ Much of the habitat of the Florida panther has been destroyed as people have drained or filled in wetlands and built on the land.

is **habitat destruction**. Habitats can be destroyed as people move into ecosystems and change them.

Throughout human history, people have changed habitats. People build houses, roads, and cities, they dam rivers to make lakes, and they lower the level of other lakes by using much of the water. Until the last 200 years, however, there was always plenty of room for other species because the human population was not too large.

Beginning in the 1800s, advances in agriculture and medicine enabled many people to live longer. Advances in technology changed the way people live. Not only are there more people than ever before, but we use more of the earth's resources than ever before and create much more waste that can damage natural habitats.

Commercial hunting, or hunting animals for profit, is another cause of species extinction. Various international agreements prohibit commercial hunting of endangered species such as alligators, rhinoceroses, tigers, elephants, and whales. In some places, however, violators are rarely punished and penalties are often lenient. Poachers, who hunt illegally, have drastically reduced the numbers of many species.

What species are endangered?

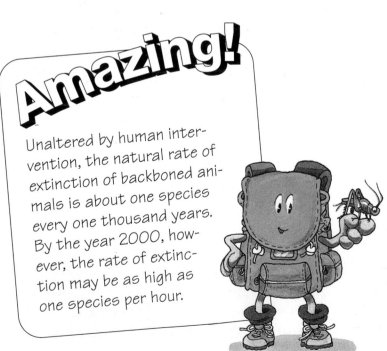

Around the world, about 25,000 species of plants and many species of animals are currently endangered. Saving these endangered species is important. The extinction of any species affects the entire ecosystem that it inhabits. For example, a cure for a disease might be found in one of these disappearing species.

The pictures on these pages show a few of the endangered species found in the United States. There are many others not shown here: tortoises, whales, other plants. How many do you know of?

▲ One of many species of pupfish that have survived for almost 50,000 years, the Desert pupfish is now endangered by habitat destruction.

Amazing!

Unaltered by human intervention, the natural rate of extinction of backboned animals is about one species every one thousand years. By the year 2000, however, the rate of extinction may be as high as one species per hour.

▲ The Knowlton cactus in New Mexico and Colorado is endangered by habitat destruction.

◀ The mission blue butterfly is a California insect that is nearing extinction.

▲ The population of American crocodiles has dropped below 500 because of hunting and habitat destruction.

Be a Scientist

MINDS-ON ACTIVITY

How do plants become extinct?

Many times when people talk about endangered species, they are thinking only of animals. Do some research to find out what plants have become extinct in the United States. Choose five and report to your class on where these plants lived and what caused them to become extinct.

◀ The manatee is an endangered water mammal. Two reasons account for this situation. Manatees swim very slowly and cannot get out of the way of boat propellers. They are also hurt by water pollution.

How can people help endangered species?

Preserving habitat is the best way to preserve species. This often involves legal protection. The Endangered Species Act of 1973 requires that all government-approved or government-funded projects that could affect endangered species be reviewed to see how great the effect will be. Thousands of projects have been reviewed under this act. Many wildlife biologists agree that this review process has preserved species that otherwise would not have survived.

Many biologists believe that large land reserves should be set aside so that habitats will not be destroyed. Such wildlife reserves have been created in 55 nations, including the United States.

The seeds of endangered plants can be stored. Many well-known and potentially useful crops already have been preserved in seed banks around the world. Today biologists are making intense efforts to collect seeds from endangered tropical forest species. However, some seeds may rot or fail to sprout after long periods of storage.

Despite many problems, habitat preservation, legal protection, and captive breeding have helped save many species, including those shown here.

▲ Habitat destruction, hunting, and pesticides greatly reduced the population of the bald eagle. Many pesticides have been banned, and the birds have been protected. The population of bald eagles is increasing, and the bird was removed from the list of endangered species.

▲ The alligator in the Florida Everglades and other southern wetlands was once endangered, but its population recovered after hunting was banned. In some areas limited hunting is now allowed as a way to control the population growth.

▲ In the past, people slaughtered wolves in the mistaken belief that wolves would destroy herds of cattle. Now that wolves are protected, their populations are increasing. The red-wolf populations in Florida and Tennessee are increasing, as is the gray-wolf population in Idaho.

▲ The California condor has been endangered by habitat destruction. Zoo workers have been raising birds in captivity and preparing them to be released. Using condor puppets, the workers are teaching the birds to recognize their own kind. This should enable them to breed naturally when they are returned to the wild.

▲ The southern sea otter feeds on abalone, competing for its prey with fishers off the Pacific Coast. Overfishing almost wiped out the otter, but legal protection has allowed the population to recover.

How are you doing?

1. List three causes of species extinction.
2. How can endangered species be preserved?
3. **Think** Suppose your family is planning on buying land to build a house. The environmental effects of this purchase are important to you. What advice would you give your family?
4. **Think** Imagine that you are a wildlife biologist. Recommend to the United States government one good strategy for preserving endangered species. Explain.

Why is biodiversity important?

You can see several plant species in the photograph shown here. Hidden among these flowers are several kinds of birds and many kinds of insects. The great **biodiversity** (bī´ō də vər´s ə tē), or variety of species, is important for several reasons. These species interact in many ways. If you remove one of these species, you affect the balance of this ecosystem.

These wildflowers are growing along a Texas highway. Texas has more than

CULTURAL CONNECTION

The Mayapple

Hundreds of years ago, American Indians discovered the healing properties of a forest plant that we call the mayapple. Cherokees used the mayapple to kill parasitic worms. Penobscot Indians used it to treat warts. Following the advice of North American Indians, potato farmers plant the mayapple to keep potato beetles away from their crops.

New studies are revealing additional medicinal properties of this wild resource. A chemical extracted from mayapples is used to treat one form of cancer. Further studies of the mayapple may yield new treatments for herpes, influenza, and measles.

Be a Scientist

Can you plan a flower garden?

MINDS-ON ACTIVITY

1. Plan a flower garden for a yard or park near your home. Include a variety of flowers in your garden. Try to find out which flowers are native to the area where you live. These flowers probably will grow best.

2. In your Activity Journal, make a diagram that shows which flowers you will plant where. Make a color drawing that shows your flower garden in bloom.

ACTIVITY JOURNAL

44,000 kilometers of highways and nearly 5,000 kinds of native wildflowers. In many places, grasses and shrubs are planted along roadsides. But in the 1950s, Texas decided to plant native wildflowers instead. The result is a roadside maintenance plan that is both economically and ecologically sound.

If you drove along the highways of Texas in the springtime, you would see hundreds of brightly colored native wildflowers in bloom. These plants need only the water they receive through rainfall, and occasional mowing, which helps spread flower seeds. Neither fertilizers nor pesticides are needed.

Because the plants need little care, the state saves money on maintenance. Because the plants grow so well, they cover the soil and prevent erosion. The plants also provide a habitat for many native species of animals, especially insects and birds.

Native species can also be used for improving crops. Sometimes crops are damaged by plant diseases. When this happens, farmers need to plant new varieties that are disease-resistant. Often, such disease-resistant plants are produced by breeding the crop plants with wild native plants that are resistant to the disease.

How can introducing new species affect an ecosystem?

Every biome has plants and animals that are native to the area. When people move from one biome to another, they often bring new plants and animals with them. Species that come from another area are called **introduced species**.

Sometimes people introduce species on purpose. Most of the food crops grown in the United States today are introduced species. In migrating, exploring, invading, and settling North America, various peoples brought in crops from other lands. Sugar cane originated in the South Pacific. Oats, rye, and grapes originated in Europe. Tomatoes and sweet potatoes originated in Central America.

Some introduced species have caused problems. If it has no competitors or predators, an introduced species can become the dominant species in an ecosystem. The new species may crowd out or destroy the habitat of native species. This decreases the area's biodiversity. The water hyacinth, native to South and Central America, has grown rapidly in the waterways of many southern states, sometimes forcing out all other native plant life.

Introduced species of insects can be very destructive. The Japanese beetle, accidentally imported into the United States on plants in about 1916, caused the defoliation, or loss of leaves, of more than 250 species of trees and other plants. The camphor-scale insect, imported on plants in the 1920s, damaged nearly 200 species of plants in Texas, Alabama, and Louisiana.

▲ These caterpillars are feeding on Balsam Poplar leaves. What may happen to the plant?

Water hyacinth plants have begun to overrun the Atchafalaya River Basin in Louisiana. ▼

Land-Use Planner

Land-use planners help people find ways to use the land without harming it. Some study forests or farms, others study land use in cities. Philip Wong is a city planner. He works with architects, builders, engineers, and others. Since the environment is an important element in city planning, he works with environmental specialists as well. To preserve creeks, wooded areas, hillsides, and other features of the areas he plans, he combines all kinds of scientific information about an area before deciding what is best for using the land wisely.

66 While we want to be sure that what is planned for a hillside follows the topography of the land and that the building design blends in with the surroundings, we also pay attention to environmental issues such as existing significant trees, the possibility of landslides, or possible changes in the area's water flow.

"Land development and environmental preservation can be compatible. We can use our land without hurting it, as long as we plan carefully and wisely. **99**

How are you doing?

1. How have people made use of native species?
2. Under what conditions can an introduced species become the dominant species in an ecosystem?
3. **Think** How can research on biodiversity benefit farmers?
4. **Think** How do you think that the introduction of new food crops into North America affected existing ecosystems? Explain your answer.

Fishing in the Northwest

Rivers in the state of Washington were once teeming with salmon. Over the years, so many fish were caught that certain species of salmon became extinct, and others were threatened. As the fish populations decreased, people became concerned about the problem. Everyone seemed to understand that some sort of limit had to be placed on salmon fishing. However, different groups did not agree on how to set such limits.

Environmentalists hoped that salmon fishing could be reduced by all people who fished. But American Indians in Washington have fishing rights by treaty. Many of the Indians and others who fish for a living felt that they should not have limits placed on their fishing. Sport fishers in the area did not want their fishing limited either.

In the late 1980s, the decline in the fish population was so serious that everyone recognized the need to join forces and solve the problem. The Northwest Indian Fisheries Commission, the Washington State Department of Fish and Wildlife, and the sport fisherman's associations decided to work together to develop a plan for maintaining the salmon population. Together, they set limits that all groups could agree on.

By working together and trying to understand one another's viewpoints, these groups found a way to share a resource. By protecting this resource, they are making it possible for future generations to continue to fish for salmon.

How are populations of endangered species changing?

Scientists have many ways of estimating the size of a population of plants or animals. By studying how the population size changes, scientists can see if preservation efforts are working.

Process Skills
Collecting data, Making a graph, Interpreting data

Observe and Collect Data

1. Select a species of endangered plant or animal.

2. Do library research to find data on the changing population of the species you have chosen. Record the population data in your Activity Journal. If your research includes information on preservation actions or changes in the species' environment, record this information, as well.

3. Make a line graph to show how the population has changed. Put the years going across and the population sizes going from bottom to top.

Draw Conclusions

1. Over the time shown by your graph, has the population of your species increased or decreased?

2. Is the change in population size constant, or does your graph show variations in the pattern?

3. Suggest reasons for the increases and decreases that you can see in the population.

Looking Back

Words and Concepts

Read each statement. If a statement is true, write *true* as your answer. If a statement is false, change the underlined word or phrase to a word or phrase that will make the statement true.

1. If the population of a species is so small that the species might disappear, it is said to be <u>extinct</u> .

2. <u>Biodiversity</u> is the variety of species on the earth.

3. Most of the food crops grown in the United States today are <u>native species</u> .

4. Species that have disappeared completely from the earth are called <u>endangered species</u> .

5. The most common cause of species extinction is <u>hunting</u> .

6. A <u>wildlife reserve</u> is a place where land is set aside to preserve habitats.

Applied Thinking Skills

Answer the following questions. You can use words, drawings, and diagrams in your answers.

7. To preserve endangered species most effectively, should a zoo protect several individuals of many endangered species or a larger population of one species? Explain.

8. Why do you think sport hunting, unlike commercial hunting, is not a major factor in species extinction?

9. Explain how the near-extinction of wolves could have been prevented.

10. **Your World** Tell about two or more different ways that, by changing your personal habits, you can help reduce species destruction.

Canis lupus—Timberwolf

Show What You Know

How does littering affect animals?

Observe and Collect Data

1. 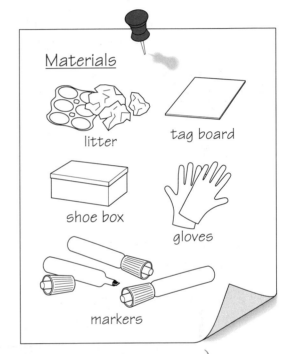 Using protective gloves and a box, collect scraps of litter from a playground, schoolyard, or other place in your neighborhood. Try to find different types of litter such as plastic wrappers, bits of plastic foam, and six-pack rings.
2. Think about how each type of litter that you collected can harm animals such as deer, squirrels, birds, and fish.
3. Using the litter, tag board, and markers, make a poster that shows the effects of littering on animals.

Draw Conclusions

1. Name one type of litter that might be left in the woods by a hiker.
2. Name one type of litter that might be thrown from an automobile onto the highway.
3. Name one type of litter that might be left on the beach.
4. Name one way each type of litter you identified can harm animals.

Process Skills

Collecting data, Observing, Communicating

Materials

litter

tag board

shoe box

gloves

markers

Chapter 3

Waste Management

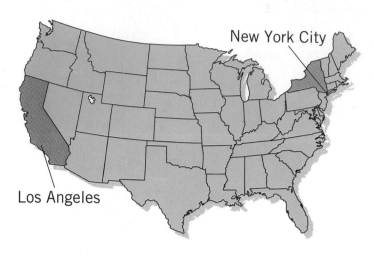

New York City

Los Angeles

As the human population grows, we produce more and more garbage. Pollutants are filling our air to very unhealthy levels in many large cities. Garbage no longer can be dumped in the sea. Landfills are becoming full. We need to find ways to manage the wastes that our society produces.

Many people have recognized the problem of waste management and have found ways to improve the situation. The key is in the three "Rs": reduce, reuse, recycle. Wastes being released into our air must be *reduced*. People can *reuse* plastic cups and plates rather than throwing them away. People can *recycle* materials so that they can be made into new products.

Do you use a lot of the things shown below? Which ones? What can you do to reduce, reuse, or recycle some of these items? ▼

SCIENCE JOURNAL

In your Science Journal, list items you turn into waste each day. Find one item whose use you could reduce, one that you could reuse, and one that you could recycle.

Aluminum

plastic

paper

Can you find pollutants in the air?

Process Skills
Predicting, Observing

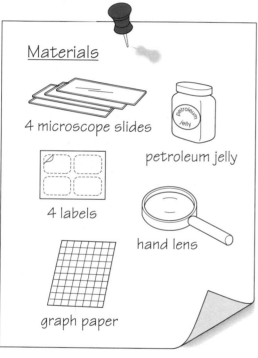

Materials

4 microscope slides

petroleum jelly

4 labels

hand lens

graph paper

Observe and Collect Data

1.  Identify four test sites where you can collect particles that are part of air pollution. **Predict** which places are heavily polluted and which places are relatively free of pollution. Write your predictions in your Activity Journal.

2. Write the name of each test site on a label and stick it on one end of the microscope slide.

3. Smear one side of each slide with petroleum jelly. Place the slides, petroleum jelly side up, in the test sites. Leave them for 24 hours.

Pollution Levels

| Location | Particles Collected | |
	Per Square	Description
1.		
2.		
3.		

4. Carefully collect the slides. Use a hand lens to examine them for solid airborne particles, such as dust. Place each slide on a piece of graph paper. Use the squares to estimate the number of particles per square on each slide.

5. Copy the table below into your Activity Journal. Record your findings on the table.

Share Your Results

Compare your table with those of two other groups. In which location(s) did students collect the most pollution particles?

Draw Conclusions

What was the source of the pollution particles that you collected?

Apply What You Know

How can the pollution that you identified be reduced?

What are the sources and effects of air pollution?

These are the main sources of air pollution worldwide. Pollutants are released by each source into the air. Some are simply dangerous to breathe. Others react chemically with sunlight and water vapor in the atmosphere to create new pollutants.

▼

After the open Texas highways, the roads in the city of Los Angeles seem choked with cars. But even in Texas, automobiles release pollutants into the air. Motor-vehicle emissions contain high levels of hydrocarbons, nitrogen oxide, carbon monoxide, and carbon dioxide. Automobile emissions, the greatest source of air pollution in the United States, are also the main source of urban smog. The photograph on page H45 shows the brown haze of smog that hangs over Los Angeles. People in Los Angeles drive just about everywhere. Traffic is very dense. To make matters worse, wind patterns and the mountains surrounding the city create

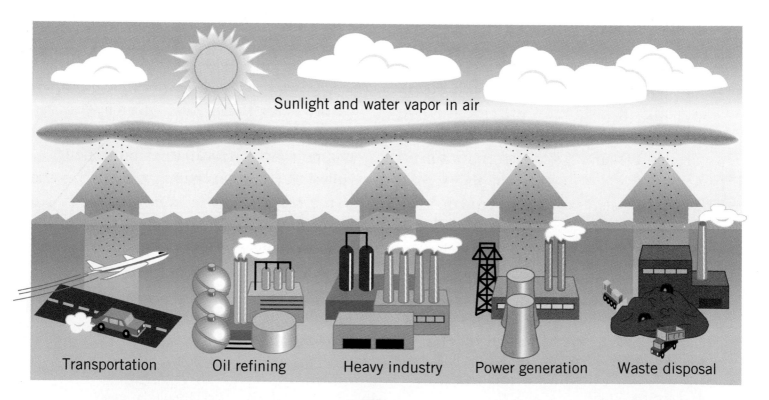

Sunlight and water vapor in air

Transportation   Oil refining   Heavy industry   Power generation   Waste disposal

◀ Not all air pollution is made by humans. Forest fires release carbon monoxide, carbon dioxide, and nitrogen oxides into the air. Decaying plants release methane and hydrogen sulfide. Volcanoes, too, produce air pollution in the form of ash and chemicals.

Air pollution in the Los Angeles basin. There are mountains in the background.

conditions that prevent air pollutants from rising into the atmosphere.

Pollutants in the air react chemically, producing nitrous oxides and sulfuric oxides. These substances combine with moisture in the air and fall to the earth as **acid rain**.

In most places, acid concentrations in rain are not high enough to kill plants. However, acid rain slows plant growth, reduces soil fertility, and raises the acid levels in lakes and rivers. The acidity of the water threatens plants and animals that live in freshwater ecosystems. Acid rain damages human-made structures, too. The Statue of Liberty and other monuments have been partially corroded by acid rain.

Air pollution also increases the **greenhouse effect**. The heat trapped by the atmosphere keeps the earth warm. This is a natural effect of the earth's atmosphere. However, pollutants have increased this effect so much that many scientists say it may cause the earth's temperature to rise. A rise in temperature of even a few degrees could produce many drastic changes in the natural ecosystems of the world.

How can air pollution be reduced?

Because automobile emissions are a major cause of air pollution, California and many other states have passed laws that require cars to have devices that reduce emissions. A special device attached to the exhaust system of an automobile changes toxic carbon monoxide and unburned gasoline into water and carbon dioxide.

Despite emission controls, smog in Los Angeles is very bad. Some people have suggested new lifestyle-changing measures to reduce it. For instance, some want to ban gasoline-powered lawn mowers and barbecues. People also have suggested banning all gasoline-powered vehicles. But people have to be able to get around in the city. Improved public transportation is needed. Los Angeles has recently opened its first subway line, and more lines are being built.

▲ To decrease automobile traffic, Los Angeles is working to improve its public transportation system by building subways.

Trees help purify the air and reduce pollution by absorbing carbon dioxide. In many cities, trees are being planted to reduce pollution. ▶

Electrostatic Precipitators

Some pollutants are small bits of solid matter, such as ash or soot. Burning coal produces gases that contain such pollutants. Many coal-burning facilities have installed electrostatic precipitators, which remove these bits, called particulates, from emissions gases. As they enter the electrostatic precipitator, the gases pass through a field of electricity. This gives the particulates a charge. The walls of the electrostatic precipitator have an opposite charge. Remember that opposite charges attract. As a result, the charged particles of gas stick to the walls.

The current that flows through the electrostatic precipitator goes on and off. When it is off, the walls lose their charge and the particulates fall to the bottom of the device.

Using a device like an electrostatic precipitator to remove toxic particulates from emissions helps control air pollution. However, that matter never goes away. The particulates that fall to the bottom of an electrostatic precipitator create another problem—hazardous wastes. You will learn more about this problem in Lesson 3.

YOU CAN HELP

Grow a plant. Remember that plants absorb carbon dioxide. This helps to reduce air pollution. If everyone in the United States planted just two seeds and tended them as they sprouted and grew, more than 500 million plants would soon be purifying the air.

How are you doing?

1. What is the major source of air pollution in the United States?
2. Describe two devices that reduce emissions that cause air pollution.
3. **Think** If the greenhouse effect caused some of the ice around the earth's poles to melt, how might other areas of the world be affected?
4. **Think** Why do some people object to even stricter antipollution standards for cars?

What is ground-water pollution?

Where does the water you use come from? Does it come from a well, a river, or a reservoir? People use water from two kinds of sources. **Surface water** flows from rivers and streams into wetlands, natural lakes, oceans, and human-made reservoirs. The relatively fast flow of surface water helps spread out and dilute contaminating wastes.

Ground water is water that has soaked into the earth. The water moves downward until it reaches a layer of solid rock which will no longer allow the water to seep through. The ground water fills the spaces in rock above the layer of solid rock.

The top surface of the ground water is called the *water table*. As more water soaks

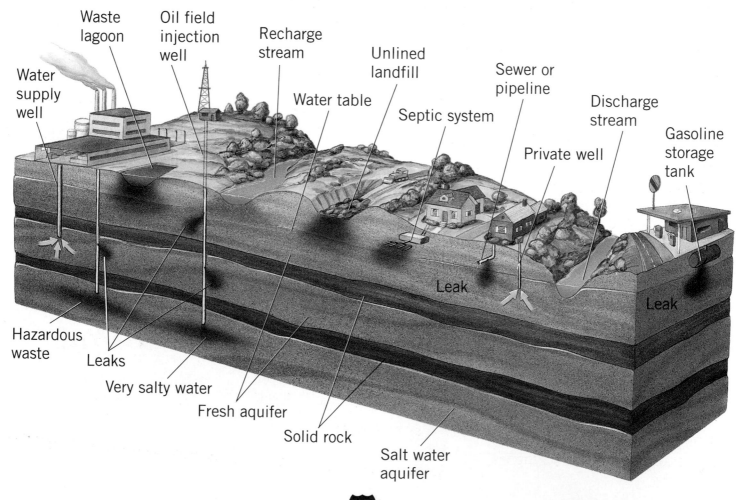

Water supply well

Waste lagoon

Oil field injection well

Recharge stream

Unlined landfill

Water table

Sewer or pipeline

Septic system

Discharge stream

Private well

Gasoline storage tank

Leak

Leak

Leak

Hazardous waste

Leaks

Very salty water

Fresh aquifer

Solid rock

Salt water aquifer

into the ground, the water table rises. The depth of the water table below the ground surface varies from place to place. Some places are swampy because the water table is near the surface.

In some places, ground water can flow like an underground stream through the spaces in a layer of rock. The water-filled layer may be sandwiched between two layers of rock that do not let water pass through. The layer of rock with water flowing through it is called an **aquifer** (aʹkwə fər). If water from an aquifer comes to the surface, a spring of fresh water flows out of the ground. One out of two Americans relies on wells drilled into aquifers for drinking water. Aquifers also provide much of the water used for irrigation on farms.

◄ The picture shows some of the many sources from which pollutants enter ground water supplies.

Ground water moves much more slowly than surface water does. This explains why many pollutants are present at much higher levels in ground water than in contaminated surface water supplies. Polluted ground water can become purified through natural processes, but this takes hundreds or even thousands of years. Today, ground-water pollution poses a growing threat to humans and other species.

Look around your yard or neighborhood to find what kinds of pollutants might be seeping into the ground water when it rains or when you wash your car or water your lawn. Think about what is on your roof, what is on the streets, what kinds of chemical fertilizers or pesticides are on your grass and garden, what is rusting, and what paints and cleaning products are lying around outside.

BACK HOME

What are some types of surface-water pollution?

▲ What signs of pollution do you see in these pictures? How would you clean these places up?

From Los Angeles, your trip takes you to another large city. New York City boasts of having some of the best drinking water in the country. An extensive reservoir system is located outside the city, and water flows to New York through large water tunnels.

Many places do not have such clean sources of water. In some parts of the world, even in some places in the United States, sewage is dumped into lakes, rivers, and oceans. Raw sewage contains many tiny, harmful organisms. When these organisms enter the water, they make it unfit for use as drinking water.

Some factories still emit their industrial wastes into bodies of fresh water. These pollutants kill plants and animals in the water, and can even make people ill if they eat poisoned fish. Some of the pollutants may also seep into ground water. In the United States, companies caught dumping their wastes like this are fined severely.

Fertilizers from farm fields are carried into streams by runoff water. Fertilizers increase the amounts of nutrients in ecosystems. At normal levels, nutrients help keep ecosystems in their natural condition. At high levels, however, nutrients become water pollutants. Nutrients interfere with the balance of freshwater

How does plant food affect fresh water?

Use pond water as a source of algae to test the effects of "plant food" on freshwater systems. Decide how much pond water you will need and how much plant food you will add. Have your teacher check your plan before you begin.

▲ High school students take a boat tour of Boston Harbor. They learn about the causes of the harbor's polluted condition and what is being done to help it recover.

A student prepares to collect a water sample from Boston Harbor. This device allows scientists to take samples from various depths. ▶

ecosystems by stimulating the growth of algae and other aquatic plants. These plants clog the water. Then, when they die, they decay. This process robs the water of oxygen. As a result, many fish die.

In recent years, water pollution has been greatly reduced by the passing of new laws. Some highly polluted lakes and rivers have begun slowly to return to life.

How is waste water treated?

Basics of the sewage and water-treatment process. Notice that some of the material removed from waste water can be recycled in a useful way. ▶

▲ Sewage-treatment plant

Although New York City has excellent drinking water, the water in the rivers in New York City once had many pollutants. The main source of the pollution was waste water, or sewage. The photograph and diagram on these pages can help you understand how a sewage-treatment plant works.

If you live in a medium-sized city or town, the waste water you generate when you wash dishes, flush toilets, and take baths or showers is probably treated in a plant like the one shown here. In New York, a system of sewer pipes links the sewage treatment plant to households, factories, hospitals, and other buildings where wastes

Be a Scientist

How can you filter water?

1. In one cup, blend water and soil to make muddy water. Set the jar aside.
2. Fill a funnel with one layer of pebbles, one layer of gravel, and one layer of sand. Make the sand layer fairly thick, about 3 centimeters. Hold the funnel over a cup and pack the layers of filtering material together by pouring a little clean water through the funnel.

Then place the funnel in another clean empty cup.

3. Slowly and carefully stir or shake the muddy water. Pour 80 milliliters of muddy water into the funnel. Observe the water that flows out of the funnel into the cup. Record your observations in your Activity Journal.

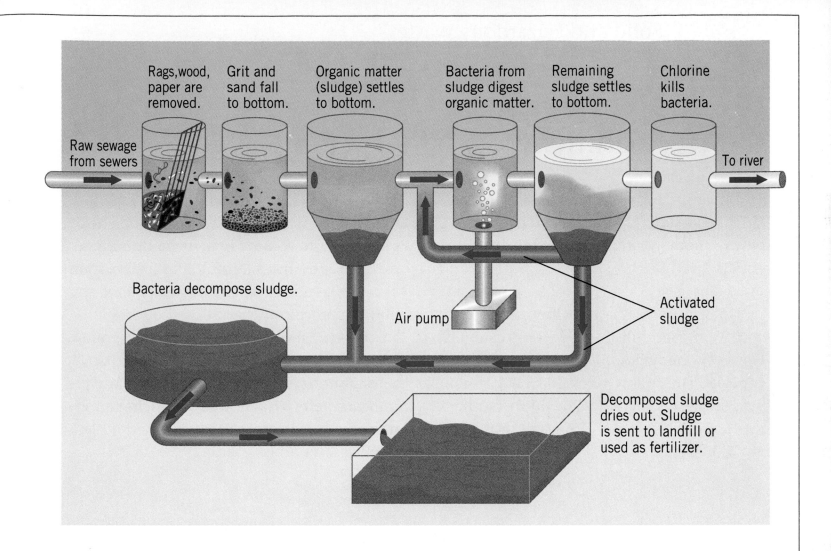

Rags, wood, paper are removed.

Grit and sand fall to bottom.

Organic matter (sludge) settles to bottom.

Bacteria from sludge digest organic matter.

Remaining sludge settles to bottom.

Chlorine kills bacteria.

Raw sewage from sewers

To river

Bacteria decompose sludge.

Air pump

Activated sludge

Decomposed sludge dries out. Sludge is sent to landfill or used as fertilizer.

are discharged into water. Storm runoff from city streets and polluted water from industry also flow into the sewage-treatment plant. At the plant, waste water is treated to remove wastes and pollutants. The clean water is then released into a nearby river.

Since New York City began using this kind of treatment plant, the water quality of the Hudson River has improved. Species of fish and other water organisms that had not been seen for many years have returned.

How are you doing?

1. What are the two sources of the water that people use?
2. How does waste water get from houses and apartments to treatment plants?
3. **Think** Many people have installed toilets that compost the wastes. In what situation would this be most helpful?
4. **Think** Imagine that you are in charge of waste-water treatment in your city. How can you convince taxpayers to pay for improved sewage treatment?

How do wastes affect the environment?

Do you know where your trash goes? Urban and suburban household wastes are either buried in landfills or burned in incinerators. Each method has its advantages and disadvantages.

Landfills have relatively low operating costs. Some landfills handle wastes carefully. However, many landfills have no pollution controls. They allow **toxic** (täk´sik), or poisonous, wastes such as paint thinner and wastes from disposable diapers to seep into ground water.

Incineration removes odors and organic matter that carries disease. Incineration also reduces waste volume by two-thirds, so less material goes into a landfill. But incineration also increases the toxicity of wastes. Like any burning process, incineration produces smoke and ashes. Smoke increases air pollution. Ash from incinerators contains toxic substances. It is very costly to dispose of these hazardous by-products of incineration properly.

A Chinese Village

Nearly half of the people on earth depend on **biomass**, plant or animal matter that can be converted to fuel, to meet their energy needs. The most frequently used fuel of this kind is wood.

Other forms include vegetable matter, manure, and human waste, but these are not used directly. Instead, the fuel is actually the gases they give off as they decay. In many Chinese villages, these gases are burned to generate electricity.

Using this gas as fuel has several advantages. It makes use of waste materials, decreasing disposal problems. In addition, it conserves energy resources. In some remote villages, this technology has provided electricity to people who never had it before.

For years, many businesses and cities used the ocean as a trash can. Growing public awareness of the threat that ocean dumping posed to marine life and people who depend on ocean food sources prompted Congress to pass laws that are eliminating this method of waste disposal. Still, illegal ocean dumping continues in the United States. In many other countries, untreated sewage is still routinely discharged into the sea.

▲ Per person per day, Americans produce more than 1.5 kilograms of household and commercial waste. Where do you think it goes?

YOU CAN HELP

Be careful what you pour down the drain. Even small amounts of paints, motor oil, unused pesticides, and weed killers can pollute the water supply. Call your town government to find out how to dispose of these and other hazardous wastes safely.

▲ Garbage barges like this regularly take New York City trash to dump or incineration sites in other states.

How can we control hazardous wastes?

▲ Residents protest the planned introduction of an incinerator in their locality.

The picture to the right shows a crew, directed by the Environmental Protection Agency, vacuuming contaminated soil in a clean-up effort in St. Louis County, Missouri. ▶

Americans are becoming more aware of the environmental damage created by the disposal of hazardous wastes. Increased public concern has prompted government and industry to reduce production of hazardous wastes and to improve disposal methods. The most effective way to control the hazardous waste problem is at the source—by reducing the amount of toxic wastes produced by industry. In addition, some hazardous waste materials can be broken down and made into chemicals that can be sold or reused.

Many industries are reducing toxic waste production by replacing toxic materials used in manufacturing with less toxic or nontoxic ones. The world's largest gift wrapping manufacturer cut its production of hazardous waste by 140,000 kilograms per year by changing the kind of inks it used. In addition, many manufacturers have changed the chemical makeup of their products for easier recycling. For example, plastics that can be recycled can be made into playground equipment or park benches.

Yet, as long as hazardous wastes are produced, even the best efforts toward recycling, reuse, and detoxification cannot eliminate the need for storage. Secured landfills, huge pits lined with plastic and thick layers of clay, may provide the best option.

DILEMMA

Exporting Hazardous Wastes

In many countries, strict regulations control the disposal of hazardous wastes. Meeting these regulations can be very costly. To save money, some companies send their hazardous wastes to countries that don't have so many regulations. Countries that import toxic wastes rarely have the facilities to manage them safely. Workers and residents are exposed to pollutants and may not know it.

Some people believe that in order to support American business, the international waste trade should continue, but with more control. They want our government to monitor, but not to ban, the international waste trade. Many environmentalists disagree. They say that as long as countries like the United States can legally export their wastes, they will not try to reduce their *production* of hazardous waste.

Think About It What should the United States decide about the exporting of hazardous wastes? Write a radio editorial expressing your opinion. Be sure to include reasons for the opinion you express.

How are you doing?

1. Name one advantage and one disadvantage of incineration.
2. What is the most effective way to control the hazardous waste problem?
3. **Think** Some people argue that deep ocean sites located near powerful currents are the best place to dispose of toxic industrial wastes. Do you agree? Explain.
4. **Think** If your neighborhood were being considered as a site for a landfill containing hazardous wastes, how would you respond?

Looking Back

Words and Concepts

Complete the following statements.

1. By banning or restricting gasoline-powered vehicles, cities can reduce a by-product of air pollution called _____.

2. High levels of hydrocarbons, nitrogen oxide, carbon monoxide, and carbon dioxide are found in _____ emissions.

3. Before being returned to the water supply system, waste water in urban areas is processed in _____.

4. Large bodies of underground water are called _____.

5. By-products of _____ are ash and air pollutants.

6. Disposing of wastes in _____ has recently been banned in the United States.

Applied Thinking Skills

Answer the following questions. You can use words, drawings, or diagrams in your answers.

7. Why do you suppose air pollution and acid rain are described as "international problems"?

8. Why is it often hard for people to tell whether their drinking water is polluted?

9. Name one place where a secured landfill should not be located. Explain.

10. **Your World** What hazardous wastes do families need to take responsibility for? How should families dispose of these wastes?

Show What You Know

Can you make recycled paper?

Observe and Collect Data

1. ⚠️ Shred some pages of newspaper. Place the shredded paper in the blender. Pour 1 liter of water in the blender. Run the blender several seconds, until the paper turns to pulp.

2. Pour about 3 centimeters of water into the pan. Place the screen in the pan. Pour 250 milliliters of pulp over the screen.

3. Spread the pulp evenly. Then lift the screen and let it drain. Open a section of unshredded newspaper. Place the screen, with the pulp on it, into the newspaper. Close the newspaper.

4. Turn the newspaper over so that the screen is on top of the pulp. Place the board on the newspaper and press hard to squeeze out the water.

5. Open the newspaper and remove the screen. Let the pulp dry for 24 hours or more. Gently remove the newspaper from the dry pulp. Then draw a picture or write a message on your recycled paper.

Process Skills
Measuring, Communicating

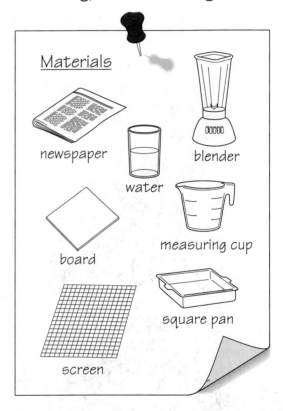

Materials

newspaper

water

blender

measuring cup

board

square pan

screen

Draw Conclusions

What are the environmental benefits of recycling paper?

The Environment

Show what you have learned about protecting the environment and managing wastes. Work with a partner, in a group, or by yourself. Select one activity.

Singer/Songwriter Write and sing a song that deals with an environmental problem in your city or town and suggests how the problem can be solved.

Mime Create a pantomime that shows either the degradation or wise management of a renewable resource such as water.

Environmental Artist Create an artwork using materials such as soil, hay, or stones, which you can find outdoors.

Print Journalist Write a feature article on an endangered or threatened species.

Radio Broadcaster Prepare and present a report on an actual or fictitious Earth Day celebration in your city or town. In your broadcast, identify one or more local ecological concerns and outline strategies proposed to address them.

Stationery Maker Design a greeting or birthday card. Then use recycled paper to create the card that you designed.

Glossary

acid rain (as´id rān´) Rain that has a higher than normal acidity due to chemical reactions between pollutants and moisture in the air. (page H45)

aquifer (ak´wə fər) A natural underground body of water. (page H49)

biodiversity (bī´ō də vər´sə tē) The variety of species. (page H32)

biomass (bī´ō mas´) Plant or animal matter than can be converted to fuel to meet energy needs. (page H54)

endangered species (en dān´jərd spē´shēz) A species whose population is so small that the species might disappear completely from the earth. (page H26)

environment (en vī´rən mənt) All the conditions around us that affect our lives. (page H3)

extinct species (ek stiŋkt´ spē´shēz) A species that has disappeared completely from the earth. (page H26)

greenhouse effect (grēn´hous ə fekt´) The trapping of heat by the earth's atmosphere. (page H45)

ground water (ground´ wô´tər) The water that seeps into the ground and is stored there. (page H48)

habitat destruction (hab´i tat´ di struk´shən) Changes in the environment that change or destroy the habitat of one or more species. (page H27)

introduced species (in´trə dōōst´ spē´shēz) A species that is not native to an area, but has been brought in from another area. (page H34)

nutrient depletion (nōō´trē ənt dē plē´shən) The loss of nutrients and minerals from the soil. (page H11)

organic farming (ôr gan´ik färm´iŋ) A style of farming that avoids the use of chemical fertilizers and pesticides. (page H12)

regenerative agriculture (ri jen´ə rə tiv ag´ri kul´chər) The use of farming methods that preserve soil. (page H12)

surface water (sər´fis wôt´ər) The water that flows on the surface of the earth. Surface water includes wetlands, rivers, streams, lakes, and reservoirs. (page H48)

sustainable yield (sə stān´ə bəl yēld) A practice of harvesting trees no faster than the forest can replace them. (page H17)

toxic (täks´ik) Poisonous. (page H54)

watershed (wôt´ər shed´) An area that absorbs and stores rainwater. (page H15)

Unit H Index

Boldface numerals denote glossary terms. Italic numerals denote illustrations.

Credits

Photographs

1BL Ralph A. Clevenger/Westlight; 1BR Larry Lipsky/Tom Stack & Associates; 1TL Tom Bean/DRK Photo; 1TR R. Kord/ H. Armstrong Roberts/Stock South; 2-3 Sharon Gerig/ Tom Stack & Associates; 4BL John Gerlach/Earth Scenes; 4BR Greg Vaughn/AllStock; 4TL Tom Walker/Stock, Boston; 5 Ken Karp*; 6 Ken Karp*; 7 Stacy Pick/Stock, Boston; 7(inset) Fred R. Palmer/Stock, Boston; 9 Elliott Smith*; 11 Ken Karp*; 12B Grant Heilman/Grant Heilman Photography; 12C Thomas Hovland/Grant Heilman Photography; 12T Byron/The Stock Market; 13 A. Rothstein/Library of Congress; 14–15 James Blank/The Stock Market; 14 Thomas Kitchin/Tom Stack & Associates; 15 Michael Fogden/DRK Photo; 16–17 Dennis Flaherty/Stock South; 20 Russell A. Mittermeier/Bruce Coleman Inc.; 21 Ken Karp*; 22 Wendell Metzen/Bruce Coleman Inc.; 23 Larry Lipsky/ DRK Photo; 23(inset) Steve Starr/Stock, Boston; 25 Elliott Smith*; 26 Tom & Pat Leeson/DRK Photo; 27 Wendell Mitzen/Bruce Coleman Inc.; 28B Stephen J. Krasemann/ DRK Photo; 28C Steinhart Aquarium:Tom McHugh/Photo Researchers; 28T Brian Stablyk/AllStock; 29B Doug Perrine/DRK Photo, 29T Thomas S. England/ Stock South; 30B Maresa Pryor/Animals, Animals; 30T Stephen J. Krasemann/DRK Photo; 31B Stephen J. Krasemann/DRK Photo; 31TL Tim Davis; 31TR Roy Toft/Tom Stack & Associates; 32 Daniel J. Lyons/Bruce Coleman Inc.; 32–33 John Elk III; 34–35 C. C. Lockwood/Bruce Coleman Inc.; 34 Ron Sanford/AllStock;

35 Anne Dowie*; 36B Bill Foley/ Stock South; 36T Ken Karp*; 36C Natalie B. Fobes/AllStock; 37 Elliott Smith*; 38 Stephen J. Krasemann/DRK Photo; 39 Wayland Lee*; 40 GHP Studio*; 41 Ken Karp*; 42–43 Elliott Smith*; 44–45 Stephen Dowell/Stock South; 45 Bob Witkowski/Westlight; 46L Michael LeRoy/ Tony Stone Images; 46R Rob Badger; 47 Ken Karp*; 50–51 Dave Schaefer/The Picture Cube; 50B Jon Lamar/The Stock Market; 50T Joel W. Rogers/AllStock; 51 Dave Schaefer/The Picture Cube; 52 Lawrence Migdale/Photo Researchers; 55BL Ken Karp*; 55BR Andy Levin/Photo Researchers; 55T Geri Engberg/The Stock Market; 56 Rob Badger; 56–57 David Ulmer/Stock, Boston; 58 Ken Karp*

Special thanks to Friends of the Urban Forest, San Francisco, California; Malcolm X Elementary School, Berkeley, California; Franklin Year-Round School, Oakland, California; Carl B. Munck Elementary School, Oakland, California; Hintil Ku Ka Child Care Center, Oakland, California.

*Photographed expressly for Addison-Wesley Publishing Company, Inc.

Illustrations

Molly Babich 10
Nea Bisek 8L, 21, 24L, 39, 42T, 59
Brian Evans 48
Jane McCreary 8B, 24B, 28, 42B

Rolin Graphics 6, 22, 40
Joanna Roy 18
Randy Vergoustraete 60–61
Nina Wallace 27, 44, 53

Text

1 "This Land is Your Land " Words and Music by Woodie Guthrie. TRO—Copyright ©1956 (renewed), 1958 (renewed), and 1970 by Ludlow Music, Inc., New York. Used by permission.

11, 54 Dr. Norman Myers, ed., *Gaia: An Atlas of Planet Management* (New York: Doubleday, 1993). Copyright ©1984, 1993 by Gaia Books Limited, London.

11 National Association of Conservation Districts, *Conserving Soil,* U.S. Conservation Service of the U.S. Department of Agriculture, 1990.

15, 16, 28, 54 Daniel D. Chiras, *Environmental Science: Action for a Sustainable Future,* Third Edition (Redwood City, California. The Benjamin/Cummings Publishing Company, Inc., 1991). Copyright ©1991 by the Benjamin/Cummings Publishing Company, Inc. Pages 172, 200, 450.

18–19 From a speech by Chief Seattle.

28 *The World Book Encyclopedia,* World Book, Inc. Copyright ©1993 by World Book, Inc.

Index

Boldface numerals denote glossary terms. Italic numerals denote illustrations.

Credits

Photographs

Cover: Kindra Clineff/AllStock

Table of Contents: iiL Guy Powers/Envision; iiR Renee Lynn*; iii Ken Karp*; ivL GHP Studio*; ivR Jane Burton/Bruce Coleman Inc.; vB Brian Stablyk/AllStock;

vT NASA; viii Geoffrey Nilsen Photography*
*Photographed expressly for Addison-Wesley Publishing Company, Inc.

Illustration

Cover: Steve Musgrave

Oregon Trail Elementary School
660 Park Avenue
Twin Falls, Idaho 83301